Justice by Consent

Justice by Consent:
plea bargains in the
American courthouse

Arthur Rosett
University of California, Los Angeles

Donald R. Cressey
University of California, Santa Barbara

J. B. LIPPINCOTT COMPANY
Philadelphia
New York   San Jose   Toronto

Copyright © 1976, by J. B. Lippincott Company

This book is fully protected by copyright and, with the exception of brief excerpts for review, no part of it may be reproduced in any form by print, photoprint, microfilm, or any other means without written permission from the publisher.

ISBN 0-397-47341-9
ISBN 0-397-47340-0 pbk.
Library of Congress Catalog Card Number 75-41447
Printed in the United States of America

1 3 5 7 9 8 6 4 2

Library of Congress Cataloging in Publication Data

Rosett, Arthur I 1934–
  Justice by consent.

  Bibliography: p.
  Includes index.
  1. Pleas (Criminal procedure)—United States. I. Cressey, Donald Ray, 1919–   joint author. II. Title.
KF9654.R66   345'.73'072   75-41447
ISBN 0-397-47341-9
ISBN 0-397-47340-0 pbk.

preface

We wrote this book to give nonexperts an idea of how the guilty plea system operates and why it is so important. What happens in our courthouses as government officials respond to people accused of committing crimes is of concern to all who value their freedom and their safety. The process of determining guilt and assessing punishment is equally significant as an occasion for ceremonially acting out a community's notion of right and wrong, its sense of justice. It seems useful to examine these procedures, processes, and values at a time when there is particularly deep conflict and widespread uncertainty about them.

The authors' association began a decade ago, when both worked for the President's Commission on Law Enforcement and Administration of Justice (the National Crime Commission). Rosett was an associate director of the Commission, charged with studying the criminal courts, and Cressey was an in-house sociologist reporting on organized crime. That was the start of a dialogue on the administration of justice by rules versus official discretion to act without constraining rules. What seemed the lawyer viewed as necessary flexibility, the sociologist then called an invitation to corruption.

The collaboration continued later at the University of California, where the authors jointly taught advanced criminal procedure courses designed to give UCLA law students some down-to-earth familiarity with how the criminal law operates in courthouses and on the street. Our disagreements continued to reflect our different backgrounds. Rosett's teaching drew upon his experience as a law clerk of the Supreme Court of the United States, an Assistant United States Attorney prosecuting federal crimes, and his familiarity with court opinions, law review articles and other lawyer's literature. Cressey called upon his experience as a researcher in a half dozen prisons, a police department, a probation department, and his wide reading of criminological and sociological theory and research. When we used the language of our respective disciplines, we found that our disagreements often were over terminology rather than substance and that the way lawyers and sociologists are used to talking among themselves frequently interferes with their talking to each other and to the larger community.

Still later, Rosett served for a summer as a Deputy District Attorney in a California prosecutor's office where Cressey was doing some research on discretionary decision making. For the better part of a summer, the sociologist watched the lawyer work and the shared experience led to new appreciation of each other's viewpoints. Cressey, who had some legal training but is not a lawyer, began pressing for the flexibility prosecutors find so essential to justice. Rosett, who had mastered a smattering of sociological principles but is not a social scientist, put more emphasis on the regularities and consistencies so dear to organizational theorists.

Somewhere along the line we began this book. Our ideas have melded to the point where it is hard to tell who first came up with an idea, who refined it and who finally put it in the form it appears in this book. We have tried to avoid the technical jargon of either discipline. As every author knows, it is harder to say something in simple and everyday language than to cover gaps in knowledge with obscure words.

This book is based on our experiences and reading concerning a number of jurisdictions, not on any rigorous study of a single courthouse. A number of good descriptions of particular courthouses have been written in recent years by both lawyers and sociologists. There has also been a steady stream of journalistic exposés of courthouse corruption. Our scholarly brethren have produced many analytical studies of one aspect or another of criminal justice administration. Bibliographic notes at the end of the book indicate the major sources for our statements in the text.

While we have tried to provide a critical framework for understanding the courthouse, this is not a reformer's tract. As will be clear from the last chapter, our final attitude toward the guilty plea system is mixed and we are surer about the folly and futility of some simplistic proposals for reform than we are about a detailed program of our own. However, we do present some ideas about what can be done about those parts of the situation that need to be changed. We think the attainment of a better system will be advanced by straightforward explanation that does not underplay the complexity of the subject.

We owe special thanks to Cherry Trumbull, who contributed significantly to the clarity of early drafts and to Julia Rider who helped to edit the later drafts. We are also deeply grateful to Elliott Studt, David Binder, Elizabeth Rossbacher and Richard De Roy who read and commented on one draft or another and donated their time and intelligence. Fortunately for us, also, Irene Jensen, Miye Narkis and Robert Ponce edited as they typed.

Arthur Rosett
Donald R. Cressey

foreword

Probably every American does something about crime every day of his or her life. Suburban residents lock their dwellings and automobiles against a potential thief. The child locks his school locker for the same reason. The ghetto mother on the way to market conceals her money somewhere in her clothing to thwart the young, fast and perhaps violent robber. We pay millions for theft insurance and billions for policemen, judges, lawyers, jail guards and prison, probation and parole personnel. People in all walks of life live in fear and change their life patterns because of apprehensions about what crime may do to them and to their children. School systems, housing projects and small retail establishments suffer helplessly as crime affects what these institutions endeavor to contribute to our society. And the price we pay for almost any product we buy is somewhat higher because of security costs and property loss suffered by businesses large and small. As with most kinds of social disorder, crime most affects the poor who live in the inner city.

Although the ebbs and flows of criminal activity have plagued America throughout its two hundred years, only recently have the Nation's politicians attempted to expend substantial resources for controlling crime. In 1965, about 4 billion dollars flowed into federal, state and local criminal justice systems. By 1971, this figure had expanded to 10.5 billion and today it probably exceeds 14 billion. The enormous expansion in private industry's investment in security measures, when added to public expenditures, means that we have expanded in the Nation's resource allocation against crime at least fourfold in the past decade.

To no avail, the crime victim would probably say. And those who bring only rhetorical observations to the problem must feel equally frustrated. The crime rate rose in the affluent, "permissive" Sixties, and after a brief decline in the annual increase, the crime rate continues to rise in the "Law and Order," recession-ridden Seventies. This rise continues for both those crimes that citizens fear the most and those that citizens fear the least.

Americans must rightfully want to know what they are receiving for their investment in criminal justice. To be sure, much of the increased investment of the past decade has been consumed by providing criminal justice personnel with better lives. Shorter work schedules, higher salaries and increased pensions have caused dramatic increases in cost with no increase in citizen safety. But every major city probably has increased significantly the number of its policemen and criminal justice courts in the past ten years.

In 1967, a national crime commission stated that "the greatest need is the need to know." The crime problem eludes solution, and fact-finding data collection and policy formulation continue to be influenced by the emotions, rhetoric and varying "hunches" emanating from general social attitudes rather than provable fact. We know that those who repeatedly commit the common, street crimes are probably arrested at least once in their lives, but we do not know who among those persons arrested for the first time will become a repetitive criminal after the first arrest. We know that the young are by far the most crime-prone age group, but only recently have studies commenced to focus upon specific deterrent effects of various law enforcement measures. We know fairly well how many robberies and burglaries are committed each year; but we do not know if there is a separate robber and burglar for each or whether, for example, one man is committing ten robberies per year and another man, five burglaries each year. And even if accurate statistical measurements were available, a sentencing judge has to deal with potential denial of freedom for the individual standing before him. That judge will always have to ponder whether or not a particular defendant represents the same criminal threat as an average defendant.

Knowing so little about deterrence or rehabilitation, those who administer criminal justice, and the citizen and the politician who try to tell them what to do, are seemingly caught in a dilemma where apparently logical solutions are unacceptable. In the 1960s, a wave of liberalism decreed that crime could be cured only by massive social upgrading of deprived communities and reintegration into the community of most adjudicated criminals. For the past seven years, a wave of conservatism has suggested that until we know more about crime, we should at least isolate most street criminals in prison so that they will be unable to prey upon victims. Either philosophy can cloak its pragmatic solutions with the term "justice": justice for the accused versus justice for the victim. Both sides of the debate also know that neither of the proposed ultimate solutions can be implemented without an unforeseeable change in the American value consensus and an improbable reallocation of resources.

The dilemma can be expressed in an oversimplified example. The criminal justice administrator—whether he be policeman, prosecutor, public defender, judge or probation officer—has little time to think about crime in general. He must deal with a particular defendant who allegedly committed a particular crime against a particular victim. In the book you are about to read, the particular defendant is Peter Randolph who is charged with burglary in the first degree. He could be sent back home or be sentenced to prison for five years up to a lifetime. No one knows exactly what harm Randolph intended for his victim and no one knows whether or not Randolph will ever commit a crime again. Even if we knew that Randolph would commit another crime, we would be unlikely to know whether or not that crime would be another burglary, a violent robbery, or a petty larceny. A general public attitude of "lock him up" or "treat him in the community" does nothing to help the prosecutor or the judge in the particular decision they face about this particular individual. How bad was Randolph's conduct, felony-bad or misdemeanor-bad? Do I deter other criminals or protect potential criminal victims by denying Randolph the right to walk freely in his community? If so, how long should I deny him his freedom? Is two months enough? Or is five years necessary?

Protect victims and potential victims, but remember that coercion and imprisonment are the ultimate, not the normal, sanctions in a free society. Society furnishes the stage, but not the script. The actors are given ultimate discretion, no factual basis for making reliable predictions, a command to do "justice," and resources and due process demands that limit the capacity for a trial about the facts of a crime to less than 15 percent of the serious crimes brought to court. Thus, plea bargaining—where the victim and the defendant become invisible spectators. Negotiated results dispose of most criminal cases. The volume of cases grows; the courtroom actors develop their own intimacy and habits; the conflicting demands become oppressive; the decision process in the exercise of discretion is cloaked from public view; and "rules of thumb" necessarily fill the vacuum of knowledge. The disposition of criminal cases becomes a bureaucratic ritual performed by professionals who feel that society has delegated to them a hopeless task. Little wonder that the victim, the defendant and the arresting officer emerge with cynicism and frustration.

There is little doubt that society expects too much from its criminal justice system. When too much deviance from stated social norms is legislated into criminal status, the enforcing system becomes a melting pot, assessing all kinds of alleged asocial conduct. Each criminal justice actor then becomes the self-appointed guardian of majority values. When an administrator cannot possibly achieve the results demanded of him, he can innovate only by setting his own priorities for his broad sweep of responsibilities. Since arrests for robbery and burglary constitute only 6 percent of the total number of arrests, these priorities may or may not help resolve the crime priority set by the city dweller huddling behind a door with five locks on it. And when a prosecutor and judge can decide whether Peter Randolph will face no time in jail or a lifetime in prison, criminal justice discretion can become almost totally subjective and therefore oppressive.

Again with little knowledge for its base, the tide of criminal justice thinking today moves towards totally constricting limitations on the discretion of criminal justice administrators. Proposals abound for mandatory minimum prison sentences for several kinds of serious crimes, abolishment of plea bargaining and required jail sentences of judicially-determined length for a wide range of crimes. These proposals are voiced with solemnity by executive branch leaders and legislators who will not recommend or vote for the billions of dollars necessary for courts and corrections personnel, and for new buildings, to implement them. Indeed, the cry for massive use of prisons persists even as state and city budgets crumble and as judges are being forced to order antiquated, crowded jails and prisons not to accept even one more prisoner until more space is available.

The temptation to seek simple solutions is enormous. Nothing seems more logical than the simple statement that if robbers were confined, they could no longer rob people. Therefore, the obvious solution is to put robbers in prison. What does this mean for the criminal justice system? Persons arrested for robbery might decide to demand a trial, and indeed who would do otherwise if plea bargaining is banned and prison sentences become required? In New York City, if all arrested robbers had to be tried for robbery without any screening by the prosecutor, and if a generous estimate of 50 percent of arrested robbers were convicted and sentenced to a mandatory, five-year prison term, the city would have to double its felony trial courts and devote all of them to robbery trials. In five years, the state would have to quadruple its prison space just for robbery prisoners coming from one-half of its general population. And then more resources would have to be found to bring to trial and imprison all the murderers, burglars, drug offenders, assaulters, embezzlers, business defrauders, corrupt politicians and other felons. Unknown costs would be incurred in building detention centers at $54,000 per cell for those awaiting trial. And no one can tell you how many individuals would be confined in prison for five years even though they would not ever have committed another robbery if returned to their own community without the cost of detention, trial and imprisonment and without the injustice of losing five years of their lives in a five-foot by eight-foot cage.

Nevertheless, would robbery be so substantially reduced by these revolutionary and unforeseeable measures that a great percentage of our population would feel and be safer? Any forecast is merely tentative because we do not know the number of persons in our population who commit robbery and studies of deterrence are only beginning to yield tentative findings. Even with no plea bargaining and with all-inclusive, mandatory five-year prison terms, potential criminals know that a robbery incidence poses only a one-in-four chance of detection (up to one-in-eight if unreported crime is as high as initial figures indicate). How many potential criminals would be deterred by a one-in-four, or one-in-eight chance of detection followed by a one-in-two chance of being convicted? No one can say. We know from one study that 6 percent of all male children born in a given year in a major city had committed by age eighteen, two-thirds of all violent crimes committed by all males born in that city in that year. What we do not know is how to apprehend and imprison that 6 percent early in their criminal careers without also imprisoning a significant percentage of persons who would not otherwise have pursued careers of violent crimes. And even if certainty of some punishment bears a significant direct correlation with the amount of violent crime, regardless of the size of that punishment, new policies and practices will have to be preceded by a resolution of the social, moral and legal judgments about what constitutes "justice."

The rising crime rate of the 1960s and 1970s has spurred, for the first time, extensive, disciplined analyses of these dilemmas and problems. But significant policy implications that should, and no doubt will, flow from these analyses have reached only the debate stage. Meanwhile, as this search for productive change continues, the criminal justice system will continue to have a distressingly unknown effect on the ebbs and flows of America's rate of serious crime. After you read what follows, please remember the dilemmas of the criminal justice system the next time a politician, prosecutor, judge or detached expert tells you the answer to the crime problem.

Henry S. Ruth, Jr.
Director of Criminal Justice Research
Urban Institute
Washington, D.C.
November 1975

contents

chapter one
The troubled courthouse

Americans expect their police departments, courthouses and prisons to demonstrate their opposition to crime and this sense of justice. These demonstrations take many different forms, and the average citizen is not likely to be aware of the inconsistencies among them. On the one hand, most citizens expect open and dispassionate criminal justice procedures. Policemen should be fair and professional. The courthouse should live up to the promise of its marble exterior. It is to be a palace of justice, with no secret closets or hidden corridors. Anyone should be able to walk in and see the rules of law being uniformly applied. Prosecutors and defense lawyers are to be vigorous advocates, but must place above all else their commitment to truth and law. Judges and juries are to wisely and justly apply the law to the particular facts of each case.

But most Americans also know that the courthouse must deal with the brutish and bloody aspects of life. Among the criminals it confronts are cheats, robbers and murderers. This reality leads to a very different set of expectations and demands. Now the public gives allegiance to a crime control system that has force and punishment at its base. Policemen are to be tough, prosecutors

1

relentless and jailers thick-skinned. When seen this way the courthouse is not a majestic palace. It is a harsh and seamy place, sometimes more cruel than just, where guilt is assumed, and men are prodded along from station to station like cattle in a slaughterhouse.

Television and movie dramas about policemen and courthouses draw upon both ways of viewing the matter and weave them into familiar plot lines. A crime is committed. The police throw all their resources into an investigation. Sometimes the investigators are led by a clean-cut, truth-seeking detective; sometimes by his more hard-boiled, tough-cop counterpart; and occasionally by a heavyset, dishonest and overbearing bad apple. Eventually, the team gets its man and uncovers the relevant facts of the case. Then the team of defense lawyers arrives. It may be brilliant and totally dedicated to finding the truth and seeing that it prevails, or it may be led by an unscrupulous lawyer who delays and distorts in order to impede true justice. The defense lawyer encounters the prosecuting attorney in a full-scale courtroom trial. The two opponents engage in ritualized combat, each spending days, or even weeks, persuading a wise judge and an attentive jury of his point of view. The combat may involve devastatingly brilliant reasoning, but this is supplemented either by clever tactics that ensure that the truth comes out, or by misleading, unsavory and dishonest tricks. In the end, however, justice triumphs. Innocent defendants go free and never resent the unjustified accusation. Guilty defendants who have been misunderstood get help. Guilty defendants who have been bad get punished.

The portraits of life in the American courthouse depicted by films and television reflect idealized views that most people have been absorbing since childhood. But rarely are these courthouse images the result of direct experience. Except for those times when he goes downtown to pay a fine for a traffic ticket or to serve jury duty, the average American has few occasions to enter the courthouse's impressive doors. So when he reads about the courthouse deals made by Watergate defendants and others he is likely to be confused, shocked and disappointed. It is likely that a citizen who spent a few days visiting a courthouse would emerge even more confused, shocked and disappointed.

Justice Behind the Scenes

Most people envision the courthouse as a judge-centered operation, typified by the image of a robed judge presiding over a solemn trial by a jury. There is a strongly expressed preference in

2

America for government by law rather than government by men. This is understood to imply that criminal charges shall be resolved by a full public trial conducted according to legal rules. Consequently, most American courthouses look as though the courtrooms were built first, and the corridors, lobbies, staircases, elevators, judges' chambers and washrooms tacked on later. The nation has its share of seedy courtrooms, but most seem designed to stress the dignity and solemnity of the public trial. The raised judge's bench and witness box dominate the room. The flags, the blindfolded lady, the high ceiling, the marble columns and dark wood panelling, the mahogany railing separating the lawyers and trial participants from the spectators—all of these symbols lead us to assume that important work is being done here, that it is being done with dignity, according to law.

But if a visitor stays in the courthouse long enough, he will get a different impression. Eventually, he will notice that part of what contributes to the majesty of the courtroom is its emptiness, its silence. Most courtrooms are vacant and dark during much of the eight-to-five working day. Some are kept dimly lit so that casual visitors—perhaps school children on a field trip—may see the raised bench, the lady with the scales of justice, the flags and other trappings. Even when the courtrooms are occupied, as they are likely to be during the midmorning rush, they are not likely to be used for trials, but rather for dealing with relatively unimportant segments of the administrative process that decides cases.

Casual courthouse observation would reveal that few trials are held nowadays, and that those few are usually conducted by a judge sitting alone, without a jury. Lengthier courthouse visits would show that judges tend to stay in the background, that defense lawyers and prosecutors only rarely get into arguments about guilt or innocence and that most cases are processed on a bureaucratic assembly line. Justice is pursued behind the scenes by professionals—policemen, prosecutors, defense attorneys, probation officers and others—who do their work and make their decisions in a closed, private system.

The citizen who manages to enter this private system will find a distressing situation. The traditional legal forms and symbols are retained, and the written values are professed, but they seem to be infrequently applied. Men charged with crimes carrying heavy punishment are treated as if they have committed only minor offenses carrying light penalties. A known rapist or mugger may plead guilty to simple assault, an armed robber to petty theft, a car thief to unauthorized use of a motor vehicle. Justice seems to be bought on the cheap.

3

The results seem only accidentally connected with what crime a particular offender has committed, what the penal codes say shall be the description of and the punishment for particular behavior, or what society thinks should be done with people who engage in threatening acts. Tactical considerations appear to dominate; prosecutors and defense attorneys dismiss or reduce charges and agree upon sentences, at times without ever consulting the accused. They rarely expect to try a case and appear willing to strike any bargain that will allow them to avoid trial. The confusion and the opportunity for manipulation seem to favor the hardened and sophisticated offender who knows how to take advantage of them, while the naive offender, relatively deserving of mercy, appears more likely to get caught in the gears of the machine. The system seems to show greatest harshness to the least powerful—the poor, the black, the young.

Selective Justice

American criminal justice is a highly selective process. Many persons are brought to it charged with crime, but only a few of them are chosen for severe punishment. Most of the others receive little or no punishment, although their crimes appear indistinguishable from those who are punished harshly. For every one hundred adults arrested on felony charges, fewer than three are sent to prison. The selective process begins when policemen decide—on the street and in the stationhouse—whether to investigate a reported crime, whether to arrest a suspect and what name should be given to the crime the suspect has allegedly committed. It continues as prosecutors decide which, if any, crime a suspect should be charged with and whether to accept a guilty plea. Selection also occurs in judges' sentencing choices, usually made on the recommendation of a probation officer.

Discretionary Justice

The full courtroom trial is rigidly governed by rules of law stating what evidence may be received, how each of the officials shall act, and even specifying what the judge is permitted to say to the jury to help it determine the facts. In practice most official decisions are not strictly governed by a rule of law. Instead, the official is free to act as he sees fit.[1] Less formal decisions are discretionary in the sense that the official who makes them can choose whether to act and often how to act in a given case. Such freedom of choice may arise from an explicit delegation of legal authority to the official—he is instructed to act as he thinks best, within broad limits. It also may exist because there is no rule concerning the action, or because the official asserts power to act despite a rule which should inhibit him.

The behind-the-scenes courthouse visitor will find that cases are not processed by the rules he has learned to expect, whether those rules be high-minded principles of justice, tough-minded slogans about getting the bad guys before they get you or illegal mandates dictated by corrupt politicians. Cases are not tried or even decided; they are settled or compromised. The system, dominated by discretionary decisions, is designed primarily to convince defendants to plead guilty.

Justice by Guilty Plea

Most citizens have had some experience with the guilty plea, perhaps from appearing in court in response to a traffic ticket. Everyone knows the coercive inconvenience of pleading not guilty rather than guilty even to a minor traffic violation—the lines are longer, another trip to the courthouse is necessary, the procedures are more complex. It is easier to plead guilty, pay ten dollars, and go home. A few years ago all America watched as the vice president of the United States pleaded *nolo contendere* (largely equivalent to a guilty plea) to minor charges of income tax evasion rather than standing trial on a more serious set of charges. Once he pleaded guilty, he was allowed to pay a fine of ten thousand dollars and go home.[2]

Whether the behind-the-scenes observer is a liberal or a conservative, a do-gooder or a law-and-order hard-liner, he is likely to be troubled by the guilty plea and the discretionary practices it exemplifies. Decisions should reflect policy, not the exercise of capricious whim. There should be equal justice under law, not haphazard and arbitrary punishment of the weak. There should be no browbeating of the guilty, not to mention the innocent. Guilty plea procedures seem capricious and unjust, and an explanation that the ordinary citizen can understand and accept has not been provided.

Perhaps it is the absence of understandable explanations of guilty plea practices that has led to current uneasiness about what is happening in American courthouses. Perhaps it is also a lack of understanding that has precipitated sweeping calls for the abolition of discretionary guilty plea practices:

—In 1971, the Nixon administration established the National Advisory Commission on Criminal Justice Standards and Goals. This group was asked to recommend to the federal government ways of waging war on crime. More specifically, it was to suggest the kinds of projects and reforms on which the states were to spend the more than one billion dollars a year in federal anticrime grants that Congress had voted. After two years of study and deliberations, the Commission published its standards and goals. These were quickly embraced as policy by the national administration. The Commission claimed that its recommendation with respect to guilty plea negotiations, formulated at the last minute, was the most far-reaching of the more than one hundred recommendations it had made concerning court procedures, although the Commission discussion of it is only slightly more than three pages long.[3] This recommendation calls for the total abolition of guilty plea negotiations by 1978.

—In 1973, at the urging of Governor Nelson Rockefeller, the New York Legislature acted in concert with the Nixon Commission's recommendation and passed laws to punish narcotic drug offenders more severely.[4] One law is designed to prevent defendants from avoiding the harsh penalties stipulated for narcotics violators in other laws. It prohibits judges and prosecutors from accepting guilty pleas to reduced charges, thus letting drug offenders off lightly. For example, a man charged with selling drugs (heavily punished) shall not be permitted to plead guilty to possession of drugs or drug use (lightly punished). In July of 1975 the New York State Legislature substantially amended and effectively repealed the major provisions of the Rockefeller scheme.

—In July of 1975, President Gerald R. Ford sent a special crime message to Congress. This message called for the reduction of judges' sentencing discretion and mandatory laws requiring prison sentences for various offenses and offenders. The message did not explicitly endorse the Nixon Commission proposal for the total abolition of plea bargaining but is consistent with it.

—Early in 1974, the late District Attorney Joseph Busch of Los Angeles County, who headed the largest prosecutor's office in the nation, announced new guidelines for substantially limiting arranged pleas.[5] Under these guidelines, one form of guilty plea negotiation is abolished. Defendants are no longer permitted to exchange a guilty plea for an understanding as to the sentence they will receive. The objective was to reduce the disparities in punishments ordered by the various courts in Busch's rather far-flung bailiwick.

—In August 1974, the Supreme Court of the United States published a number of amendments to the Federal Rules of Criminal Procedure.[6] One pertains to guilty plea procedures. It is "designed to give recognition to the propriety of plea discussions, to bring the existence of a plea agreement out into the open in court, and to provide a method for court acceptance or rejection of a plea agreement." These new rules, which are similar to those recently adopted in some states, will apply to all criminal cases in the federal courts.

Our principal objective is to show that the first three proposals, and the versions of them that are proliferating in cities and counties across the country, are unrealistic and likely to reduce rather than improve the quality of justice. Guilty plea negotiations are negotiations about proper punishment, and our objective, stated positively, is to suggest how these negotiations may be improved. The last two proposals face in this direction, but we shall offer compelling reasons why they are unlikely to attain their stated goals in the absence of additional substantial reforms.

Abolishing the negotiated guilty plea in America would be disastrous. Plea negotiation is the central technique for settling cases in American courthouses. Without it, policemen, prosecutors, judges, defenders and probation officers would be unable to perform their crucial duty—to do justice.

One reason why there are so few trials in the courthouse is that Americans who favor government by law also favor government by men. They want strict rules that will restrain oppressors and bigots, but they also want flexible rules that will enable sensible officials to soften harsh laws in individual cases. Further, Americans want full trials, but they also want low taxes—they expect courthouse workers to compromise, to save money by developing procedures that are less costly than trials. For reasons of both justice and economy, then, most of the handcuffed suspects who enter the courthouse are persuaded not to exercise their right to be tried. The majority who are convicted are persuaded to plead guilty. Plea negotiation is the visible symbol of a discretionary system which serves important social goals. Prohibiting it by law, as the New York State Legislature did in drug cases, and as President Ford proposed in his crime message, merely evades the difficult question of why it is so prevalent and how it can be improved. When the New York State Legislature recognized this it substantially modified the Rockefeller laws relating to narcotics.

We share the critics' distaste for the devious and underhanded dealings that go on in guilty plea negotiations. We believe that

7

many current practices are unacceptable and should be changed. We favor a system of justice more impartial than current plea-negotiating procedures allow. We want to prevent the travesty of the guilty escaping punishment for high crimes, as they now do by means of the plea-negotiating process. More generally, we want better procedures for ensuring that the punishment fits the crime. All informed Americans want these things. But before they can frame and bring sensible reforms into being, they must have a clear sense of what must be changed. Much more than mere "plea bargaining" is at stake.

We will try to describe what we have observed taking place in courthouses, explain it and in some cases justify it. Our discussion moves back and forth between the specifics of the guilty plea and the more general concern for official discretion in the criminal justice system. We have invented fictitious characters whose careers closely resemble those of people we know. Our aim is to provide different perspectives on the same experience, the prosecution in a state court of a routine burglary charge. The process looks different to each of the participants—the accused, the judge, the prosecutor and the defense lawyer—because each stands in a very different pair of shoes. The descriptions also vary from chapter to chapter because, inevitably, there are important differences between what an outsider thinks courthouse people do, what courthouse people think and say they do, and what, in fact, they do.

The complexity of the significant values, interests and perspectives is a major barrier to understanding the courthouse process. First, it is essential to become familiar with the basic sequence in the prosecution of a criminal case in a state court. This process varies somewhat from state to state and in the following chapter we present a typical example. Courthouse professionals usually see only a segment of this process; only the defendant sees it whole, and so it is his perspective that we take in Chapter 2.

Next, in Chapter 3, we examine the courtroom itself, which reflects the accumulation over centuries of legal ideas that shape the process we propose to examine. In Chapter 4 we discuss the most central of these ideas—the concept of justice—the most important value that the courthouse seeks to embody. We view justice from the special perspective of the judge, not because he is the only courthouse official concerned with justice, but because traditionally he is seen as its guardian.

At this point our examination of discretion and the guilty plea must go beyond familiar issues of legal process and justice values to include other important perspectives. In Chapter 5 we suggest that the courthouse is a special community, a subculture, with values and attitudes distinct from the larger community. We explore the importance of this special community to the operation and function of the guilty plea system. These forms and procedures are viewed from the perspective of the prosecutor, an official specifically charged with exercising his discretionary powers in ways that are responsive both to the larger and the special courthouse communities. In Chapter 6 we focus on the impact of courthouse organization on the operation of discretion and the guilty plea. Organization reflects and influences the goals and methods of courthouse work and is the source of demands upon officials which are met by the discretionary system of justice. Courthouse organization is examined from the viewpoint of a public defender.

In Chapter 7 we focus on two political dimensions of the problem: the extent to which the guilty plea system meets deeply rooted needs for the acquiescence of the criminal as a precondition to punishment, and the relation between the need to escape from the written law by means of discretion and the unjustified severity of the penal law.

These last four conditions, subcultural influence, organizational pressures, the need for acquiescence and the avoidance of severity limit the possibilities for simple reform or abolition of the guilty plea. In the final chapter we suggest what might be involved in changing the system. This task remains what it has always been: the continuous struggle to give justice meaning, not in some abstract definition, but in the daily activity of making decisions about guilt and appropriate punishment.

chapter two
The odyssey of
Peter Randolph

Arrest is not a rare event in America. Each year there is one arrest on a nontraffic criminal charge for every eight adults in the arrest-prone ages between eighteen and thirty-nine. Of course, a small number of people are arrested a large number of times, but the statistical likelihood that an American male will be arrested sometime during his life is very high, particularly if he lives in a city and is a member of an ethnic minority. Most individuals arrested are young men; more than half are under age twenty-four. Specifically, fifteen- and sixteen-year-olds account for the largest number of the most serious class of arrests; but in most jurisdictions criminals under age eighteen are treated as juveniles, and are processed differently than adults.[1]

Millions of the arrests made each year are not for serious crimes. Most are related to drinking: public drunkenness, disturbing the peace, disorderly conduct. Others grow out of family and social fights. Many are made on petty theft or shoplifting charges. The most serious crimes are called felonies, a classification that includes all offenses which carry one year or more in prison as possible punishment. In California about 90 percent of those arrested for a felony are charged with offenses in one of five broad groups: drug offenses make up about 40 percent; burglary about 15 percent; robbery 6 percent; assault 10 percent; and other property offenses (thefts, embezzlement, forgery and fraud) 20 percent.[2]

One can find every type of person among those who are led into the police station in handcuffs, although as might be expected, there is a disproportionately high number of the poor, the jobless, the disadvantaged, blacks, Mexican-Americans, problem drinkers and drug abusers. A large number of those arrested for criminal behavior abuse alcohol, drugs, or both. Peter Randolph's case is typical.

During the early morning hours of August 3, Gus Simmons was awakened by the noise of someone moving things around in the garage attached to his house. Then he heard the scratchy noise of someone prying at the latch on the kitchen door. Simmons reached for the bedside telephone and dialed the police.

When, a few minutes later, two young police officers entered the garage with drawn guns, Peter Randolph, age twenty-one, was still clumsily at work trying to pry open the kitchen door. The policemen handcuffed and arrested him, advised him of his rights and took him to the stationhouse. There he was booked on the charge of burglary in the first degree. This meant that he was accused of unlawfully entering an occupied dwelling at night with intent to steal, a serious offense carrying punishment of five years to life in the state prison.

During the period between arrest and the beginning of the court process in such cases, an administrative official screens the serious criminal charges made against the defendant. In many cities, this official may be a senior police officer, an assistant district attorney or a judge. In some communities there is a sequence of reviews of each case involving both police and prosecutorial officials.

Screening is necessary because it is not always certain that the events reported to police patrolmen by citizens and to senior police officers by patrolmen constitute a crime. For example, a policeman arrested a middle-aged lady on a store owner's complaint that she had walked out of the store without paying for the shoes she was carrying. He charged her with petty theft. The stationhouse watch officer listened to the report. He also listened to the woman's claim that she had become confused and excited when she could not find her wallet in her purse and had rushed out to the parking lot to find it, forgetting that she was carrying the shoe box. The watch officer decided the matter was "a misunderstanding" and released the woman. Perhaps he made his decision because the legal evidence was not clear, because the store owner did not press his complaint once the shoes were returned, or because the woman appeared respectable and had no history of prior theft. Perhaps the whole incident seemed too minor to make a case of.

When Peter Randolph was taken into the police station immediately after his arrest, he stood confused and frightened, listening to the arresting officers describe his case to their watch commander. The commander glanced at Randolph a couple of times but never spoke to him. He just listened impassively to the policemen's oral report and ordered Randolph booked on burglary in the first degree and put in a stationhouse cell pending transportation to the jail.

When the station detective arrived later in the morning, he found on his desk a roughly typed arrest report prepared by the two officers. This two-page document included a checklist of the elements of the crime—unlawful trespass, occupied dwelling, nighttime, intent to steal—followed by a brief personal history given by Randolph, the officers' observations at the scene and a narrative of what Gus Simmons had told them. Also included was a short inventory of the power tools and other property which the officers had found piled outside the entrance of the garage, and photographs of the pry marks and scratches on the kitchen door. There was a property receipt which noted that when arrested Randolph was carrying on his person $2.35, a billfold, a bottle of wine and a one-inch wood chisel. On top of the pile of papers was an index card indicating that Randolph had twice been detained, counselled and released while a juvenile, once for breaking windows and another time for being drunk at school. At age eighteen he had been put on probation for joyriding with friends in a car that did not belong to them. The detective picked up the papers and ordered Randolph checked out of the jail and transported to the courthouse. There the detective locked him in another holding cell and went upstairs to the district attorney's office.

Most of three or four thousand district attorneys' offices in the United States are one- or two-man operations. But the bulk of the nation's criminal business is handled by a few large offices in big cities. In a large office, a single assistant district attorney is likely to act as complaint assistant, although this duty may be rotated periodically among different attorneys, and everyone may be expected to help during busy periods. The complaint assistant is likely to be a young lawyer, out of law school a few years. It is his job to review the case to decide whether the evidence is adequate and the offense is serious enough to justify prosecution. He also decides, on the basis of the accused's personal circumstances and record, whether the accused deserves light or severe punishment.

In many jurisdictions well over one half of all felony arrests are likely to be screened out very early in the process and either dismissed outright or filed as less serious misdemeanor charges.[3] In time, the complaint assistant learns what kinds of cases the judges tend to throw out, which ones his boss and colleagues want vigorously prosecuted, and which are likely to become headaches if accepted for prosecution. He is also likely to be sensitive to the attitudes of the police, his major client. He develops an intuitive feel for which cases the department wants pressed and which ones it does not really care about. He also learns the technique of authorizing an inflated charge in the hope of gaining a conviction later by reducing the charge in exchange for a guilty plea.

Randolph's case looked like a good one to the complaint assistant. It contained the elements of a serious crime, strong evidence, the report of a good witness and professional police handling of the matter. The police detective had no quarrel with the prosecutor's decision to file a complaint charging Randolph with burglary of a dwelling at night. Neither he nor the complaint assistant was sure that Randolph should get a five-to-life prison term. However, it seemed to both of them that the documents on the desk made the case look like first-degree burglary. If the punishment seemed too severe later when more was learned about Randolph, the charge could be reduced or dismissed.

The Initial Court Appearance

Between 10:00 A.M. and 11:00 A.M. the next day, Randolph, dressed in a pair of garish orange jail overalls, found himself, along with several other recently arrested men, in a big cell-like room behind a courtroom waiting to make his initial court appearance. Through the half-opened door he could see the remnants of the morning's court business, mostly traffic violators paying their fines.

When court recessed, Randolph and the other men were manacled together and ushered to seats in the rows of chairs lining the jury box. These prisoners were accused of felonies, and they rose and then sat silently as a judge came in to give them their first hearings. But they had to sit patiently, in bored silence, while the

14

judge first went through the calendar list of other defendants who, dressed in street clothing and accompanied by friends and relatives, had replaced the traffic violators in the seats reserved for the public. These men also had been charged with felonies, but they were the lucky ones who had raised bail money.

The criminal court judge has power to set the amount of bail at first appearance. In some cities, including Randolph's, the fixing of bail has become so routine that the police accept bail at the stationhouse, using a schedule which lists the amount of bail required of anyone charged with a particular offense. For example, a person charged with burglary may be released if he posts two thousand dollars bail, while a person charged with assault can be released for one thousand dollars bail. Few arrested persons are able to deposit two thousand dollars with the police sergeant, but some can afford to pay a bail bondsman his premium, which is likely to run from one hundred to two hundred dollars on a two thousand dollar bond. The bondsman figuratively deposits the two thousand dollars with the police in the form of a surety bond, a legal promise to pay that amount if the suspect does not appear in court.[4] Like most defendants, the prisoners who sat in the jury box with Peter Randolph were unable to raise either the necessary bail, or the 10 percent bondsman's premium.

Eventually, Randolph's name was called. The burglary in the first degree charge was read to him, a public defender was assigned to serve as his attorney and bail was fixed at one thousand dollars, a sum Randolph could not hope to raise. A preliminary hearing was scheduled for several days later. It all took ninety seconds. Randolph, unable to pay for freedom, was sent back to jail.

As he sat with the other prisoners and waited to be transported back to jail, Randolph had his first chance to speak to his assigned lawyer.[5] As the proceedings in other cases droned on, the lawyer came over, took a seat in the row in front of Randolph, squirmed around and whispered the tired introduction he used a dozen times a day.

"My name is Vincent Long. I am a lawyer, a public defender. I am a criminal law specialist. I am a winner. I want you to know that I fight like hell to win. I don't care if you killed your grandmother, I'm going to fight for you if that's what you want me to do.

"You've probably heard a lot of talk about deals around here. Well, I don't make deals. I don't cop anybody out. If the DA offers a deal, I'll pass it along to you. It's your deal, and you can take it or leave it.

"You control this case. This is your file. You can read anything in here; there are no secrets. You make the decisions.

"One more thing. I can't help you unless you play it straight with me. I don't care what you did, but I've got to know all the facts. If you try to con me, you haven't got a chance. Any questions?"

"Well, no," said Randolph. "See, sometimes I don't know what I do. I was drunk, you know, but—well I wasn't drunk but I had some wine in me. I just went in there. It seemed like a pretty good idea at the time. Sometimes I drink just to think, you know. I would like to do the best I can; I wish I can be somebody. I was sitting in the park drinking this wine and thinking like that, you know, and then I said to myself, 'Oh piss on all that,' and I went for a walk. I saw this garage, and I just went in there. It was more or less on the spur of the moment, I don't know. . . ."

As Randolph spoke, several people nearby turned their heads. The court clerk looked up from his pile of papers and glanced reprovingly at Long.

Long interrupted Randolph by putting his finger to his lips. "Shh. Not so loud. We can't get into that now. Just let me get some background information on you."

Long then recited a list of general questions concerning where Randolph lived, what he did for a living, and whether he had a criminal record. Randolph, having been through similar lists a dozen times, answered politely and routinely. Then Long handed Randolph a copy of the complaint.

"Why don't you start by telling me where this place was that you broke into?"

"I don't know for sure," answered Randolph. "I think it was on 13th Street or around there some place."

"What were you going after?"

"I don't know, whatever there was, so I could get a little cash."

"Was anyone with you?"

"No, I was by myself."

"Were you drunk?"

"No. Like I said, I had some wine in me, but I wasn't drunk or anything like that. When I do this kind of thing I say to myself, 'Why did I do this for?' I don't like to do it. I say to myself, 'I wish I wasn't this kind of person I am. I want to. . . .'"

Long interrupted again. "Look, I've got to go. If anything comes up, I'll contact you, OK? But I'm not going to come to the jail and hold your hand. You follow me? Your preliminary hearing will be in five days. If you are bound over we will have an arraignment in a couple of weeks; I'll see you then."

Then Long launched into his "close out speech," as he named it when he first memorized it. "If I don't see you at the preliminary hearing, it means I am in a trial defending someone else. I handle dozens of cases at a time. I'm busy. I might not see much of you, but that does not mean I'm not working on your case. If another public defender comes to see you, it will be because I sent him. I'll tell him all about you. But when it comes down to trial, I'll be there. Don't worry about that. I'll put all I've got into it. Understand? Don't worry. OK?"

Without waiting for a response, Long got up and left the courtroom. His tone and patter reminded Randolph of all the teachers, social workers, hospital workers and missionaries who had lectured him about one thing or another over the years. He began to wonder about himself, wishing he had a drink, and he pictured himself back in the park. His daydreaming was shattered by the prisoner chained to his left wrist.

"You got a asshole," he said. "That guy's just a messenger boy for the DA."

The Preliminary Hearing

The preliminary hearing process tests whether there is enough evidence against the accused to justify holding him for trial.[6] It provides a look at the prosecution's case which often persuades the prosecutor or the judge to dismiss a weak case, or the defendant to plead guilty to a strong one. It enables the defense lawyer to cross-examine prosecution witnesses and to prepare intelligently for trial in contested cases.

The precise form and content of the preliminary hearing vary from place to place, but the central issue is always whether there is cause to hold the suspect for trial rather than whether he is guilty or innocent. However, evidence of guilt is significant, because before a court orders that a suspect be held to face trial and his freedom be restricted, it must have sufficient evidence that he has committed an offense. Most people assume that the police have inherent power to arrest and jail, but this power is limited to confinement only long enough to bring the accused before a judge for a hearing. The decision to confine for a prolonged period pending trial must be made by an independent judicial officer, not by a policeman.

In a number of states and in many federal courts, the preliminary hearing has virtually disappeared. In these courts, defendants charged with felonies are encouraged to waive their rights to preliminary hearings in return for a reduction in the charges or the amount of bail. But in other states, the preliminary hearing remains an important stage of the process because it provides the setting for assessments and negotiations which often lead to the reduction of charges, and ultimately, either to dismissal of the charge or to the guilty plea.

Preliminary hearings on serious charges usually are held in a lower court by a judge who is authorized to dismiss cases or to order the arrested person to be held for trial at a later date.[7] A trial is then scheduled to be held in a different and superior court, presided over by a different judge. Substantial numbers of cases are dismissed at the preliminary hearing, some because the complaining witnesses do not appear, some because the judge decides that the police evidence is legally insufficient or was obtained by unconstitutional methods.

Standards of proof and persuasion become more exacting at each successive stage of the criminal justice process. The policeman in the street must act on the spot, so the law requires only that he have reason to believe that a crime has been committed and that the accused is the person who committed it. The judge at the preliminary hearing, however, must be more exacting. He adheres to a standard that requires more substantial evidence. If the accused is ordered to stand trial and is tried, his guilt must be proved beyond a reasonable doubt. It is not surprising, therefore, that in many cases there is adequate evidence for a policeman to arrest, but not for a lower court judge to bind over for trial.

But factors other than the technical quality of the evidence also influence judges holding preliminary hearings. These factors cannot be given legalistic labels. For example, on the morning of Peter Randolph's preliminary hearing, the judge dismissed an armed robbery charge against an old man who had stumbled drunkenly around a liquor store demanding a bottle of whiskey and waving a toy pistol over his head. Clearly the evidence contained all the legal elements defining the crime of robbery. Nevertheless, the judge ordered the man released. The judge did not give explicit reasons for dismissing the charge, but he obviously did not consider the incident serious enough to justify the potential expense of a trial to the state and to the defendant. He also was impressed by the prosecutor's lack of enthusiasm, as well as by the complaining witnesses's apparent amusement now that the episode was over. In most courthouses, such cases are called "cheap"—a cheap robbery, a cheap burglary and so on.

At the preliminary hearing, the prosecutor plays a vital role in the final decision as to whether or not a case should move to the superior court.[8] He, like the judge and the stationhouse watch officer, has broad discretionary powers. As he studies a case ordered to trial on the basis of a preliminary hearing, he might, like the judge on the toy pistol case, decide that it is not serious enough to justify full felony treatment. He is authorized to let the case drop at that point and allow the accused to go home a free man, and he might do so. It is more likely that he will file a lesser charge, perhaps a misdemeanor charge such as disorderly conduct, disturbing the peace or trespassing. Or, if the accused is charged with several felonies, the prosecutor may exercise his discretion and not file the most serious charges. Further, even when a judge decides at a preliminary hearing that there is not enough evidence to proceed with felony charges, the prosecution may file misdemeanor charges.

On the day set for Peter Randolph's preliminary hearing, five days after his initial appearance, he was again moved from the jail to the courthouse. Another public defender was in court instead of Vincent Long. Randolph watched this lawyer glance over his file. The lawyer then asked Randolph one or two questions about his arrest and told him to sit next to him at one of the long counsel tables that faced the judge's bench.

The preliminary hearing in the case of *People* v. *Randolph* was quick and clean-cut, consisting of testimony by Gus Simmons and one of the arresting officers. The public defender asked a few questions, but made no great effort to bring out Randolph's side of the story. The judge and the prosecutor also ignored Randolph. But within one-half hour he found himself bound over for trial in felony court.

The Formal Accusation

Until completion or waiver of the preliminary hearing, a criminal case is based on a complaint, a brief written statement of charges sworn to by a policeman or complaining witness. Minor misdemeanor charges are usually tried and disposed of on the complaint—the suspect is brought to court, pleads guilty or has a short trial, and the case is closed. Felony cases are more formal. A precise statement of the charge must be filed with the superior court. This may be done either in the form of a grand jury indictment or in an information containing a precise statement of the charges filed by the prosecutor.[9]

The indictment or information presented to the trial court sets forth in a separate count each of the offenses the defendant is accused of. Theoretically, he may be separately punished on each count. Occasionally a newspaper story tells of an accusation carrying potential punishment of one hundred years or more in prison. For example, if the penal code specifies that embezzlement shall be punished by five years in prison, and a company bookkeeper alters the books and takes money on twenty different occasions, he could be sentenced to imprisonment for one hundred years. But this potential is rarely, if ever, realized, and the embezzler is likely to be sentenced to five years at the most. Many counts will be dropped by the prosecutor or judge. Moreover, in most cases the judge will impose concurrent sentences, even if the defendant is found guilty on all counts, and the punishments merge into the longest term imposed.

In Peter Randolph's case, an assistant district attorney filed an information specifically accusing him of three crimes: one count of burglary in the first degree (occupied dwelling at night), which carries a penalty of imprisonment for from five years to life; one count of simple burglary (any building any time), which carries a lesser punishment; and one count of grand theft, which is also a felony. By law, an information also automatically contains charges of all lesser included offenses in the specified charges. For example, Randolph's burglary charges implied misdemeanor charges of unlawful entry because it is impossible to commit burglary without entering unlawfully. The burglary charges also included misdemeanor charges of trespassing—it is impossible to burglarize without trespassing. For that matter, it is impossible to enter unlawfully without trespassing. The grand theft charge automatically accused Randolph of misdemeanor petty theft as well—it is impossible to steal a lot (grand) without inevitably stealing a little (petty).

The rules governing the wording of felony accusations are very technical and legalistic, particularly those for indictments, in which even a misplaced comma can be a prosecutor's undoing. The technicalities have developed over the years as lawyers have found loopholes in formal accusations and other lawyers have closed them. They reflect a constitutional concern that the accused have precise and definite notice of the charges against him. He must be told exactly what it is that he must defend himself against.

On the other hand, the automatic inclusion of lesser offenses reflects administrative interests. Permitting inclusion of misdemeanor charges enables a prosecutor to say, "If I can't get him on the formal charge, I'll get him on something else." Or, "If I formally charge him with a felony or two, maybe he'll plead guilty to a misdemeanor." Further, the rules encourage prosecutors to play it safe, saying, "I really don't know whether to charge him with a serious crime or a minor one, so I'll hit him with the serious one and wait for developments."

It is nearly impossible to determine which of these concerns, if any, a prosecutor has in mind when he files an information. Is he merely trying technically to make the accusation fit the evidence? Is he using the accusation of serious crime as a bludgeon for persuading the defendant to plead guilty to a lesser charge? Is he looking for justice, hoping that later he will be better able to match the punishment to the criminal and his behavior?

The prosecutor filing the information in the Peter Randolph case knew that his three accusations were technically proper. He also suspected that they were mere window dressing. He was not convinced that Randolph was dangerous enough to be sent to prison for a minimum of five years or a maximum of life. He knew that the serious accusations might push Randolph into pleading guilty to one or more of the misdemeanor charges, but he did not believe that he was overcharging Randolph to the point of terrorizing him into a confession of guilt. Randolph was no pillar of the community, but he did not seem all that bad either. It appeared as if Randolph should go to a misdemeanor court, plead guilty and receive a short jail sentence. Perhaps the case should have been dismissed at postarrest screening—the whole episode was extremely amateurish and no actual harm was done.

The prosecutor decided to look for conviction on one of the lesser included counts silently charged in the information. However, he still did not have enough information to make a final decision. Randolph had been fingerprinted at the police station when he was arrested, but the full report on his criminal record based on these fingerprints had not yet arrived. The detectives on the burglary detail were following up on the Randolph case, but it would take a while to link him with any other burglaries. It was possible that Randolph was an experienced criminal; more likely he was just what he appeared to be.

The Uses of Delay

Once the formal charge is filed, time is a major weapon used by both sides to bring about the settlement of cases without trial. The defendant frequently gets caught in the middle. Time runs against the prosecutor and the judge. Both work for organizations which demand that the steady flow of incoming cases be kept moving. As cases grow old, the administrative pressures to dispose of them increase, even if this must be done at a discount. As time passes, it becomes more difficult to make witnesses appear, and trials of stale cases based on hazy memories are hazardous for prosecutors because they are less likely to end in conviction. Public defenders are under comparable organizational pressures to move their cases, to dispose of them before they become "old dogs."

Curiously enough, the outcome of these time pressures is delay.[10] Defendants are shunted aside for weeks while lawyers try to take up the opposition's time. A defense lawyer whose client is free on bail is able to manipulate time pressures to keep his client free. Typically he does this by pleading the client not guilty, by pretending that he is going to trial, or by creating scheduling problems and trial preparation burdens which cut into the time budget of the prosecutor. A number of the less reputable members of the private criminal defense bar are retained by their clients more for their known ability to "buy time on the street," to keep their clients free on bail, than for their prowess in the courtroom. Some defense lawyers use ingenious technical stalls, even when there is no hope of acquittal, because they know old cases are settled more cheaply than fresh ones.

But a man in jail awaiting trial is stuck, punished by each day of delay. His suffering is used by prosecutors to pressure him into pleading guilty. Statistical studies have shown that the detained defendant is more likely to plead guilty as the time spent in jail awaiting trial increases.[11] If he stays in jail for six months or a year, which is not unusual, a judge is likely to sentence him to "time served" if he pleads guilty to a minor crime like unlawful entry. He goes home free. But if he insists on his right to be tried, he lies in jail until the prosecutor and court find time to try him.[12]

Arraignment

Three weeks after his arrest, Peter Randolph appeared in court for arraignment on the information filed against him. Arraignment is a ritualistic procedure seemingly based on the assumption that defendants and their attorneys cannot read. The charges contained in the indictment or information are read aloud, and the defendant is asked to plead guilty or not guilty. That is it.

In the three weeks following his arrest, Randolph's mood and position had changed substantially. He had lost his job; his landlord had evicted him from his rooming house and seized his personal possessions; and life in the jail had been grim. The jail was old, overcrowded and dirty, and it smelled. As an unsentenced prisoner, Randolph had been at the bottom of the stack, subject to maximum-security regulations with his freedom extremely limited. He had been kept in a cell around the clock except for a short break at meals and one hour's exercise each day. As there was no work or school or recreation hall, he had had nothing to do except to sit with his cellmates. His aunt had come to see him once, but she had not returned. She had been both angered and saddened by the arrangements for visiting—a thick screen separating her from Randolph through which she had had to yell to make herself heard. Her job as a waitress had made it impossible for her to come to the jail frequently during the posted visiting hours (2:00 P.M. to 4:00 P.M. daily except Saturdays, Sundays and holidays). As a result, Randolph was lonely. Moreover, he was frightened. Tough convicts who know their way around run most jails. Within the social system of the jail Randolph was in the lowest class, controlled not only by the guards, but also by convicted and experienced prisoners.[13]

When Randolph reached the courtroom for his arraignment, a man he had not seen before introduced himself as a public defender. Randolph did not catch his name. He asked about Mr. Long, but the lawyer just shrugged. Then he said that he supposed Randolph was going to plead not guilty. Randolph, bewildered, said, "Well, they tell me I never knew what I was doing, so . . . ." The defender interrupted, "OK. We'll plead not guilty, and I'll see what I can do." He walked away and took a seat at the defense attorneys' table.

When Randolph's name was called, the lawyer motioned him to come forward and stand before the bench. In a singsong voice, the court clerk recited the charges and asked Randolph to respond by pleading guilty or not guilty. He pleaded not guilty as instructed. After consulting a calendar for a few seconds, the judge announced that the case was assigned to Judge Perkins for trial. A few days later Randolph was brought to another courtroom where the judge called his case and announced that trial would begin in one month.

Offer and Acceptance

Shortly before the date set for trial, the jailhouse public address system ordered Randolph to report to "the lawyers' room," a crowded place with four desks at which attorneys conferred with their clients. When Randolph entered the room he expected to see Vincent Long. Instead, he met Steven Ohler, the public defender who had been present at the arraignment and trial setting, and who either assumed that Randolph knew his name, or did not care. Without wasting time, the defender said, "Look. I've talked to the DA and he seems willing to drop the felonies if you'll cop to unlawful entry."

"What is it?" asked Randolph. "What'll happen?"

"If you'll plead guilty to going into the house, they'll take it easy on you. The DA will ask the judge to let you off for the sixty days you have already served, plus probation. You go home. You can insist on a trial if you want to, but that'll keep you here longer."

"Can I trust him?"

"Trust me. I advise you to plead. What could you say to a jury? You wouldn't have a chance. Five to life is a long time."

Randolph knew he was guilty of something—breaking into an occupied dwelling, walking into an unoccupied garage at night, trying to steal some tools, or wandering around drunk and up to no good when he should have been home. But he was not sure just what he was guilty of. And as time had passed it made less and less difference to him. He was quite shaken by the threat implicit in the defender's advice. He had been thoroughly worn down by his experience in jail. His cellmates had told him many stories about what went on in the courthouse, and he now saw that the prosecutor's offer was a pretty good deal. Randolph agreed to take it.

The Ceremony of Justice

Early in the afternoon of the day set for trial, Randolph was brought into the courtroom and ushered to the defendants' table. One-half hour later the bailiff arrived, followed by the court stenographer, who set up his transcribing machine at a desk just below the bench, tested it and opened his newspaper. At about 2:00 P.M. the court clerk and a probation officer appeared, and a short time later, the assistant district attorney arrived. They took seats at their desks and waited. The public defender came in, shook Randolph's hand, sat down, and thumbed through Randolph's file. A buzzer sounded. The bailiff cried "All rise." Everyone stood as the robed judge entered and sat on the high-backed leather chair behind the bench. The actors were all in their places, and the drama began.

Court Clerk: "People versus Randolph for trial."

Assistant District Attorney: "Your Honor, with leave of the Court, the People move that the information in this case be deemed amended by adding Count Four thereto alleging that on or about the date alleged in the other counts the defendant, Peter Randolph, did unlawfully enter the premises in question, a misdemeanor."

Assistant Public Defender: "If Your Honor please, at this time the defendant Peter Randolph consents to the amendment proposed by the assistant district attorney and tenders a plea of guilty to this Count Four of the information charging the misdemeanor offense of unlawful entry.

"I should inform Your Honor that I have discussed this matter with Mr. Carbo, the assistant district attorney, and he has indicated that he will ask the Court to dismiss the remaining counts in this information, charging first-degree burglary, simple burglary and grand larceny, at the time sentence is imposed on this charge."

Assistant District Attorney: "That is correct, Your Honor."

The Court: "Mr. Randolph, do you understand what your attorney has just said?"[14]

Peter Randolph: "I do."

The Court: "Have you been furnished with a copy of the information and discussed the charges contained in it with your lawyer?"

Peter Randolph: "Yes, sir."

The Court: Have you discussed all the facts and circumstances of the matter with your lawyer?"

Peter Randolph: "Yes, sir."

The Court: "And do you understand that you are charged with entering the real property of Augustus Simmons at 568 Hope Street in this city on August 3 of this year without the consent of the owner or person in lawful possession?"

Peter Randolph: "Yes, sir."

The Court: "Under the Constitution you cannot be required to incriminate yourself. You may remain silent at all times, and your silence may not be commented upon or used against you. Do you understand that?"

Peter Randolph: "Yes, sir."

The Court: "And do you further understand that you are entitled to confront your accusers, to require that they testify in open court at a public trial and to cross-examine the witnesses against you, as well as to call by compulsory process witnesses on your own behalf?"

Peter Randolph: "Yes, sir."

The Court: "And do you further understand that by your plea of guilty you are waiving all of these rights and subjecting yourself to sentence and punishment without a trial?"

Peter Randolph: "Yes, sir."

The Court: "Were any threats, promises or inducements made to cause you to offer this plea?"

Peter Randolph: "No, sir."

The Court: "All right, I will accept the plea, but I want a presentence investigation. Sentencing is set for two weeks hence in this courtroom. The defendant is remanded to jail pending sentence. Next case."

The Informed and Voluntary Guilty Plea

The ritual of questions by the judge and answers by the accused is required by law. In principle, it is based on common sense. Surely a guilty plea should not be entered or accepted if the accused does not understand what he is admitting or is browbeaten into making the plea. If he knows what he is doing and does it voluntarily, his confession is a particularly reliable kind of statement. No one knows better than the defendant himself whether he is guilty, and men do not lightly confess when they know the confession will bring punishment. A statement made in the face of such disadvantages is generally reliable. The problem, of course, is deciding whether a defendant really knows what he is admitting and whether his guilty plea is indeed voluntary.

In California and other states, police and courthouse workers go by the numbers: "Harry James Smith, you are charged in seven counts with violations of Sections 288(a), 241 and 238 of the Penal Code. How do you plead?" The quality of any admission that might follow is seriously limited if Smith does not know in detail what these sections of the penal code prohibit. Before he is able to give an informed answer, he must be taught what the numbers mean, what the elements of each crime are, what it takes to be guilty of an offense, and what the possible defenses may be. Put more generally, he must realize that he has a moral and legal right to plead not guilty even if he believes himself guilty.

A guilty plea is of little help to a legal system interested in its own legitimacy unless the accused knows that self-defense is justification for homicide, or that it is not theft to carry away property which he mistakenly believes is his own. Further, a guilty plea smacks of injustice if the accused does not understand the consequences of his admission. A guilty plea is not merely a

26

statement of fact; it is an admission of culpability and responsibility. As such, it is acceptable only if made by a person aware of the consequences of guilt, the punishments that may be imposed, and the price of confession.

Courthouse procedures are technical and confusing, and, therefore, for a guilty plea to be made knowingly, it must be counselled by a competent attorney who has carefully investigated the technicalities of the case and discussed them fully with his client. In other words, the defense lawyer is supposed to teach each client the fundamentals of criminal law and procedure. Yet there are many distinguished lawyers who would find it difficult to recite the specific elements which make up such common crimes as burglary or robbery. Even fewer are aware of the actual or even likely consequences of conviction for trespass or unlawful entry. Seasoned practitioners working in the criminal courts know something of these matters, but even they must turn regularly to the library to research fine points of the rules defining offenses and punishments. And when sentencing is left entirely to judges, even topnotch prosecutors and public defenders are unable to predict the penalties that will be imposed in a given case. Moreover, prosecutors, defenders and judges alike are unaware of the reality of how much hurt is imposed by a jail or prison term.

As a result, many guilty pleas are the product of uncounselled decisions by defendants. Some are offered by defendants who have not been told the likely consequences and without any assurances of a bargain. Others are entered after a hurried conversation with a public defender in a courtroom or a holding cell. The lawyers representing the majority of those accused of crimes in most cities are young, inexperienced and low-paid. The quality of counsel available to indigent defendants casts serious doubt on whether many guilty pleas are made knowingly.

Consequently, many defendants plead guilty, take a chance, and afterward feel cheated. It would be naive to take literally the rationalizations and explanations of prisoners who have been through the system and have lost. Nevertheless, every jail guard and prison warden knows that at least one half of their wards deny the justice of their punishment, claiming that they were convicted on a "bum rap." Many of these prisoners admit vaguely that they were guilty of something, but they assert that the guilty plea system never gave them an opportunity to bring out all the facts: "I didn't have a chance to tell my side of the story"; "I didn't have enough money to hire a good lawyer"; "The prosecutor was out to get me"; "The judge didn't know what he was doing."

Prisoners and prison workers also commonly hear other remarks: "I did it for convenience"; "My lawyer told me it (plead guilty) was the only thing I could do"; "You can't beat the system"; "I wanted to get it over with"; "They have you over a barrel when you have a record." Such responses obviously cannot be taken at face value. Nevertheless, it is at least suspicious that only 95 out of 724 (13 percent) of the defendants questioned in a study by Abraham Blumberg, Professor of Sociology and Law at City University of New York, admitted their guilt to a probation officer shortly after pleading guilty in court.[15] This suggests either that the criminal justice system fails to ensure that the accused knows what is going on, or that the workings of the process so obscure this knowledge that 87 percent of those accused feel free to deny responsibility later.

Coerced Guilty Pleas

Modern Americans are easily convinced that involuntary guilty pleas are undesirable. Yet until two hundred years ago, the system of justice in most countries depended heavily on legal torture, and even today in some nations physically or psychologically coerced confessions are still a dominant feature of the criminal law.[16] In the United States, it was not until the 1930s that the Supreme Court outlawed "third-degree" methods of coercing confessions.

Americans are shocked by coercive tactics because they are inconsistent with respect for human dignity. It simply will not do to beat people, to inject them with drugs, to harass them, to force them to affirm as true that which they deny. In the last century, American law has severely narrowed the circumstances in which it is permissible for one person to injure another physically. Whippings by teachers, beatings by parents and husbands all have been drastically curtailed. In the realm of criminal law, also, beatings by police and physical tortures by jailers have been outlawed.

Americans also sense that it is especially wrong to terrorize people into confessing to a crime.[17] Confessions given after beatings or prolonged psychological torture are notoriously unreliable. If enough pain is precisely applied, innocent men will confess, even to the most outrageous and absurd crimes. In short, a coerced confession is a very dubious piece of evidence. Beyond that, the use of force to obtain confessions deprives the law of its moral power. The very word "confession" implies that the confessor accepts moral responsibility for what he did. A moral progression from accusation, to confession, to expiation and redemption has little meaning in a system that coerces confessions from the unwilling accused.

Most importantly, Americans know that any fact-finding system which depends on the extraction of confessions inevitably becomes a victim of its own methods. Writing about the courts of sixteenth-century England, Lytton Strachey put the matter this way:

> It was, of course, an essential feature of the system that those who worked it should not have realised its implications. Torture was regarded as an unpleasant necessity; evidence obtained under it might be considered of dubious value; but no one dreamt that the judicial procedure of which it formed a part was necessarily without any value at all. The wisest and the ablest of those days—a Bacon, a Walsingham— were utterly unable to perceive that the conclusions, which the evidence they had collected seemed to force upon them, were in reality simply the result of the machinery they themselves had set in motion. Judges, as well as prisoners, were victims of the rack.[18]

Many guilty pleas submitted in American courts are not free acts of the accused; they are gained by psychological coercion through threat of severe punishment. Sometimes the sale of a light punishment for a guilty plea is explicit and overt, giving rise to an image of the courthouse as a Mexican marketplace filled with haggling and bargaining small-time merchants. However, overt bargaining is neither popular nor often necessary in the American courthouse, because the entire criminal law system—from the framing of statutes by the legislature through the organization of the police, the structure of bail practices and the rules of the parole board—is purposely aimed at inducing the guilty plea.

Criminal codes create grades of offenses for similar conduct, ostensibly so that judges can match punishment and circumstances. If the defendant is judged to have committed burglary in the first degree, the judge is supposed to send him to prison for from five years to life or to put him on extended probation for his serious felony. If the defendant has committed burglary in the second degree, the judge is supposed to make the punishment less severe, but still more severe than the punishment for unlawful entry. In addition, this grading permits policemen and prosecutors to match accusations and crimes. The different grades further enable judges and others to reduce serious charges to lesser included charges in the interest of justice.

But grades of offenses also function, subtly and not so subtly, as threats to encourage defendants to buy mitigation with a guilty plea. For example, such crimes as unlawful entry and the unlawful use of a motor vehicle are typical misdemeanors. They are also "knocked down" counts, meaning that they are thrown out as bait to persons who have burglarized a house or stolen a car. Considered practically, lesser included offenses are inserted in criminal codes to encourage defendants charged with serious crimes to buy relief with a plea of guilty to a knocked down charge. The California legislature, concerned about labeling marijuana users as felons, first revised its penal code to allow court officials, including both judges and prosecutors, to knock down marijuana use from felony to misdemeanor status.[19] But the legislature did not eliminate the *possibility* that marijuana possession would result in a felony charge. As a result, to avoid being labeled a felon, the defendant had to plead guilty to a misdemeanor. In 1975 as public attitudes developed further, the second stage in changing the law was taken, and the simple possession of small amounts of marijuana was further reduced to a misdemeanor punishable only by a fine of up to one hundred dollars, eliminating the possibility of felony conviction in these cases.

There are other legal pressures aimed at inducing the guilty plea. Recent court decisions practically abolished capital punishment. Until those decisions, federal law and the law in many states provided that a defendant who went to trial for murder could be executed, but a man who pleaded guilty to murder could not. A young man who pleaded guilty under such circumstances appealed his case on the ground that he literally would have risked his life to assert his right to a jury trial. Despite the obvious truth of this claim, the conviction was upheld by the Supreme Court of the United States.[20]

In addition, there are laws which require severe, mandatory sentences for some crimes; for example, all persons carrying guns while committing a crime must go to prison for a minimum of five years. In his 1975 crime message, President Ford endorsed incorporating such mandatory sentences in the federal criminal code. The effect of such law is to stimulate accused robbers to plead guilty to unarmed robbery, in exchange for which the prosecutor "swallows the gun." Other laws impose more severe sentences on repeated offenders and thus motivate them to plead guilty to almost any serious charge if the prosecutor will not invoke the habitual criminal law. When combined with discretionary charging processes, such mandatory sentence laws put a high price on a plea of not guilty.

We have questioned judges and prosecutors about such tacitly coerced guilty pleas. The almost inevitable response is as follows: "But that isn't plea bargaining. We never promise defendants anything. They act merely on their hope of leniency. There's nothing wrong with that." This response misses the point completely. It fails to recognize the degree to which the criminal justice system from beginning to end threatens all defendants with severe punishment if they do not plead guilty. Consequently, there is no need to ask specific defendants to bargain for leniency.

Underlying many of the concerns about the uninformed or involuntary guilty plea is, of course, the fear that on rare occasions an innocent man is coerced into making a false confession. Another concern is that prosecutors will arbitrarily decide that an offender should be punished in a certain way, find a crime to fit the punishment and persuade the defendant to plead guilty to that crime. We shall see later that this last process is not all bad—it can improve the quality of justice in the face of a harsh criminal code. But the same process casts doubt on the legitimacy of the official system. Law and order lose all meaning unless justice is dispensed with dignity to men who have an opportunity to know the basis of justice administrators' actions.

The Presentence Investigation

Following his guilty plea, Peter Randolph spent another two weeks in jail awaiting sentencing. One day a probation officer called him to the lawyer's room. He seemed friendly, and he explained that he was writing a personal history of Randolph, to be used by the judge in setting Randolph's sentence.[21] Most of his questions were routine requests for the same information Randolph had already given to others. After ten minutes of such questions, Randolph was asked for his version of the crime. The probation officer seemed to listen carefully as Randolph explained that on the night of the crime he was feeling sorry for himself, disappointed, fed up and drinking too much wine. On his note pad the probation officer wrote: "Subject says he doesn't know why he committed the burglary. Was drinking wine in the park and just wandered in the house. Inadequate personality."

Then he asked Randolph what he thought a proper sentence would be. Randolph replied that a public defender had told him that a district attorney was going to let him out of jail and put him on probation. That seemed OK. The probation worker seemed unconcerned. He made some notes.

"That's the deal, ain't it?" Randolph asked.

"The DA and PD don't have the final say. That's up to the judge. He'll read my report and decide what to do."

When Randolph stalked out of the interviewing room a few minutes later, he loudly slammed the door. His guard growled, "Take it easy, kid. Take it easy."

The Sentencing Ceremony

Imposition of a sentence is the grand finale of a criminal proceeding.[22] When the judge stipulates the punishment to be imposed, all hopes and understandings that led to the guilty plea are either realized or dashed. After all, it was pain that defendants, defenders and prosecutors had been negotiating all along. For most defendants, conviction is a foregone conclusion. Each knows that he violated the law. The only question is "How long will I have to serve?"

In virtually all cases, the sentencing judge has broad discretion. Even when the penal code sets a mandatory sentence for a crime, the judge usually has effective power to decide what crime the defendant is to be convicted of. In some states this means he is able to decide whether the defendant is to be handled as a felon, a misdemeanant or a youthful offender. And what he decides automatically determines the limits of the sentence. If he chooses to imprison a defendant, usually he sets the minimum and maximum sentence and stipulates the date of parole eligibility.

There is a sentence hearing on every case in which there has been a conviction, whether after trial or after a guilty plea. In some states, the judge is required by law to order a probation or presentence report before he sends a man to prison, and in an increasing number of states, presentence reports are written in most felony cases. The report is supposed to provide the judge with background information on the offender and his offense. Sometimes the officer assembling the presentence information is a trained social worker who includes psychological evaluations in the reports. But frequently the probation officer has no special training, and the reports are nothing more than moralistic statements or gossipy accounts. In some states, the person preparing the presentence report must testify about the report in an open hearing, and may be cross-examined. More commonly, the report is confidential and may be given only to the judge. Its contents may not be revealed to either the defendant or his lawyer.

At Peter Randolph's sentencing hearing the prosecutor addressed the judge first.[23] "If it please the Court, since Your Honor has the presentence report in hand, the People at this time have no further statements or recommendations to make. Thank you,

Your Honor." It was easy for the prosecutor to speak so briefly and with such confidence in the outcome. He had spent ten minutes with the probation officer before the report was written, describing the arrangements he had worked out with Randolph's lawyer. When he was given a copy of the final report, he glanced through it to make sure that it recommended the disposition they had agreed upon. He skipped the parts dealing with Randolph's background, personality and probation plan.

Steven Ohler, the public defender assigned to Randolph at arraignment, made a slightly longer speech. "Your Honor, in the interests of justice, I would like to take just a minute to make a few remarks concerning my client, Mr. Randolph. I would remind Your Honor that this is my client's first adult conviction. He has never been in any really serious trouble before, and the offense he has pleaded to, unlawful entry, was committed in such a way that it is clear we are not dealing with an experienced criminal. In fact, I feel sure that in this case we are, so to speak, nipping a criminal career in the bud. I would also remind the Court that my client has already served more than sixty days in the county jail. He has expressed to me a deep and sincere remorse for his behavior, and this is, more than anything, what leads me to believe that this is a case in which the mercy of the Court would be most appropriate and just."

The judge then asked Randolph if he wanted to add anything. The bailiff motioned him to stand before the bench.

"No, Your Honor."

"Nothing to say?"

"Well, Judge . . . I don't know, but I sure wish you would let me out."

This the judge did, as everyone but Randolph was sure he would do. He sentenced Randolph to a jail term equal to the time already served, plus a year on probation.

The Flow of Cases

Although the case of *People* v. *Randolph* is imaginary, it closely resembles in important respects hundreds of ceremonies acted out in American courthouses each day. Official statistics indicate that more than two out of three adult felony arrests are disposed of or are lost somewhere in the system before formal charges are filed in any felony trial court. At the point of arraignment, less than one third of the persons arrested for felonies still face felony charges. About 85 percent of those who face felony court charges

33

will be convicted of some offense, but only about 10 percent will be tried before a judge or jury. In California, over 40 percent of the persons arraigned on a serious felony charge plead guilty to a misdemeanor only, and many more plead guilty to a lesser felony.[24]

The selective process continues when sentence is pronounced. Only 13 percent of those convicted in California's felony courts are sent to state prisons. Another 41 percent are sentenced to serve time in a county jail. Seventy percent of those convicted are placed on probation, either directly or after a short jail sentence.

In summary, of the one hundred adults arrested on felony charges and arriving at the front door of an American courthouse, as Peter Randolph did, only two or three will be escorted out the back door to a van waiting to carry them to a state prison.

Selectivity and Discretion

The tremendous drop in cases from step to step in the courthouse process cannot be explained merely in terms of a lack of evidence necessary for conviction. Such an explanation would mean only that the police are doing a shockingly bad job of deciding whom to arrest.[25] They are not. Observers of the process are unanimous in concluding that the drop occurs because at each stage there is a broad area of discretion which enables officials to decide who shall be prosecuted and on what charge.

But these observers disagree about why discretion is necessary and why it is pervasive. Is it because of a need to shuck off some of the workload of an overburdened system? Is it because the traditional system has collapsed, smoothing the way for the exercise of personal bias, prejudice, whim or even corruption on the part of the decision maker? Is it because courthouse workers are lazy, inept, bureaucratic? Or is it because of a need to arrive at a better brand of justice than that provided by the statutes and law books? We recognize the influence of workload, bias and bureaucracy, but the dominant factor seems to be a sincere and pervasive, if unstated, desire to improve the quality of justice. To see why this is so, it may help to pause and consider the demands of economy and justice.

Discretion and Economy

Punishment is expensive. If the courts sent to prison everyone legally deserving such punishment, there would be little of the gross national product available for anything other than prison maintenance. Beyond the economic need to keep the size of the system down, there must be some way to decide which cases deserve expensive time and attention. Formal court procedures are also costly. No sensible court wants to spend its time finding petty shoplifters guilty if there are a number of murder-rapes or commercial narcotics sales waiting in line to be heard. Somehow the system must have the capacity to allocate its limited resources by concentrating on important cases and dropping petty ones.

A major asset of the guilty plea process is its promise of speed and economy in sorting the unimportant cases from the important ones. It avoids the belaboring of the obvious that marks so many trials. In most trials, the only genuine dispute between the prosecution and the defense is not guilt or innocence; it is what the punishment shall be, and this can be settled outside the courtroom. Trying cases in which there is no real dispute is a waste of vast resources and tedious for everyone involved except the accused. Moreover, for the innocent as for the guilty, justice delayed is catastrophic. Speed in the resolution of a criminal matter is necessary for fairness.

But formal rules and procedures cannot weed out unimportant cases or assign priorities among the cases. If judges were required to announce formal rules about priorities, each judge would have to hold a trial to decide which cases were most important and should be tried first. Such an approach would be unacceptable, cumbersome and expensive. It would prevent the system from deciding that more than a few defendants were indeed guilty. The option is to leave the sorting out to responsible officials who have been provided with guidelines for their exercise of discretion.

Settling cases by guilty pleas and other discretionary procedures produces other savings. Important and unimportant cases of all kinds are disposed of in a few minutes by the routine entry of a guilty plea. On the other hand, trials and hearings often involve the extended presence of at least a dozen persons: the judge, the clerk, the stenographer, the bailiff, the attorneys, witnesses and jurors. It is extraordinarily difficult to schedule court proceedings; someone is always waiting. Too many contemporary courts place undue emphasis on the convenience of court personnel, particularly judges. In such courts, large numbers of defendants, attorneys, witnesses and jurors are likely to be left sitting and waiting for a judge to hear their cases. This could be changed by setting a different kind of appointment schedule. Then the judges and clerks would be the ones left sitting and waiting. But even if a computer were used to coordinate appointments, the logistics problem would persist, because a large number of trials and hearings are necessarily settled or postponed at the last minute. For example, a witness, attorney or defendant might be ill, or a prosecutor might have an automobile accident on the way to court.

The guilty plea system has developed and flourished, at least in part, because it helps move cases through the courthouse rapidly and inexpensively. Witnesses, jurors, and complicated scheduling are unnecessary. Prosecutors and other officials may safely predict that any case will be disposed of in five to ten minutes. If a snag develops, only a few additional minutes are needed to straighten it out, or the case may routinely be held over to another day without inconveniencing many people. Attorneys may come into court and enter the guilty plea twenty-four hours after they have reached an agreement. Most cases may be handled by essentially the same speedy procedure. The clerk does not even need to make detailed entries on the docket; rubber stamps will do.

Yet there is substantial reason for doubting the economy and efficiency of the informal process as it now operates. Cases sometimes drag along to a plea because time and delay are used as tactics by both the prosecutor and the defense counsel. Justice in these cases is by no means speedy. Time and talent are invested in relatively unproductive matters, such as determining the number of counts to which the defendant will plead guilty. The guilty plea eliminates cases, but the time invested is poorly spent.

It seems quite economical to dispose of cases by diversion, dismissal or plea, but in the long run the system may be expensive. It throws criminals back into the same social milieu that produced them, where their problems tend to grow and become chronic. It does nothing to change either the criminal or the society that spawns him. In the existing system, if a case is not dismissed outright, it becomes valuable to the organizational needs of the criminal justice agencies. The punishment secured by an arranged guilty plea provides food for the bureaucracy employed to deal with criminals. There is an organizational prejudice in favor of retaining power over criminals. This may result in state prisons and county jails filled with individuals who should be in some other program. Thus, a discretionary system using the guilty plea may actually increase the costs and size of the criminal justice system. The police, the prosecutor and the court serve as a series of gates limiting the system's business. A slow, laborious process serves to

36

prevent overcrowded jails and prisons, but the guilty plea system creates a bypass around these barriers. Discretionary decision may permit economy at the court stage, but it is likely to do so by shunting too much work downstream, thus increasing the workload of the total system.

The Balance of Justice

Aside from the claims of economy, discretion in criminal justice is needed to balance the system's commitment to the individuality of guilt with its commitment to a general set of rules for everyone. Words are blunt tools at best. There are inherent limits on the capacity of human beings to state in advance general rules which will be appropriate in a variety of cases. No legislature that is far removed from the conduct it defines as criminal is able to incorporate enough justice-producing nuances and behavioral clues in its statutory statements. No two robberies are the same. No two defendants charged with robbery are identical either. A brutal armed holdup and a scuffle in which one boy in a schoolyard takes a basketball from another are both defined as robberies by statutes prescribing punishment for the offense. Yet these two robberies bear little resemblance to each other when criminal intent, degree of guilt and personal character are taken into account. The National Crime Commission described the problem this way:

> Before the criminal courts come many offenders who are marginal in the sense that, although they are guilty of serious offenses as defined by the Penal Code, they may not be habitual and dangerous criminals. It is not in the interests of the community to treat marginal offenders as hardened criminals, nor does the law require that the courts do so. Framing statutes that identify and prescribe for every nuance of human behavior is impossible. A criminal code has no way of describing the difference between a petty thief who is on his way to becoming an armed robber and a petty thief who becomes one on a momentary impulse.[26]

Professor Frank W. Miller has noted the following relationship between legislative prohibitions and discretionary adjustment of these laws to individual cases:

> The wide variety of situations which may arise, including important differences in the characteristics of particular offenders, as well as inherent limitations in the use of language, force legislatures to proscribe conduct in broader terms than might be considered ideal. Indeed, there is evidence that full enforcement apart from resource limitations is not consistent with legislative expectations in some situations. . . . [D]iscretion is necessary to transform broad legislative proscriptions into pragmatically satisfactory social policy.[27]

Actually, modern criminal codes represent a rather crude attempt to satisfy both the sense of justice which demands that similarly situated people be treated alike, and the sense of justice which demands that each man be treated according to his deserts. They make room for both uniformity and diversity in three principal ways. First, they stress equality by outlawing all robbery and other crimes, but they also stress individual differences by subdividing and grading offenses in terms of a range of culpability. For example, most criminal codes make the punishment for robbery with a gun more severe than that for unarmed robbery, and the penalty for burglary of someone's home more severe than burglary of a warehouse. Second, criminal codes universally ask for punishment of the guilty, but they also set only a range of minimum and maximum punishments for particular offenses. One kind of robbery may be punishable by a prison term ranging from five years to life, another by from one to ten years, another by from one to three years. Third, criminal codes make all criminal acts punishable by law, but they also authorize judges to suspend punishment and place the criminal on probation.

All three aspects of the codes—the grading of crimes, the range of permissible punishment, and the possibility of suspending punishment—become the subject matter of official, but discretionary decisions. The first gives tremendous power to prosecutors who can decide what crimes to charge a man with. The second gives power to parole authorities who can decide whether a man stays in prison for five years or for a lifetime. The third gives tremendous power to judges who can suspend punishment.

Moreover, the definition of justice is complicated by uncertainty about the content of criminal statutes. Everyone agrees that the state should forbid the unlawful killing of human beings, but is a fetus a human being? Everyone agrees that the state should forbid stealing, but what is stealing? The concept has changed over history as society's concept of property and its values have changed, and it continues to change. If a factory worker takes tools home from the plant it is stealing, but is it stealing if he loafs on the job? If a legislator or a city councilman sells favors it is stealing, but is it stealing if he profits politically by flouting the will of the people? If a student takes a library book and puts it on his own shelf it is stealing, but is it stealing if he takes the book without properly checking it out, reads it and returns it? Is it stealing if he takes the book, photocopies it and then returns it? Did Daniel Ellsberg steal government property when he took the Pentagon Papers, duplicated them and returned them to the files?

Such questions must be decided by someone. Justice is the process by which such decisions are made. When prosecutors decide that a case does or does not involve stealing, or some other crime, they are doing justice. It is not a mechanical matter whereby an abstract set of rules is uniformly applied to all cases. It requires wisdom, sensitivity and a sense of balance. Any wise judgment as to guilt or punishment inevitably involves discretion.

A system of criminal justice that did not take into account people's uniqueness and personality would be so unmerciful and wasteful of human lives that few thinking citizens would support it. There is a real likelihood that if the federal government or state government succeeds in minimizing officials' discretion, the quality of courthouse personnel would deteriorate. Few talented and sensitive people would want to be a prosecutor or judge if they were foolishly required to treat equally a member of an organized band of persistent robbers and an eccentric grandmother who flashed an antique pistol at a bank teller and demanded a paper bag full of money.

Criminal justice workers want the power to control, or at least to bend, the process of catching and disposing of offenders. They want it because, put simply, it allows them to do justice, to do good. Citizens of democracies would be appalled by officials who did not feel this need. Strict compliance with severe and rigid laws abstractly resembles justice, but it is not just in effect.

A commitment to legislative and judicial rules is central to doing justice, yet other compelling considerations of justice demand the capacity to make decisions without the constraint of rules. For example, most citizens are not ready to repeal the laws forbidding the use of marijuana, but many of them no longer support full enforcement of these laws. So the courthouse makes adjustments. Prosecution is limited to a relatively few aggrevated cases, thus satisfying the politically powerful "death on narcotics" groups which define officially what crime is and what it is not. At the same time, discretion quietly reduces the total amount of punishment actually imposed, thus keeping the law tolerable to the young, their fearful parents and the more permissive groups in the community.

Informal discretion on matters of guilt and punishment promotes flexibility, and flexibility in turn lends itself to discretionary decisions that grow and change with experience, rather than being determined by a binding ideological choice. The development of the values of the criminal law goes forward without being subjected to undue and premature public pressure. Inconsistent aims of various community interest groups are quietly reconciled.

But this same quality of discretion presents the ironic danger that the discretionary system itself will become mere routine, that it will lose contact with society's highest goals and serve as neither a moral demonstration of justice nor an effective program for community response to criminality. As contemporary American experience suggests, there is a real risk that the courthouse will lose all sense of purpose and will become totally preoccupied with itself and the institutional and professional interests of those who run it. There is a potential for monstrosity, because any system permitting routine exercise of discretion also permits routine exercise of whim.

Those who think that the courthouse can implement a unitary scheme of values by enforcing the law are likely to be unsettled and disillusioned by the suggestion that courthouses operate through discretion, for this means that the values are never totally realized. But this nonfulfillment is not necessarily a vice. Although it is impossible to find an absolute set of values being implemented in the courthouse, it is possible to find a system of compromises which accommodates many different values and acts them out in the ceremonies of justice.

Discretion and Guilt

The pain of confinement and loss of status that accompany criminal conviction should be imposed only when ample proof of the facts has been provided. In other words, conviction must be preceded by proof beyond a reasonable doubt. No one expects a policeman to arrest or a prosecutor to charge any person against whom there is only *some* evidence of criminal behavior. There must be a judgment that there is sufficient persuasive evidence upon which a conviction can and should rest. In fact, however, such assurance is often lacking, for circumstances often are uncertain. Many occasions for the exercise of police and prosecutorial discretion arise because there is an expectation of highly persuasive proof but only limited capacity to collect and present such proof.

The process of doing justice often is seen as one of deciding who is right and who is wrong. Typically, this is an all or nothing choice. A lawsuit arising out of an automobile collision is likely to involve a whole series of ways in which each driver could have performed better than he did. If the first driver had been going slower, and had braked as he approached the intersection, if his headlights had not been slightly obscured with mud, if he had reacted more promptly when the second car came out of the side street, the collision would have been avoided. On the other hand, if the second driver had looked more carefully in each direction before he pulled on to the main road, if he had accelerated more quickly, the collision would not have occurred either. Yet in most states the result of a lawsuit between the two drivers will be a verdict either for one or the other, or for neither, but not for both. The uncertainties and imponderables of this assessment of the accident may explain why most collision cases are settled out of court.[28]

In criminal trials, too, the defendant is either guilty or not guilty. The formal criminal law treats guilt as a black or white matter of fact. But in criminal cases as in automobile accidents, justice is rarely an all or nothing matter. More often, the process involves adjustment and compromise. Whether the defendant is guilty always depends in part on knowledge of what the consequences of the guilty verdict will be and on a sense of whether the punishment will be proportionate to the defendant's wrongdoing. Frequently such issues cannot satisfactorily be decided by the processes used in formal criminal trials. Another advantage of the discretionary system is that it helps to avoid insoluble questions of fact, evidence and proof in deciding what to do.

Preoccupation with problems of proof is an ancient vice of lawyers, resting on the assumption that there is only one truth and, for that matter, frequently insisting that there is only one morality. Too often the subtle process of persuading a judge or jury about guilt is not essentially captured in the lawyer's concepts of evidence and proof. Humans regularly make excellent decisions by means which are rational and systematic, but alien to courtroom evidence. The probabilistic approach of the scientist is used in a commonsense way by most citizens but stands in stark contrast to the lawyer's demand for proof beyond a reasonable doubt:

Is it necessary to decide . . . as to the existence of an absolute truth? If we once overcome the childlike notion that every act is either right or wrong, that every statement is either true or false, that every question may be answered by a "yes" or "no," we will recognize that with our present knowledge there are some statements which are more probable than others.[24]

The law's rules of evidence are designed to serve as guardians of the truth, but they frequently serve to prevent the full examination of many circumstances relevant to guilt. For example, evidence of habit or propensity is not generally admissible as evidence that a person committed a crime, but every judge would be helped in deciding whether Mrs. Jones stole the shoes from the store if he were allowed to know that she had been arrested and convicted as a shoplifter on twelve other occasions. Similarly, official and clinical files—evidence based on statistical inference or derived indirectly from the testimony of observers—are excluded from court consideration under doctrines relating to hearsay, best evidence, authenticity and opinion. Often evidence is excluded from courtrooms for reasons wholly unrelated to its reliability and usefulness. Very persuasive evidence is excluded because society's commitment to personal security and privacy demands that courts not use evidence obtained by improper search and seizure or intrusion into a confidential relationship.

Expectations about what is proper courtroom evidence sometimes lead lawyers to be hostile to proof that does not fit comfortably into the examination-cross-examination method of production and challenge. Trial lawyers love to challenge doctors and other witnesses who come to court to testify. The courtroom is the lawyer's territory—it is run according to rules that reflect his prejudices, and many a competent witness has been made to look and feel like a fool, although everything he said was eminently sensible when judged by noncourtroom standards.

Before making a decision, the discretionary system allows consideration of material which a judge might refuse to hear, and consideration of such "inadmissible evidence" often allows more complete fact-finding and a closer approximation of the truth. The flexibility accompanying discretionary processes can lead to more accurate decisions than are possible in the comparatively rigid courtroom. Freed from the necessity for formal fact-finding, the judge can ignore the indeterminate and try to reach a decision on whatever basis seems to work best.

But there are real costs associated with informal fact-finding. If justice is to be visible, facts must be demonstrated, not merely asserted. Society places a high value on these demonstrations, and its confidence in the fact-finding aspects of the trial contributes greatly to the acceptability of the results. In contrast, the guilty plea system proves few visible and persuasive procedures. There is no point at which the parties to the agreement, particularly the judge, examine the arrangement objectively to determine whether or not it conforms to the evidence or to policy goals. Because the process of decisions is invisible, deviations from norms are not apparent.

The criminal justice system is supposed to teach. Through the ceremonies of law enforcement, society's values are affirmed and made visible to everyone. Citizens are instructed by the application of the law and told what happens to individuals who misbehave. But this affirmation of values does not occur in a guilty plea system, when the decision as to guilt is made behind closed doors and the agreed level of conviction is the product of negotiation, not the ceremonial playing out of values. Armed robbers are convicted of attempted assault in the third degree; car thieves with unauthorized entry into a motor vehicle; child molesters with loitering in a school yard. None of these dispositions reinforces the sense that violations of basic rules carry with them stated penalties.

The open public trial also serves as an opportunity to review the behavior of the police and of the prosecutor trying the case. Judicial review has been increasingly influential in exposing police and prosecutorial malpractice and in formulating the rules that are to govern official behavior. But the guilty plea deal sometimes involves the dropping of motions to suppress confessions or evidence seized in the course of a search. These questions never come before the court for public review and evaluation, and the potential for audit is lost.

Even when they are relatively rare events, public trials allow all interested persons to see what crimes are occurring in the community and what the official response to crime is. In this way there is a constant opportunity to reevaluate the criminal law itself. Does it make sense to send young men who are found in possession of a small quantity of marijuana to prison for five years? Should men who engage in strange sexual behavior be sent to prison, should they be let alone, or should they be treated in some more therapeutic program? These questions do not arise for public review.

In practice, discretionary justice processes are not now equally available to all defendants. When the opportunity to avoid conviction and punishment for a serious offense by pleading guilty to a less serious one depends on the degree of overcrowding of the trial calendar, justice is not done. When this opportunity depends on the friendship between defense counsel and the prosecutor, the tenacity of the former or the political ambitions of the latter, justice is not done. When time in prison depends on paternalistic, autocratic and even bigoted ideas about what is good for poor, black and unsophisticated defendants, justice is not done. When the sophisticated and calculating offender, who knows the ropes and is represented by a knowledgeable criminal attorney, fares much better than the less dangerous, naive, or guilt-ridden defendant, justice is not done.

Justice is not a matter of grace. Every person is entitled by right to a fair determination of his culpability and punishment. No person should have to demand, let alone pay for, a trial. Rather, such a determination is a precondition to the state's right to inflict punishment. One of the most telling criticisms of the guilty plea system as now administered is that it violates this principle by placing a price on a defendant's right to trial.

The informed citizen is likely to be most outraged at guilty plea negotiations because they take place in settings where justice occurs almost randomly. When the pain of punishment is the result of tactical concerns and individual biases, it does not reflect a coherent execution of policy. When the punishments meted out to criminals reflect no sense of the seriousness of their offenses, their past records or even the appropriateness of punishing them, it is time for a change. But these conditions cannot be modified significantly by abolishing plea bargaining and by replacing it with rigid rule enforcement. They can be changed only by introducing procedures which permit all the parties, especially the defendant and the judge, to examine the proposed arrangements and voluntarily consent to their implementation. Such procedures are the essence of justice.

Who Runs the Courthouse?

No courthouse looks precisely like the picture we have painted. In different courthouses, different officials dominate the process.[30] In some cities, the police department is very strong politically, and its officials do much of the selecting. We have already pointed out that in some cities the complaint officer is a senior policeman. He sits in a courtlike room and is addressed by lawyers, who presumably know his true status, as "Your Honor." In other cities, older patterns persist. Built on the justice of the peace system, many of the discretionary duties performed elsewhere by policemen and prosecutors are performed by a magistrate.

In most large cities—New York and Los Angeles, for example—the prosecutor is dominant, sometimes dealing directly with arresting officers and making choices almost at the moment of arrest. Telephone calls from policemen seeking guidance on whether an accused person should be held often awaken the complaint assistant in the middle of the night. But such spontaneity is tempered by bureaucracy. The usual practice in large cities is to go through channels. In Los Angeles, for example, the police department uses a professional specialist to deal with the intake prosecutors. Ordinary patrolmen and sergeants must route cases through this specialist, who deals only with specialists representing the district attorney's bureaucracy. The diplomatic relations between the specialists may take on the complexity of international negotiations. The policeman on the beat and the courtroom prosecutor are insulated from each other by several layers of intermediaries.

There are also great variations in what the complaint officer does, or says he does. In some courthouses, officials claim that they are mere agents of the law with little decision-making discretion. In others, they claim that all their choices are made on the basis of the sufficiency of the evidence and the availability of witnesses. Some officials more candidly recognize the reality of discretion but try to formulate policies that state how different kinds of cases will be handled—first-time minor offenders should be fined, first-time serious offenders should go to jail and be put on probation, bad men should go to prison and so on. But in all of these courthouses, and others, the basic principle is the same: The complaint officer must use common sense.

The subject matter of negotiation also varies from place to place. In some courthouses, the issue is drawn primarily in terms of whether to file charges or not, while in others many charges are freely filed but are later reduced or dismissed. In some places, the primary concern is which felony charges the accused will be convicted of, in others, whether the final conviction will be deemed a felony or a misdemeanor. In still other courthouses, the issue is explicitly what the sentence will be.

These variations are less significant than the processes that are shared by every courthouse. Despite different structures and procedures, the results are surprisingly similar. Informal discretionary choices, rather than formal courtroom choices, determine the outcome of all but a small portion of criminal cases. Even in nonmetropolitan courthouses that are by no stretch of the imagination overburdened with work, whether an accused man goes home rather than to a state prison depends on relatively fine factual or legal points or on no factual basis at all.

The discretionary and selective process characterizing the American courthouse always has a potential for great severity. Almost all of the cases flow easily through the discretionary system to dismissal, probation, a fine or a short jail term. But for those few individuals who have the book thrown at them, the results are disastrous. They may be imprisoned under sentences that run the full length of a man's vigorous years. They become pariahs, permanently excluded from social and economic opportunities shared by free men and forced to wear forever the stigma of felon status.

The Difference It Makes

Americans who commit serious crimes usually share the values of law-abiding citizens, including the sense that crime should be punished, that the process of justice should be fair and that its operation should be visible. Peter Randolph was offended by what happened in the courthouse, to say nothing of what happened to him in jail. The problem was not the matter of his guilt. It was his discovery that he was a case to be processed by a mindless machine. The system treated him as less than a person, as an annoyance to be gotten rid of. Nobody was interested in who he was and how he got into trouble.

On his first night of freedom, Randolph sat in the park where he had sat on the night of his crime, again drinking wine, but this time with two friends. He told them about his hassles in jail and in the courthouse. One friend asked if he had had a lawyer. "No. I had a public defender. I hardly saw this guy. They said he was just a messenger for the DA. You know, you're a public defender—you don't care what happens to me. You don't know me, and I don't know you. So you go up there and say a little bit and make yourself look good, but you don't give a damn."[31]

"What about the DA?"

"Just saw him in court. 'Give that guy five to life.' You know, make yourself look good. He never saw me. The judge neither."

"Who'd you get?"

"Perkins. He just sat there. He's supposed to be the head man, but he ain't nothing. Ah, it's all fixed ahead of time. The PD come over to the jail and tells me what they're going to give me. So it's fixed someplace—maybe the DA. Perkins just sat on his ass and took orders."

Randolph took a long pull on the wine bottle before he continued. "It's all a phony fucking game."

chapter three
The story of the courtroom

Even a silent courtroom tells a story about the past and the present. The chamber is strictly ordered. The placement of objects reveals important assumptions about how justice is supposed to be done. A high judge's bench dominates the room, its position fortified by a flag and seal, the ultimate symbols of governmental authority. The jury box, counsel table and witness stand show specialized activities and organization which have evolved over the years. The open area between the bench, counsel table and the jury box, the well of the court, is available for movement but tends to be empty and avoided, like a magic circle reserved for special ceremonies. Perhaps most eloquent of all is the bar across the middle of the room, separating all the official participants from the mere spectators, the public for whom justice is to be done in this room.

Courtroom proceedings have a genteel and archaic tone consistent with the physical setting. The lawyers speak formally, using foreign words and phrases—Latin and French relics of legal ceremonies of the past. Everyone must look up to "His Honor," a

47

robed judge who is called "the Court" and is said to "sit" and "preside" as well as to "order," indicating that he is both an impartial arbiter and a man with the authority of high rank. He is addressed deferentially by lawyers: "If the Court please, at this time the defense would ask leave to conduct a *voir dire*." The jurors are addressed as "ladies and gentlemen," and they are treated as important outside observers, not as high-ranking participants.

The courtroom setting is so formidable that the observer is led to believe that it is here that the work of justice is done. The proceedings are so quaint that it is easy to conclude that they have changed little since the days of the Magna Charta.

These impressions are doubly misleading. The symbolism distorts contemporary reality. The criminal trial was many generations ago displaced in most cities by a system based on administrative discretion exercised by police and prosecutors. Courtrooms continue to be dominated by judges, but in most cases the judge responds to and ratifies the decisions of others. Moreover, the modern criminal trial, around which courtrooms are designed, took shape more recently than the venerable symbols and procedures suggest.

The Beginnings of the System

Anglo-American criminal justice began in the English Pleas of the Crown. In the centuries following the Norman conquest, punishments were ordered and imposed by the king's royal entourage, his "court," his jurisdiction was limited and episodic, the methods just a short step from trial by combat. No clear distinction was made between crime as a private wrong to the victim or his kin, crime as a sin and crime as a public wrong against the community and its king. Those were disorderly times. Communities lacked the protection against violence now provided through the criminal law. Men's lives were constricted; the world went dark when the sun went down, and for the average man living on the land, the border of his life was the first big hill beyond the village. The state claimed no monopoly on the use of force; people were left to take care of themselves. Self-help, limited warfare, feud and vengeance were only slowly displaced by a public system of community security. A criminal charge could be privately brought by the victim or his kin and decided in a trial by a battle of champions. This sounds very primitive to modern ears, yet the possibility of trial by battle persisted for centuries. It was not completely abolished in English law until the nineteenth century.

Citizens of the twentieth century are likely to take the presence of government for granted, but in feudal times the king's power was limited, and he shared it with a variety of church and secular authorities.[1] Some of the problems now dealt with in state criminal courts were treated as sins by the courts of the church. Others were handled in the court of the local baron or by the borough court of the town. The king's obligation to administer justice was related to his interest in military control of the countryside, but no administrator of royal justice was continually present in the community. Judges rode in circuit throughout England holding court in each county several times a year. These royal officials would summon (or sometimes physically corral) a number of local citizens, who would be put on their oath to tell of all the crimes and serious breaches of the peace that had occurred since the justice's last visit.

The early judge was an active agent of the king; he was not expected to be neutral or impartial. Only slowly did lawyers and judges develop a sense of professional identification and a commitment to values independent of their duty as the king's servants. The jury trial system which developed from these beginnings retains to this day its preference for the use of amateurs drawn from the community as crucial actors in the process of determining guilt or innocence.

Early juries were accusers and witnesses as well as deciders of fact. They could seek information from others to supplement their own knowledge, but primarily they were on their own. Gradually it became accepted that the Crown, in the person of a prosecutor, would submit evidence and bring witnesses to testify before the jury. But it was not until the seventeenth century that the accused was permitted witnesses to rebut the Crown prosecutor's charge. This right was granted reluctantly, and it was only in the eighteenth century that defense witnesses were allowed the added credibility of the oath. There were few rules of evidence; the judges and counsel for the Crown were quite free to bully and intimidate witnesses and jurors. If a judge did not like a jury's acquittal or refusal to convict, he could jail and fine the recalcitrant jurors. The practice of allowing the accused a lawyer to ask witnesses questions was not accepted until shortly before the American Revolution and was then written into the U.S. Constitution and most state constitutions as a protective right. In England, full right to counsel was not given the defendant until 1836.

Thus, until recently, the law of crime and punishment and its administration was simple, if severe. There was no coherent criminal code. In England there is still no such code. The law was a collection of traditionally defined crimes (muder, mayhem, burglary) supplemented by a crazy quilt of statutes enacted over the centuries. The general punishment for all serious offenses was death and the forfeiture of all property and titles. The theft of as little as two shillings was punished by hanging, and more serious offenses led to drawing and quartering and other lingering tortures. This criminal justice apparatus reflected the relatively simple, brutal and short life that typified both medieval England and later frontier America.

The Constitutional Revolutions

During the seventeenth and eighteenth centuries, treason, sedition and religious nonconformity were commonly prosecuted crimes. The American revolutionaries were deeply impressed with the dangerous potential of criminal prosecution as an instrument of political and religious repression. They made important changes in the system of criminal justice through constitutional provisions, statutes and judge-made rules which reflected special attitudes toward the role of the law, the function of the judge, the participation of the community in the justice process and respect for the personality of the accused.

The cornerstone of this constitutional system is its emphasis on the value of legality, which in this context is summed up by the rule of Magna Charta and the Bill of Rights: No person shall be deprived of life, liberty or property without due process of law. Volumes could be written about the definitions given "due process of law" over its long history; it develops and changes in meaning for each generation that grapples with it.[2]

But one strand of meaning it has carried for generations is that coercive government action is permissible only when exercised in conformity with a previously stated legal grant of power. In other words, no government official has general power to kill, confine or seize the property of those who offend him; he gains this power only when it is granted by the law. The citizen has a right to know in advance what the law requires, what acts are punishable and what demonstrations of legitimate authority the official must make before punishment may be imposed. To give reality to this conception that power shall be governed by law, there must be a mechanism to ensure that officials obey the rules. The potential abuses of investing absolute power in the king are avoided by giving the power to make laws to one body, and the power of administration to another. Also, the idea that power shall be governed by law is to be monitored by independent, law-trained judges, who review the legality of the exercise of coercive power and thus moderate it. The executive may not carry out punishment until an independent court has issued a formal judgment.

But law is not the only limitation on power. Government is legitimate only if it reflects and acts with the consent of the governed community. Both the judge and the jury originated as the absent king's watchdogs on the local community. But over the centuries the judge's personal commitment to the king has changed into a professional commitment to the law, and the jury's role has been modified from that of witness and informer for the state to that of assessor and weigher of evidence. In time, judge and jury have become intermediaries between citizens and their governors. Instead of serving as the king's watchdog on the community, the jury has become the community's watchdog on the state, guarding against abuse by the all-powerful and continually present government. The judge has developed a unique position as the law's watchdog on both the government and the community, guarding against abandonment of legal values under the pressures of the moment.

The constitutional model of the criminal justice process contains a radical view of the personality and place of the individual whom the state seeks to punish. In the medieval process and in the church inquisition that existed alongside secular criminal law, the accused occupied a subordinate and passive position. He was an object of inquiry, to be subjected to inquisition; he was not an independent actor. He was questioned but could not question. If he insisted on challenging the officials and asserting his innocence, he was tortured until he desisted and confessed.

But underlying the Anglo-American system is the concept, perhaps derived in part from the old trial by battle, that the accused is an equal contestant. Therefore, he is to be given competence and opportunity to challenge the legal basis for any action proposed against him. Judge and jury are arbiters deciding the points between the equal adversaries, and the government must demonstrate the accuracy of its charge. The accused is not a tool who may be used to accomplish his own condemnation. He is an independent personality. He must be respected, not abused, and is permitted to stand silent without his defiance being taken as proof of his guilt.

It is an unanswerable question whether this magnificent concept would have been invented if the framers had not been exposed to blatant political abuses of power. Would the authors of the Bill of Rights have become so involved with the details of criminal procedure if, in their minds' eye, they had seen the system being used only to punish ordinary thieves, burglars, drunks and addicts, rather than free thinkers and political dissidents? It is surely to their credit that they saw the indivisible nature of the problem of power. They insisted that all exercises of coercive authority to confine and punish had to be governed by law and administered by an independent judiciary, with a community check and an opportunity for those accused to challenge the action. But the undesirable and unjust alternatives remain all too familiar—the commitment of dissenters to mental hospitals, the administrative deportation of potential troublemakers and the jailing of children who have run away from home. Even when all political elements are removed, there is a real danger that unwanted and despised members of the community will be shunted to warehouses to be confined in subhuman conditions by mental hygiene doctors, juvenile court probation officers and parole board executives who operate independently of the legal structure just described.

As this adversarial and accusatorial view of the relationship of the individual to the state emerged, it proved a profoundly revolutionary idea, one which carried within it the seeds of most of the current problems in the administration of criminal justice. For despite these laudable philosophical assumptions, the person accused of crime is unlikely to be the equal of the state, nor is he likely to be in a position to effectively challenge its accusation. It has not been easy for the community to accord the same degree of legal recognition to the rights of the poor, the immature, the addicted and the mentally afflicted that it gives to other people. These persons are unable to champion their own cause and do not make a good showing for themselves in adversary judicial proceedings. On the contrary, it has been easy to conclude that citizens with little power deserve to be rendered more powerless; society unfailingly tends to reject, commit and cage them.

The ideal constitutional system was visualized by men who lived in a predominately rural society in which there was no sizable governmental bureaucracy and no professional police force or prosecutor. Their articulation of a due process system was a reaction to tyranny and an evil reality which its creators knew well. Like all utopias, the ideal continues to exist in the mind, and it is not certain that it will ever be fully realized. Nevertheless, the unique worth of this constitutional model has been demonstrated by its two centuries of existence, not because it has been applied fully, but because attempts to do so have led in wise directions.

The Rise of Professional Discretion

The society to which the legal model was to be applied changed rapidly and radically with the political and industrial revolutions of the nineteenth century. Professional criminal police had long existed on the European continent but were resisted in England and its colonies until 1830. As the police forces grew, so did the size and professionalism of courts and prosecutors. As the American continent was settled, urban centers developed the now familiar agencies of the criminal law. The court process ceased to be episodic; the four sittings a year by a traveling judge and local jurors grew into a resident court in which a full-time judge sat continuously hearing a high volume of cases initiated by policemen and processed by a district attorney.

During the nineteenth century the new professionals gradually obtained power. They created courthouse bureaus and invented techniques for serving them. The courthouse was transformed from a center of community culture into an office building. The private citizen complainant was replaced by the policeman, the part-time squire justice of the peace was replaced by the full-time magistrate and release of the accused on bail promised by his family or clan was supplanted by his release on a bond insured by a corporation and posted by a professional bail bondsman. The grand jury continued to be composed of amateurs drawn from the community, but it became largely the tool of police and prosecutors. Imprisonment replaced whipping, hanging and exile as the most common punishment for serious crimes; the first attempts were made to state a rational and comprehensive criminal code; and the first probation and parole systems began to appear.

In the twentieth century, imprisonment has been increasingly perceived as a means to reform, correct or isolate offenders rather than as an opportunity to take revenge or to make an example of the criminal. In keeping with this development and especially as treatment pretentions grew, greater discretion was given to the sentencing judge and the parole board to enable them to individualize punishment, to fit it to the situation of the particular offender.

In a real sense the early English criminal law was totally discretionary. Few rules were specifically stated, the law itself was largely unwritten and many of those who administered it were illiterate. The king's power was used whimsically, episodically and very uncertainly. What was predictable about its application was that it was an instrument of the king's political power and was to be used to promote his authority and to fill his purse. It is also safe to assume that the community's grand jury accused those it abhorred and swallowed the derelictions of those it loved.

The constitutional revolution sought to bridle this naked power by demanding universal and prestated rules, applicable to everyone and knowable by all. The administrators of the system were expected to be servants of the law alone, not to pursue their own or the king's interests. The process by which a decision to punish was made had to be open, structured by rules and subject to inspection and review. The legality of the constitutional model largely disallowed discretion in the application of its universal rules. The system was expected to run like a clock, marking its own time.

But the social changes of the last century and the growth and professionalization of the criminal justice system that accompanied these changes created new needs for discretion. The very universality of the legal rules demanded discretionary opportunities for interpretations and exceptions. The organizational needs of the professionals inevitably asserted themselves in demands for discretionary power to make the system work. Attempts to narrow this power by stating laws more specifically only produced more rules for the professionals to interpret. Over time, the professionals developed their own group sense of justice, their own values, a subculture distinct and coherent. The vindication of these group values depended on discretionary power to apply the legal rules as the professionals believed they should be applied. This new-style discretion flew in the face of constitutional ideals as surely as did ancient arbitrariness.

It is difficult to trace with certainty how this conflict between legal values and discretion gradually came to be recognized. It is not even clear when administrative disposition of criminal cases without trial became the accepted practice in most American communities. Most likely there were some communities in which the preference for disposition by trial never was strong. It is known that most authoritative books, commentaries and judicial opinions of the first half of the nineteenth century were familiar with, but tended to be hostile to, disposition by arranged guilty pleas, while those later in the century seemed more accepting of convictions obtained without trial and proof.[3]

The presence of police, prosecutorial and judicial discretion surprised and embarrassed most judges. The independence of the judiciary isolated judges from the administrative aspects of the matters that passed through their courts. Then as now, most of the business of the criminal courts involved poor people who did not have funds to retain attorneys. Most defendants did without lawyers, and most court-appointed lawyers were of distinctly inferior quality. As a result, few appeals were taken in criminal cases, and many basic problems, of which the discretionary practices are only illustrative, did not rise to the view of the courts of appeal. It was easy to turn a blind eye toward the gap between how the system worked and how it was supposed to work.

Judges and other officials simply denied the existence of discretionary practices and insisted that policemen and courthouse officials were merely enforcing the law as written. Sometimes the high rate of police and prosecutorial charge dismissals was explained as exclusively the result of judgments about the quality of evidence. Officials claimed that their discretion was limited to deciding whether there was sufficient legal proof to justify court trial. The system piously maintained its insistence on constitutional and adversary values.

This hypocrisy still can be observed in courthouses. It comes into sharpest focus in the court ceremony during which the administratively arranged guilty plea is offered and accepted. As the Peter Randolph case illustrates, the judge inquires whether the plea is free and voluntary, and whether any coercion, threats, or promises were used to obtain it. To each question the accused makes the expected reply and the answers are solemnly recorded, although everyone in the courtroom knows that the plea has been arranged, that the realistic choices open to the accused are few and that the entire process up to that moment, from the structure of the penal code to the whispered assurances of the prosecutor and defense lawyer, has been structured to create threats and rewards leading to the plea.

By the second quarter of the twentieth century the discretionary system was so widespread that it blended with the landscape, so familiar that it was virtually invisible even to those in the system. Courthouses became increasingly dependent on this way of doing business. Every part of the process became colored by the expectation of and the need for discretionary disposition without trial, usually through the guilty plea. The symbols of adversariness and the trial process remained in place, but they were harnessed to serve the needs of the administered courthouse.

The Response to Discretion

The times are bad, but they are not as bad as they were in the good old days. The past forty years have produced profound changes in American criminal justice. A more urbanized nation has been chastened and educated by the sour experience of Prohibition, the social reforms of the New Deal, the civil rights movement, the Vietnam War and the Watergate scandal. The last generation has been marked by national interest in equality of treatment of the poor and disadvantaged before the law, and in concern about official misbehavior. The central institution in this revolution in the criminal law has been the Supreme Court of the United States.

It is remarkable that in its first 150 years the Supreme Court decided few criminal cases. In the early 1930s a typical year's work for the Court included approximately two hundred full opinions, only five of which were likely to involve criminal cases. There was no significant intervention by the federal courts in the criminal law or procedure of the states, which, of course, handled virtually all the criminal cases.

Ironically, it was the conservative, pre-New Deal Supreme Court that set in motion the chain of reform and indicated the directions for later development. The Court did this by deciding cases concerning brutally coerced confessions and inadmissible evidence, and a defendant's right to counsel. These decisions showed twin concerns for reducing official misbehavior and for equal protection of the poor, later elaborated in a series of Court decisions which, for the first time, gave the majority of criminal defendants an opportunity to challenge the operation of the system.[4] The new rules excluded from use in criminal trials any evidence obtained through official misbehavior (coerced confessions, illegal searches and seizures). They also stipulated that defendants without funds were to receive, at state expense, a lawyer to represent them and a transcript of trial proceedings in order to press an appeal.

Perhaps most importantly, the Court's decisions focused increased attention on criminal matters. As the criminal courts attracted more lawyers, and as vigorous defenders of the accused became more common, championing due process became more respectable. These changes in attitude were reflected in American literature. The fearless defense lawyer—as typified by the fictional protagonist Perry Mason or by glorified real men, such as Daniel Webster or Clarence Darrow—became a familiar American folk hero. Appellate courts increasingly provided a more sympathetic forum in which the defendant could press his claim. Every aspect of the criminal processing system, from the moment of arrest to discharge of the parolee, came under critical scrutiny. In such a setting, the operation of the discretionary system could not escape unnoticed.

How could the courts, which so vigorously attacked confessions coerced through force or trickery by the police, tolerate confessions by guilty plea coerced through force or trickery by prosecutors or judges? How could any confession obtained by threat of punishment or promise of leniency be a voluntary act of free will? How could a judge, charged by the law to be neutral and dispassionate, participate actively in the negotiation of a plea? All of these questions arose with increasing frequency as the new order in criminal justice took shape. Yet until very recently the courts themselves did not rule on the important due process problems presented by plea bargaining.

The Supreme Court has broad power to decide what cases it will hear. In the 1950s and 1960s the Court several times went out of its way to avoid considering cases raising guilty plea problems. One reason for this judicial reluctance was the fear of announcing a constitutional rule that would require a wholesale opening of prison gates. That would be the likely consequence of upsetting the practices by which nine out of ten criminal convictions were obtained. Generations of failure to measure practice against stated values left the legal system a prisoner of its own inconsistency, fearful of dealing with the present lest past errors return to haunt it.

A foundation for change was laid by a series of observational studies of the administration of criminal justice which began to appear in legal and sociological journals during the 1950s.[5] These studies focused on exposing rather than explaining the informal and discretionary methods by which most criminal charges were resolved. They showed, also, that social science techniques could be used effectively in the study of courthouse affairs.

Based on these studies, reports by the National Crime Commission and the American Bar Association Project on Minimum Standards for Criminal Justice expressed a new set of legal attitudes toward the guilty plea.[6] Neither of them condemned or denounced plea bargaining out of hand. Both placed heavy emphasis on the potential value, usefulness and justice of a negotiated guilty plea system. Both stressed the need to devise legal reforms to make plea negotiation an open part of the criminal justice system. Both recommended that denial of negotiation be replaced by a process in which prosecutor and defense counsel openly and candidly discuss possible dispositions as an expected and regular part of trial preparation.

These proposals shifted the debate over the guilty plea from such questions as "Is it constitutional?" to "How can the existing negotiated plea system be modified to make it work more fairly?" Beyond that, the Crime Commission and Bar Association reports made the problems of the guilty plea a fashionable subject for debate within the legal profession. Judicial attention was inevitable and soon followed.

The Supreme Court Acts

As of early 1968 little law concerning the guilty plea had been announced by the Supreme Court. There had been scattered cases, dating back to 1926, stating the principle that the plea must be voluntary and uncoerced, but few cases had related this principle to the realities of the means used to motivate defendants to plead guilty. The first case arose out of an indictment charging one Charles (Batman) Jackson with kidnapping under a federal law which provided that when the kidnap victim is not liberated unharmed, the kidnapper can be punished by death "if the jury so recommends."[7] For defendants pleading guilty or otherwise avoiding a jury trial, the statute had no provision for the death penalty. Jackson asked the trial judge to dismiss the indictment, claiming it unconstitutionally forced him to risk death if he asserted his right to a jury trial. The trial court agreed, but the government appealed the decision directly to the Supreme Court, an unusual procedure that is permitted in rare cases in which a federal statute is declared unconstitutional. In the case of *United States* v. *Jackson*, the Supreme Court thus found itself confronted with issues it had long avoided.

The majority of the Court, speaking through Justice Potter Stewart, agreed that the Kidnapping Act did create impermissible pressures upon defendants to plead guilty and to give up their right to a jury trial. This aspect of the statute therefore was declared unconstitutional, and the case was sent back to the lower court for trial without the possibility that Jackson would receive the death penalty.

In the context in which the *Jackson* case arose, this decision seemed satisfactory. But in resolving its immediate problem, the Court opened for consideration a much broader and more difficult to answer set of questions. In particular, what of the defendant, now in prison, who had earlier pleaded guilty and thus apparently yielded to the threat of death which the Court in *Jackson* found impermissible? May he now be relieved from his guilty plea? The *Jackson* decision soon produced a number of petitions from federal prisoners seeking this relief. It was to take years for these cases to work their way up the judicial hierarchy to the Supreme Court. As they did so, the Court turned its attention to other aspects of the guilty plea problem.

The cases that next came before the Court in 1969 concentrated on the procedures by which the guilty plea is to be entered in court, rather than on the pressures and negotiations that may motivate it. In many courts the ceremonial tender of the plea was extremely brief, while in others a ritual set of questions and answers concerning the voluntariness of the plea was exchanged. The accused formally denied that threats or promises had been made to induce the plea, even when everyone in the courtroom knew that the plea had been arranged. Other courts avoided this charade by not asking any questions.

Speaking through Chief Justice Warren, the Court in *McCarthy* v. *United States*, held that a trial judge had failed to comply with a requirement of the Federal Rules of Criminal Procedure when he accepted a guilty plea without personally addressing the defendant and questioning him to make certain that he understood the technical elements of the tax evasion charge to which he was pleading, the rights he was giving up by his plea and the possible penalties that might be imposed.[8]

This decision is significant for what it says about the attributes of a valid guilty plea and the role it assigns the trial judge. The Court continued to emphasize voluntariness as the hallmark of a valid plea; the defendant's understanding of the elements of the offense and the consequences of the plea are important because they are necessary ingredients in a voluntary choice. But no lawyer would find that a contract was enforceable, even if the party who signed it understood it, if his only options were to assent or to be hung. The emphasis on voluntariness inevitably casts into doubt any guilty plea induced by explicit threats of severity or promises of leniency, as well as the threats and promises of an institutional character.

The Supreme Court in *McCarthy* emphasized the part of the Rules of Criminal Procedure that assigns to the trial judge the job of "addressing the defendant personally and determining that the plea is made voluntarily with understanding of the nature of the charge and the consequences of the plea."[9] But the opinion did not indicate how this is to be done in the common situation, in which there have been reduced charges, time spent in jail awaiting trial and corridor negotiations leading to the plea. The Court emphasized that in announcing these requirements, it considered its task to be merely interpretation of the rules of procedure. It denied any intent to announce a constitutional rule that would be binding on the state courts and could not be easily modified.

Despite these disclaimers, the rules were placed on a constitutional footing later that same year by the Court's decision in *Boykin* v. *Alabama*.[10] In this case a poor Negro, with no prior criminal record, pleaded guilty to robbery on the advice of appointed counsel. He received the death sentence, an unusually harsh sentence for robbery in any circumstances. At the time the plea was entered, the trial judge did not ask Boykin any questions, nor did Boykin ask the judge any questions. He remained silent. In an opinion by Mr. Justice Douglas, the Supreme Court held that the trial judge's acceptance of Boykin's guilty plea without an affirmative demonstration that the plea was intelligent and voluntary was so basic an error as to violate the constitutional requirement of due process. Voluntariness and the intelligent waiver of rights may not be inferred from silence; the judge is obligated to explicitly inquire into the matter.

The same factors that had stimulated the Supreme Court to pay attention to the guilty plea began to influence the state and lower federal courts. Major decisions in several federal courts of appeals and in the highest courts of New York, Pennsylvania, Illinois and California, among others, fortified existing doubts as to the basic legality of plea-bargaining practices and their consistency with the principle that guilty pleas must be intelligent and voluntary.

In three cases decided together in May 1970 the Supreme Court resolved many of the remaining questions. The first case, *Brady* v. *United States,* was a logical sequel to the decision in *United States* v. *Jackson*.[11] Brady had pleaded guilty to a federal kidnapping charge and was sentenced to imprisonment. He was fully questioned by the trial judge before the plea was entered. But later he sought relief from his plea, on the ground that it was induced by fear of a death sentence if he had demanded a jury trial. The court of appeal had denied him this relief. The Supreme Court affirmed this denial of relief.

In the second case, *McMann* v. *Richardson*, the court reviewed a decision by a federal court of appeals in New York granting a new trial to three state prisoners, each of whom claimed that his guilty plea was the product of an unconstitutionally coerced confession.[12] At that time New York law permitted a defendant to challenge the validity of his confession only by going to trial. If a defendant was in doubt as to whether the court would agree with him that the confession was unconstitutional (and he usually was), he ran a great risk in going to trial. The prisoners claimed that, lacking any way to suppress the confessions, they each were forced to plead guilty. The Supreme Court rejected this claim.

The third case, *Parker* v. *North Carolina*, involved a fifteen-year-old boy who pleaded guilty to burglary and rape and was sentenced to prison for life. He claimed that the plea was involuntary because under North Carolina law he had to plead guilty in order to avoid a possible death penalty. The Supreme Court affirmed Parker's conviction.

Each of these cases presented a situation in which the law was structured to place the most extraordinary pressures on a defendant to plead guilty and not to challenge by trial the charges against him. Each was an instance in which it was most questionable whether the law complied with the standard that a guilty plea must be a free and voluntary act. The Court was faced with the choice of abandoning the voluntariness standard, stretching its meaning beyond the range of common usage, or declaring invalid many thousands of the guilty plea convictions for serious state crimes, and releasing or retrying large portions of the prison population.

The political climate in the nation had shifted sharply in the preceding few years. "Law and order" was a consuming political issue, and the President had been elected in 1968 on a platform that promised basic changes in the direction being taken by the Supreme Court. Chief Justice Warren had retired and Chief Justice Burger now sat in his place. While more profound changes in personnel lay ahead, there were perceptible shifts in the viewpoints of the remaining justices as they accommodated to changing times.

The opinions in the *Brady, McMann* and *Parker* cases were all delivered by Mr. Justice White. The basic argument running through each opinion proceeds from a recognition that "The State to some degree encourages pleas of guilty at every important step in the criminal process."[13] While the State's agents cannot produce a plea by actual or threatened physical harm or by mental coercion overbearing the will of the defendant, the decision was that there is nothing inherently wrong or compelled by a plea "motivated by the defendant's desire to accept the certainty or probability of a lesser penalty rather than face a wider range of possibilities extending from acquittal to conviction and a higher penalty authorized by law."[14]

Justice White described the guilty plea system as an exchange of benefits between the state and the accused. The state gets the benefit of a conviction without the trouble of trial and the accused receives certainty and, usually, leniency. The appropriate standard of voluntariness is whether the defendant is aware of the direct consequences, including the actual value of any commitments made to him, and, therefore, a plea is not involuntary simply because it is induced by a desire to avoid execution.

Turning specifically to the *McMann* case, the Court further elaborated these concepts. The defendants in that case had been presented with the dilemma of pleading guilty or risking at trial the possibility that coerced confessions would be used against them. Oddly enough, the Supreme Court equated this unpleasant choice with the routine kinds of predictions, guesses and evaluations defendants and their lawyers make in every case. "Questions like these [whether to go to trial or not] cannot be answered with certitude. . . . Waiving trial entails the inherent risk that the good faith evaluations of a reasonably competent attorney will turn out to be mistaken. . . . That a guilty plea must be intelligently made is not a requirement that all advice offered by the defendant's lawyer withstand retrospective examination."[15]

The effect of these decisions was profound, both for the very limited concept of "voluntary and intelligent" they proclaimed and, more significantly, for their insulation of the guilty plea from later attack. As long as the defendant has a lawyer, the prosecutor does not publicly beat him in the courtroom, and the judge asks the right questions and receives the predictable answers, the arranged guilty plea is now beyond challenge.

Later in 1970, the logic of these cases was carried even further in *North Carolina* v. *Alford*. Henry Alford was charged with murder. Faced with strong evidence of Alford's guilt, his lawyer recommended that he plead guilty and eliminate the risk of a death sentence. As part of the process of taking the plea, Alford was questioned in open court, during which he said:

I pleaded guilty on second degree murder because they said there is too much evidence, but I ain't shot no man, but I take the fault for the other man. We never had an argument in our life and I just pleaded guilty because they said if I didn't they would gas me for it, and that is all. . . .

Well, I'm still pleading that you all got me to plead guilty. I plead the other way, circumstantial evidence; that the jury will prosecute me on—on the second. You told me to plead guilty, right. I don't—I'm not guilty but I plead guilty.[16]

This case raised more than the question of whether the plea was voluntary. By asserting his innocence, Alford cast doubt on the factual accuracy of the plea and raised the possibility that an innocent man was being convicted because of the threat of capital punishment. The Court, again speaking through Mr. Justice White, restated its position: "An individual accused of crime may voluntarily, knowingly and understandingly consent to the imposition of sentence even if he is unable or unwilling to admit his participation in the acts constituting the crime." Alford weighed the risks of trial against the risks of plea, and decided that the dangers presented by the trial were too great to bear, despite his asserted innocence. Once he made that choice and successfully avoided the risks of trial, he was not permitted to change his mind.

The cases discussed so far do not involve plea bargaining as narrowly conceived. When the pressures on the defendants flow directly from the statutes or rules of procedure themselves, as they did in all of these cases, there is no need for the prosecutor or the judge to negotiate anything. Late in 1971 the Supreme Court considered a case that did involve explicit bargaining. The prosecutor in *Santabello* v. *New York* had agreed with defense counsel to accept Santabello's plea to a lesser charge and to make no recommendation to the court as to the sentence.[17] The expectation clearly was that without a specific recommendation from the prosecutor, the judge was unlikely to send Santabello to jail. A series of delays followed, and by the time the case was heard for sentence a new defense counsel and a new prosecutor appeared in the courtroom. The new prosecutor recommended the maximum sentence. Despite protests from Santabello's lawyer, the judge imposed it. The Supreme Court unanimously reversed the decision. In the words of Chief Justice Burger:

> This record represents another example of an unfortunate lapse in orderly prosecutorial procedures, in part, no doubt, because of the enormous increase in the workload of the often understaffed prosecutor's offices. The heavy workload may well explain these episodes, but it does not excuse them. The disposition of criminal charges by agreement between the prosecutor and the accused, sometimes loosely called "plea bargaining," is an essential component of the administration of justice. Properly administered, it is to be encouraged. If every criminal charge were subjected to a full-scale trial, the States and the Federal Government would need to multiply by many times the number of judges and court facilities. . . .
>
> This phase of the process of criminal justice, and the adjudicative

element inherent in accepting a plea of guilty, must be attended by safeguards to insure the defendant what is reasonably due in the circumstances. Those circumstances will vary, but a constant factor is that when a plea rests in any significant degree on a promise or agreement of the prosecutor, so that it can be said to be part of the inducement or consideration, such promise must be fulfilled.[18]

In *Santabello*, the court explicitly put its seal of approval on explicit plea bargaining at the same time that it tried to keep the marketplace honest. Pleas may be bargained, but bargains must be kept.

The law as announced in the decisions since 1968 is relatively clear. A guilty plea is legal only if it is voluntary and knowing. The requirement has two practical effects. Statutes which penalize those who insist on a trial by subjecting them to more severe punishment are invalid. And before a judge accepts a guilty plea, he must personally question the defendant and make a record of the "free and knowing" nature of the plea. Yet the voluntariness requirement does not allow a defendant to later attack the validity of his plea on grounds that he was forced to plead by the threat of potentially more severe punishment following trial, even if the greater severity threatened was death. If the "free and knowing" requirement is met and there is evidence to support the plea, the defendant need not admit his guilt when he pleads guilty. He may plead to limit his risk while maintaining his innocence. Finally, as a corollary to the Court's legitimation of the bargained plea, the decision in the *Santabello* case requires that if the bargain is not kept, the accused must be given an opportunity to withdraw his plea.

The net result of the Supreme Court's rulings on the guilty plea process is this: The discretionary system that hinges on the guilty plea is lawful. Whether it is fair as well as legal remains to be seen. The Court did not demand significant progress toward a better justice process in exchange for its stamp of approval as it had in cases involving police interrogations, search practices and juvenile court procedures. The decisions require judges to observe the niceties of ritualistic questions and answers about the voluntariness of the plea. Further, they installed some protections against consumer fraud, particularly prohibiting the prosecutor from welshing on a deal. But the nuts and bolts level of courthouse operation is not substantially affected by these decisions.

For good or for evil, pervasive discretion and the use of forceful incentives to plead guilty are still permitted and are now positively sanctioned by the Supreme Court of the United States. The business of the courthouse has officially been shifted out of the majestic courtroom and into the offices and corridors, where punishments are arranged. Sadly enough, the Court has not helped Americans to decide whether this informal system of convicting and sentencing is more or less just than the one which implemented the due process concerns of our forefathers.

chapter four
Judge Perkins
considers the law

A major function of the criminal law is to influence the behavior of men like Peter Randolph. The system of justice must be seriously flawed for Randolph to have drawn so puzzled an impression from his experience in the courthouse. The job of educating and discouraging criminals is not done well if the signal they receive is garbled and unclear. It is done badly when those at whom the signal is directed come to hate the criminal law, to reject its values and to perceive as an enemy the society which established it. If the ceremonies of the courtroom do such a poor job of communicating their message to men like Randolph, it is reasonable to ask whether they are similarly unsatisfactory for the other participants, particularly the judge, the prosecutor and the defender.

Judge Perkins Ascends the Bench

On the morning he sentenced Peter Randolph, Judge Edward J. Perkins's business day began early, as usual. Although the superior court convenes at 9:30 A.M., Judge Perkins arrives in his chambers by 8:00 A.M., and sees his clerk at 9:00 A.M. He very much enjoys the quiet early morning hour, alone in his chambers, and feels that he does his best work then. During the three years he has been sitting on the superior court bench, he has made the room very much his own. He is at ease with the dark wood panelling, the heavy drapes, the high-backed leather chair and his huge desk, which is usually piled with papers and law books. The walls are lined with his judicial commission, bar admission certificate and law school diploma, as well as plaques and pictures of friends and events in his twenty-five-year career as a lawyer.

Like most lawyers, as a young man Ed Perkins had a secret yearning to be a judge. Fresh out of law school, he had gone into the district attorney's office to learn the trial lawyer's trade. After gaining sufficient experience, he had entered private practice with three other lawyers. At first this had been an office-sharing arrangement, in which Perkins was actually the tenant of an older attorney, but paid his rent in services rather than in cash. The practice prospered, and the relationship grew into a partnership.

Ed was politically active during this period. He became involved in numerous political campaigns, usually on behalf of friends, but sometimes for the party. He continued these activities when he entered private practice. After all, it was good for business to be known as a man with some political contacts, particularly as his law firm's practice grew to include a sizable amount of zoning and real estate law, as well as a steady flow of probate matters.

Perkins also took an active part in the affairs of his bar association. While these activities were not exactly like those of partisan politics, the two had much in common. Both provided good opportunities for lawyers to become known to potential clients and to each other. The bulk of a trial lawyer's business comes through referrals from other attorneys. Also, Perkins's ability to settle nine out of ten cases out of court, which was essential to his success, depended on his knowing and having good relationships with the attorneys he was likely to be opposing in court.

But Ed Perkins's bar association activities were not merely a crass search for business contacts. An idealist, he viewed his committee work as a real public service. He served two terms on the important committee that screened judicial candidates for the governor. In his state, judges are elected by the people.[1] However, most judicial appointments come up in midterm and, therefore, are filled on an interim basis by the governor. The man appointed almost certainly runs as an incumbent at the next election and usually is elected.

Five years ago the bar association president asked Ed Perkins to consider accepting an appointment as a lower court judge. Ed knew that the question really was an offer. He and his wife spent a long weekend thinking about it. To go on the bench was the fulfillment of a dream, but it also meant a substantial cut in income and giving up much of the excitement that he had enjoyed as a successful lawyer. The old dream of being a judge was still sweet; Perkins decided to accept.

Soon his days were filled with bail hearings, preliminary hearings, traffic court cases, misdemeanor criminal charges, landlord and tenant disputes, and small claims lawsuits. The volume of business was staggering. A single day's calendar of small civil claims or misdemeanor criminal charges might include several hundred cases, most of which fell by the wayside. One of the parties would fail to appear in court and, therefore, would default. Most misdemeanor defendants would plead guilty and would pay their fines without protest. In both civil and criminal cases, a compromise settlement often would be reached in the hall as the parties waited for their cases to be heard. Nevertheless, there was never enough time for Judge Perkins to stop and to work through the technical questions a case might present because the cases had to be kept moving. Sitting on the bench, Perkins would sometimes ask himself whether he should stop the machine long enough to hear and to worry through a particular legal point that interested him but that involved only a ten-dollar lawsuit or a five-dollar fine. Occasionally he bowed to boredom or to his legal background, carefully getting together all the arguments on a fine point of law or fact. More frequently, he simply made quick, almost intuitive, decisions. When he chose to be careful rather than quick, he was unable to plow through his long calendar by the end of the day. Plaintiffs, defendants, witnesses and lawyers were required to come back another day.

After six months in lower court, Judge Perkins found himself becoming increasingly mechanical in his handling of cases. He developed routine techniques and strategies for cases that fit a particular pattern—the sweater that went to the dry cleaners and came back with all the fancy buttons missing, the landlord's repossession of an apartment, the department store charge account run up by a wife shortly before or shortly after she separated from her husband, the park bench drunk, the Saturday night country club party drinker, the marijuana user, the petty thief and so on. The novelty wore off. The work became boring.

When a superior court judge died three years ago, Perkins telephoned the bar association president and the county chairman of his political party to express his interest in being nominated to the higher court. The word was passed, and soon the governor, acting on an enthusiastic report from the bar association committee, appointed Perkins to the superior court bench.

Judge Perkins is happier now than he was in the lower courts, but he confides to his friends that being a judge in any court is not without problems. One problem is isolation. Because he must guard against accusations of favoritism, he is no longer able to be politically active or to spend time with his close friends from the bar association. His social contacts are more and more restricted to other judges and their spouses. In the courthouse, each judge sticks to his own baliwick. Judge Perkins has never seen another judge at work, and he has never visited the district attorney's office or the public defender's office. Formerly an active man of affairs, he now finds himself in a very small world.

Perkins's work in superior court involves fewer cases than it did in lower court. Previously, in the solitude of the early-morning hour in his chambers, he had reviewed all the pleadings and technical points of the cases he was to hear later in the day. But he soon found that even in superior court most of the cases never came to trial. The parties to civil suits usually compromised and settled out of court, and defendants pleaded guilty, just as they did in the lower court. So Perkins decided that reading the files was largely a waste of time.

Now he spends most of his moments of solitude considering the sentences he will hand out. Because he has more time, he has become more introspective and deliberate. These traits, of course, are precisely what the community wants in its judiciary. Judge Perkins was given independence and tenure, and a distance was set between him and other men in order that he might develop them.

Now when he arrives in chambers, Perkins quickly reads his mail and looks over the folder of advance sheets reporting recent appellate court decisions. He may dictate a short letter or two, or draft a decision in a case he has recently heard. Then he settles down with a cup of coffee and studies the cases of men who soon will be before him for sentencing.

The law gives Judge Perkins broad discretion on what sentence to impose. He can sentence a defendant to the county jail but then suspend the sentence, letting the man go free. He can place the defendant under the supervision of the probation department for up to five years, fine him as much as several thousand dollars, or send him to county jail for up to one year. He can work out some combination of probation, fine and jail. Or he can sentence the same defendant to from one year to several decades in state prison. There are few guides to exercising this discretion.

Law books are full of technical rules that control the ways in which a judge runs a trial—what evidence he must admit or exclude, when he must hold a special hearing on a point of law, what his instructions to the jury must be. But these rules avoid the issue of punishment. The law gives judges very few instructions on how to use their awesome power over defendants. As a result, they may impose grossly disparate sentences on similar defendants.[2]

In the final analysis, a judge is never certain exactly what is expected of him. The police ask him to be tough, and the social workers ask him to be soft. Other pressure groups are also involved. But the law itself gives him little guidance. An army general would not be sent into battle with orders saying only "Be brave, and be victorious." Yet judges' official orders only ask them to do justice. Judges do not swear that they will take revenge on criminals, set them up as bad examples, try to rehabilitate them or try to protect society from them. They swear that they will do justice. But to define justice is another matter. To understand what Judge Perkins means by doing justice, it is necessary to step behind the courtroom facade and examine social values.

The Balance of Justice

Defining justice has been one of the primary tasks of jurisprudence, philosophy, ethics and the social sciences since civilization began. Thoughtful men always have found it difficult to make clear and comprehensive statements of what justice is. Contemporary ideas can be traced back to the philosophy of ancient Greece, and to the Near Eastern wisdom expressed in biblical and rabbinic traditions and such early law codes as that of Hammurabi. As a judge does justice, two ancient but competing approaches come into play. Justice is done when like situations are treated alike. Each individual is to be subjected to general rules, regardless of who he is. But justice also is done by giving each person what he deserves, by making the punishment fit the crime and the criminal.

71

This principle of adjustment requires recognition of differences in persons and circumstances. It conflicts with the first principle, equality in punishment.[3]

Every person's sense of criminal justice includes these two opposing principles, and it is difficult to express in words how the balance should be struck between them. Rather, communities rely upon legal ceremonies to act out symbolically the sense of justice they find so difficult to put into words.

The courtroom trial emphasizes the principle of equality. Like cases are to be treated alike, and questions of guilt decided according to universal rules. But sometimes this emphasis on equality produces decisions that do not seem just because individual differences are overlooked. Two defendants may justifiably be found guilty of burglary in the first degree, but are they equally guilty? A crime is defined not merely in terms of a physical act. Criminality is a complex mixture of action, thought and effect, including a requirement that the action be accompanied by a particular mental state on the part of the actor. This mixture varies from defendant to defendant, and the adjustment principle demands that the variations be considered.

Whether a guilty defendant is *really* guilty usually depends on an assessment of his intent. Yet intention and motivation are always problematic. They do not lend themselves to the black or white treatment of courtroom question-and-answer testimony. How is it possible to know with what intent a man entered the premises he is charged with burglarizing? Even a most sensitive and intelligent person would have great difficulty in describing clearly why he behaved in a particular way. People tend to attribute their own conduct to circumstances and situations, while observers tend to attribute other people's conduct to characteristics of the actor. Undue stress on the equality principle, to the neglect of the adjustment principle, minimizes these important differences. Concern for motivation and intent complicates decisions about just punishment as well as decisions about guilt. At best, the criminal statutes which prescribe degrees of guilt provided only a broad framework.

To Judge Perkins, sentencing is an effort to make the best of a bad situation. He knows that men are rarely reformed in jails or prisons and that caging men often damages them beyond repair. Yet he also represents the community, and, as he sees it, his community would not tolerate his dismissing criminals with a pat on the head and a warning not to do it again. One compromise is to give short jail terms. Another is to give probation whenever possible. In the last twelve months Judge Perkins has put on probation about seven out of ten defendants convicted of felonies. He reserves prison for the few criminals—approximately one in ten—he considers violent and dangerous.

Why Society Punishes

Judge Perkins assumes that criminal law is a means of regulating behavior, and he worries about its efficiency. But like most judges, he rarely asks why there is a system of criminal law. It is so much an expected part of the landscape that few people question its place. Most other government programs have clear goals, even if they are general—they are trying to get a specific job done, be it building roads, running a post office or providing schools for children. In contrast, criminal law is expected to do a variety of conflicting jobs, the most widely mentioned of which are retribution, deterrence, rehabilitation and isolation.

Punishment for crime is retributive. The state inflicts pain and suffering on men who have harmed others by their criminal behavior. The pain of punishment is widely considered a most appropriate response to the guilt of crime. Yet from ancient times, religious leaders have also emphasized the virtues of forebearance and forgiveness. Both of these limit, but do not eliminate, retribution as an acceptable goal of the law. Perhaps retribution has become less acceptable because lawmakers and enforcers want the law to reduce crime, and retribution smacks too strongly of revenge, the useless returning of evil for evil. Revenge is insatiable and always demands more. The princple of retribution, therefore, is of little help in deciding how much punishment to impose.

Beginning with the Age of Reason in the eighteenth century, the function of law has gradually changed from punishment for its own sake to punishment as a means to improve man's social behavior. Punishment is designed to deter future crime by making an example of each defendant, thus frightening society at large so that others will not do what the defendant did. Beyond this, punishment is designed to educate and, therefore, to reform the criminals subjected to it. As optimistic theories of human improvability and new psychological theories of behavior have become popular, education for punishment has given way to programs of rehabilitation and treatment of criminals.

There are two possible ways of achieving education through punishment: deterrence and rehabilitation. Deterrence has given some ground to theories of rehabilitation and treatment for criminals which propose that the law be used to heal the social and moral sickness within men. Criminals are to be rehabilitated so they can lead productive lives. Many of the defendants appearing for sentence are without skills and are dissolute; some are emotionally disturbed. Therefore, it makes sense to suggest, as Judge Perkins often does, that these individuals must be taught a trade and how to get along with other people.

In addition to its other functions, criminal law still provides a measure of social defense, seeking not to punish, deter, educate or cure, but to isolate human predators. Not long ago, social defense was an important factor in most sentences. In England, it was the basis of banishment to the American colonies, and later to Australia. In early America, concern for simple security was behind extensive imprisonment. Gradually, lawmakers and criminal justice administrators learned that wholesale isolation of criminals was both unnecessary and quite costly. So they asked for imprisonment of only the dangerous defendants. Now criminal law is supposed to make the community safe by removing and warehousing those persons who have demonstrated by their behavior that they are too dangerous to have around.

Many judges are aware of the weaknesses of each of these ideas about the criminal law. Idealized statements about what people hope the system might do usually are not followed in practice. The failure of rehabilitation cannot be cured by spending more money on various programs. There is no one type of treatment which has been proved effective; in fact, correctional workers are unable to demonstrate that they rehabilitate any more men than they could "save" by leaving them alone. It is true that the behavior of some probationers and prison inmates improves, but it is not possible to attribute this improvement to correctional programs. All men have the capacity to change, and many who at one time had engaged in predatory, damaging, violent behavior no longer do so. They have changed, have reformed, have become rehabilitated or, as some psychologists are fond of saying, have become adjusted. But there is little factual support for the idea that such change is created or even fostered by the incarceration and treatment imposed upon those convicted in the courts. The depressing evidence is that the very notion of treating or curing criminals is based on very poor psychology—it is impossible to treat people for immorality.

Judge Perkins is most cynical about deterrence. As does everyone, he knows that in some situations fear of punishment keeps people from committing crimes. Yet he also knows that family, group, religious, philosophical and other moral pressures prevent crime with much greater force than the small statistical chance that a person will be arrested, convicted and punished. So the test questions Judge Perkins asks repeatedly are these: How much reduction in crime do I gain with how much punishment? How do I measure the punishment necessary in this case to deter others from behaving this way?

About once a month, Perkins sees a defendant he considers dangerous. Such men should be isolated from the community, but it is difficult to decide what degree of dangerousness must be found before the state can justifiably spend the money, energy and democratic spirit necessary to strip a man of his liberty. Perkins knows that no one can demonstrate that all of the thousands of men now in prison are dangerous enough to be locked in steel cages. Nor has anyone been able to predict future dangerousness.

Many released prisoners commit further crimes, but Perkins has no reason to believe that persons released from prison are more likely to commit serious crimes than are persons who have never committed serious crimes. It seems obvious that even if all of those convicted of crime were killed or permanently removed to prisons, those remaining at liberty would still have the potential to keep the crime rate flourishing. Whether one believes that criminals are born bad or that it is society that spawns them, there is no basis for believing that society will stop creating criminals just because all of those who have been identified have been killed or jailed.

The criminal law system assumes that we know much more about how to predict, control and change human behavior than we actually do. The theory of deterrence does not work because very little is really known about how to discourage people from committing crimes. The theory of rehabilitation does not work because most criminals are not sick, and those who are suffer from ailments we know very little about. The theory of isolation does not work because, except in a few extreme cases, it is impossible to predict accurately who should be isolated and for how long. When all of the rhetoric is peeled away, the criminal law lies exposed as a procedure for hurting people who commit crimes, rather than for understanding crime or reducing its incidence

Doing Justice

Judge Perkins usually receives a probation officer's presentence report on a case several days before sentence is to be imposed. He reads it carefully, then puts it aside and lets his ideas jell until the day of sentencing. Frequently he meets with the person who prepared the report on a troublesome case. They discuss the defendant's background and what might be done with him. Occasionally Judge Perkins is also visited by the police department's chief of detectives. The chief does not make sentencing recommendations, but now and then he lets Perkins know that a defendant coming up for a sentence is an important police informer, who has been providing useful information on drug cases, that a burglar with a minor record is believed to be a professional, or that, in his opinion, there must be a crackdown on a specific crime, such as robbery. Such visits are technically improper if defense counsel is not present, but Judge Perkins knows that they are sometimes necessary. He also listens when a private defense lawyer comes around seeking leniency for his client. Assistant district attorneys and assistant public defenders rarely call.

On the day Peter Randolph was due to be sentenced, two other men were also scheduled for sentencing by Judge Perkins. Defendant Robert Hollows was charged with aggravated assault as a result of a brawl with a fellow tenant over the loudness of a radio. Hollows, a factory worker in his forties, had blackened the victim's eyes, broken his nose and opened his scalp with a gash that took twenty-five stitches to close. Hollows had been in a lot of trouble in his youth and once had been committed to the state reformatory for car theft, but he had not been in criminal court in fifteen years. He had been drunk at the time of the crime and at first had claimed that his vicious attack was in self-defense. He was charged with attempted murder but pleaded guilty to assault after his lawyer had assured him that Judge Perkins would not send him to prison. The probation officer had recommended ninety days in the county jail, to be followed by a year on probation.

The second defendant was Thomas Dunham, whom a jury had found guilty of holding up a liquor store. Dunham, age twenty-eight, had spent most of the previous fifteen years behind bars, having first been adjudged a delinquent at age thirteen. He had no significant work skills or employment record. This was his first charge of robbery, although he carried prior convictions of car theft, burglary and possession of dangerous drugs. The jury had found that while Dunham was on parole from the state prison he and a friend had begun a series of late-night holdups of liquor stores, markets and small restaurants. During the holdup he was convicted of, Dunham had carried a loaded revolver and fired a shot, apparently accidentally, over the head of the store proprietor. Dunham claimed that he was only a lookout, carried no gun, and fired no shot. The probation officer summarized his presentence report with these words:

All the personal and social data suggest that Thomas Dunham is unable and unwilling to play a productive role in society. I therefore have no alternative to recommending that he be returned to prison for a further term of institutional rehabilitation.

Neither the Hollows nor Dunham recommendations bothered Judge Perkins. Hollows had settled down. He was a good family man with a steady job. To send him to the state prison would destroy everything he had worked for. But a man cannot go around beating up neighbors, no matter how drunk and frustrated he may be. The probation officer's recommendation made sense and would get Hollows back on his job in three months. Nor did the Dunham case seem difficult. Dunham had to go back to state prison. He had graduated to the big time. Sooner or later, a man who sticks a pistol in someone's face is going to commit murder. A short term in county jail would not do; Dunham was too dangerous to remain loose.

Of the three cases, it was Peter Randolph's that troubled Judge Perkins. He felt that the probation program was not helpful for this kind of case. Although the probation officer's report did not suggest it, this looked like a case for the new Young Adult Offender Program. Judge Perkins was impressed by this program— "guided interaction, structured setting, group work—all aimed at gradually reintegrating the boy and putting him out on his own." Under this program, Randolph would go to a correctional facility for nine months, be diagnosed and given vocational training and rehabilitation. Then he would move to a halfway house for eighteen months, after which he would be put on straight parole. It made sense to Perkins. If Randolph were to make it on parole, the conviction would be expunged. Perkins decided to get the probation officer's views. He picked up the phone, dialed the probation office, and asked Bob Pollitzer to stop by chambers for a minute when he was free.

Bob Pollitzer is an old and experienced probation worker.[4] In college, he had majored in sociology, but his grades had not been high enough to make him eligible for PhD work. Upon graduation, just after the Korean War, he had taken a job as probation trainee, and a year later had made high scores on the civil service examinations for probation officer. He has been in probation work ever since. For the first six years he had supervised probationers, and he was good at it. His guiding philosophy was that probationers needed vocational guidance, employment opportunities and a helping hand. In those days he had occasionally loaned probationers money from his own pocket.

But things had changed. His department had pushed through legislation requiring each senior probation worker to have a master's degree in social work. Bob had gone back to the university on a part-time basis, and after four years of grinding night classes had won the advanced degree. The hard work paid off. He became a true professional, with knowledge of the ins and outs of nondirective counselling and individual psychotherapy. He was promoted to senior probation officer and for ten years has specialized in conducting presentence investigations and writing reports and recommendations to superior court judges, Ed Perkins among them.

It took Pollitzer less than five minutes to respond to Judge Perkins's circumspectly phrased order that he appear. The Judge motioned him to a deep leather chair along the panelled wall. After they had chatted casually for a few minutes, the Judge mentioned the Hollows and Dunham cases. The presentence reports were well prepared, and the sentencing recommendations seemed reasonable. No problems there.

Then Perkins brought the conversation around to the Randolph case. The Judge asked Pollitzer why he had not recommended that Randolph be sent through the Young Adult Offender Program.

Pollitzer's response was routine, "There's no record, no violence or heavy stuff. He's been in jail two months. Longer confinement would appear unnecessary. Time served seemed like enough."

"I doubt it. He's a loser. He's got psychological problems. You say so yourself. He's got alcohol problems. 'Inadequate personality,' you say. That calls for more intensive programming than your probation staff gives to ordinary petty offenders."

Pollitzer was unprepared for the Judge's comments because he had assumed that Joe Carbo, the assistant district attorney, had cleared the sentencing with the Judge. The deal was time served. It was a reasonable sentence—sixty days—just the kind that Perkins usually imposed on men like Randolph. Perkins was putting him on the spot. The public defender would not buy the Young Adult Program at this late date. Neither would Randolph, even if he was told that it was for his own good. It meant at least nine more months in a cell and a couple of years on the string. Pollitzer shifted uneasily and then spoke formally, like a lawyer.

"Your Honor, it is my understanding that there were discussions between the district attorney's office and the public defender's office. The plea was offered with the understanding that the felony counts would be dropped and that the defendant would be sentenced to no more than time served and probation. It seems reasonable. Randolph is young and has a future."

Now it was Perkins who felt pressured. The prosecutor, public defender and probation officer all assumed that he would go along with what they had agreed to. He could call off the deal and insist on the rehabilitation program. That was his right, his duty. But if he interfered now, he would have to give Randolph a chance to withdraw his guilty plea. That would mean more work for everybody, and Randolph would have to stay in jail until there was a trial or a new guilty plea.

"If I send him to the youth program he'll claim he was tricked," Perkins said. "But your recommendation is wrong. It puts him right back where he started."

The Judge paused to give the tense probation officer a reassuring smile. "Understand, Bob, I'm not dumping this on you. When you made the recommendation you were just doing your job. It's all right. I'll work it through."

The Power to Do Justice

Whatever a person's feeling may be about the operations of the courthouse generally, he is not likely to defend a system which puts undue pressure on defendants to plead guilty. The dangers of the purchased guilty plea are particularly strong when the "for sale" sign is erected with the active help of the trial judge. The prosecutor has tremendous power to coerce guilty pleas, and there is reason to worry about abuse of that power. When the coercion comes from the judge, there is even greater concern because the process of forcing a plea is so basically inconsistent with the judge's role as an impartial arbiter, a powerful but neutral supervisor. A distinguished federal trial judge, Edward Weinfeld, has put the matter this way:

> The unequal positions of the judge and the accused, one with the power to commit to prison and the other deeply concerned to avoid prison, at once raise a question of fundamental fairness. When a judge becomes a participant in plea bargaining, he brings to bear the full force and majesty of his office. His awesome power to impose a substantially longer or even maximum sentence in excess of that proposed is present whether referred to or not. . . . Intentionally or otherwise, and no matter how well motivated the judge may be, the accused is subjected to a subtle but powerful influence.[5]

Judge Perkins is very conscious that people view him as an

authority figure in a long black robe. He knows that he has power, and that if he uses his influence he is usually able to get whatever he wants in his courtroom. But he also knows that the wise judge avoids overuse of power.

Practically speaking, neither the defendant nor his lawyer is in a position to resist the judge effectively if he wheels and deals. Noncooperation almost inevitably assures harsher treatment. Any attempt to prolong charging discussions and plea negotiations by detailed examination of special factors can produce irritation, whether the delay is caused by the prosecutor, the defender or the judge. But the judge comes into a case only briefly; it is one of a large number of matters he must dispose of on a given day. He does not have time to assess and evaluate facts. When he intervenes by calling the lawyers in and forces a guilty plea by getting involved in deciding what the defendant should plead to, or what the sentence should be, he is likely to find himself only causing trouble. In these circumstances, the judge can too easily use the power of his office to make take-it-or-leave-it propositions to defendants and their attorneys—take this deal or go to trial and face a much more severe result.

At the same time, the judge knows how important the steady rate of guilty pleas is in his court and how crucial his cooperation is in enabling the system to work. It makes no sense for him to sit in court all day deciding cases in which there are no substantive issues. If a case is clear-cut, it should be disposed of by a guilty plea or a dismissal. Otherwise the lawyers are not doing their jobs. But for a guilty plea system to work there must be some reliable expectation of what the sentence will be if the defendant pleads guilty, and this expectation inevitably must come explicitly or tacitly from the judge who will impose sentence.

Whether the issue is stated in terms of what charge, how many counts, or even felony versus misdemeanor, the heart of all negotiations leading to a guilty plea is the question of punishment. An agreement may be reached that the defendant will plead guilty to a reduced charge on the understanding that he will receive probation or merely a county jail sentence, and not be sent to state prison. In fact, agreements on charges or counts are agreements on how serious the case is, and therefore "what it is worth." In some courthouses, there is a general rule that prosecutors will not discuss punishment explicitly. Such a rule is the essence of the guidelines recently put into effect by the District Attorney of Los Angeles County. The aim is to reduce direct prosecutorial bargaining on sentence in most cases. Sentencing is the judge's function, and this prerogative is not to be undercut by the prosecutor's bargaining. While this may reduce the ambit of explicit sentence bargaining, it seldom eliminates arranged punishments. When a crime is negotiated into a misdemeanor rather than a felony, the sentencing alternatives of the judge are automatically restricted. By selecting charges and counts, the lawyers establish limits to the case that will greatly influence how the judge sees it at sentencing time. In the extreme, a prosecutor and a defense attorney may agree to call a criminal act malicious mischief rather than armed robbery. They thus make it impossible for any judge to punish the accused for robbery. In some states, when a defendant pleads guilty to a felony, the judge may impose a sentence as light as a one-dollar fine or as heavy as life imprisonment. But if the defendant pleads guilty to only a misdemeanor, the judge cannot treat it as a felony. Severe punishment becomes impossible.

No matter how aloof a judge may think he is and no matter how eccentric others may think he is, he shares in a framework of understandings, expectations and agreements that are relied upon to dispose of most criminal cases. As does a prosecutor or a defense attorney, he can deviate from this consensus only slightly; otherwise he threatens the whole working structure of the courthouse. When he strays too far from expectations by imposing a sentence either substantially more lenient or more severe than the one agreed on by defendant, defense lawyer and prosecutor, it becomes more difficult for the prosecutor and defense counsel to negotiate future agreements.

Judge Perkins tries to stay within the narrow area left to him. He refuses to take any part in negotiating the terms of a bargain, but if the lawyers come up with a proposal, he is willing to discuss it with them in chambers and to give them his reactions to it. If the deal sounds reasonable and the presentence report does not contain any surprises, that is the sentence he will impose. In many cases, the lawyers do not discuss the plea with Judge Perkins. This may be because they know his views and his likely reactions to the kind of case in question. Thus, there is no need to ask him explicitly. Sometimes Judge Perkins suspects that the lawyers negotiate a guilty plea to keep him from hearing the facts of the case. If he were to hear in detail at the trial what was involved, he might not agree to the easy disposition they had settled on. Arlen Specter, former District Attorney of Philadelphia, described this aspect of bypassing the judge:

The strategic position of the defendant is often never better than before the state's witnesses have been heard at trial. Police reports . . . are often terse and frequently omit unsavory facts which are developed at trial. . . . Comparing a guilty plea, a non-jury trial and a jury trial, the conclusion is inescapable that judgments are ordinarily more harsh in direct proportion to the fuller disclosures involved in those proceedings. . . . After a jury trial with lengthy summations by counsel and charge by the court, the trial judge is very likely, at least subconsciously, to consider the case more serious, when it comes time to sentence, than he would have if he had thought about it for only a few minutes on a guilty plea.[6]

Whether he actively participates in the negotiation of the plea, limits himself to merely approving or rejecting the deal reached by the parties or refuses to even be informed of the content of the negotiations, the judge is involved in the bargain and is bound by it. Judges do go along with tacit and explicit deals, although some of them still claim to have no knowledge of these bargains in their courthouses. If there is a conviction after trial, the judge has heard the facts and knows something about the person before him for sentence. However, when there is a guilty plea, the judge's view at sentence is largely determined by the probation officer's investigation report. Judges accept probation officers' recommendations in more than nine out of ten cases; in some courts, 98 percent of the time.[7] Prosecutors can and do influence probation officers' reports and recommendations.

If the judge's position is delicate when he is explicitly presented with a proposed bargain before the guilty plea is offered, he can be even more uncomfortable when presented with a *fait accompli*, at sentence. Judge Perkins's practical options in the Randolph case were limited. If he reopened the issue of the appropriateness of the deal, he would likely upset both sides, and in the confusion the settlement might well fall apart. If he decided that the agreed sentence was incorrect, Randolph might be forced to go to trial and face the substantial risk of conviction of burglary in the first degree and a long prison term. On the other hand, his judgment might be accepted, but at the cost of creating a disgruntled defendant who knew an agreement had not been kept, or a dismissal by a furious prosecutor who angrily denounced judges who would not let criminals plead guilty even when they wanted to.

Judge Perkins was torn. The doer of justice in him wanted to know more—to learn more about Randolph, his crimes and his potential, and why the prosecutor, defense counsel and probation officer all seemed to think time served was the right disposition of the case. Yet the prudent and experienced administrator in him told him to stay out of the matter and to let them have their way. As do all judges, in the end, he had to share his sentencing power with others.

Discretion and Ceremony

Perhaps the most significant comparison between the trial process and the discretionary process is in terms of what it does to judges. The common-law trial exalts the role of the judge, who sits at the center and above the proceedings, actively supervising and by his dignity casting the solemnity of the law over the proceedings. An ideal trial judge is completely caught up in this ceremony of justice. He is calm, dispassionate, fair and dignified, even when the arguments he must listen to are silly, and much of the testimony he hears is either ridiculous or an outright lie. He makes his job seem more important than it really is. He is not bored by cases that contain no substantive issues and could be disposed of quickly. He is imbued with the importance and the seriousness of the judgments he must make, and his seriousness is infectious.

In contrast, much of the daily work of the judge in a court dominated by the guilty plea can be stupefying. He goes to the courtroom to accept guilty pleas arranged by others. He is inhibited from participating too actively in the negotiation of these pleas and can only cause trouble for himself by injecting himself too forcibly into the proceedings. He is rarely involved in determining degrees of guilt and is able to make few concrete choices about appropriate action. The cases flow past him with unremitting sameness and soon even he begins to see them in stereotypical form.

The common-law judge, with his majesty and his robes, developed out of a king's functionary many centuries before. The guilty plea has completed the cycle, converting the judge back into just another bureaucrat, charged with disposing of a certain number of indistinguishable cases a day, going through the ritualistic mumbo-jumbo of the guilty plea, shuffling the papers and moving the caseload on to the next stage in the process. He must once again be charged with doing justice, and in ceremonies as fitting to modern urban life as common-law trials were to the life of their times. This means, basically, that discretionary judicial processes must be made meaningful.

83

Judge Perkins Goes Along

After Bob Pollitzer left chambers, Judge Perkins sat silently for a few minutes. He drummed his fingers angrily on his desk, but then the tension passed. His shoulders rose in the barest hint of a resigned shrug. He realized that Carbo and Ohler had made a deal and had assumed that it would be agreeable with him. Pollitzer went along and wrote the report to fit the deal. If their guess about Randolph was wrong, he would be back in court again, whether he was on probation or not. The system would catch up with him the next time. Judge Perkins decided not to force the issue but to go along with the recommendation. He mulled it over for another minute, glanced at his watch and rose to enter the courtroom.

chapter five
Joe Carbo
negotiates the facts

Judge Perkins was disturbed by the disposition of the Randolph case because he felt that by not consulting him the courthouse staff had taken over his function. He was distressed because under the law it was his job to match punishments and crimes; yet Peter Randolph's fate was decided before the case came to him.

Perkins's feelings were understandable, but not totally justified. It is true that no one spoke to him about Randolph's guilt or punishment until the settlement had been reached. Nevertheless, he had played a part in that settlement because his performance in past cases and his likely views in this one were in the minds of the prosecutor and defender when they reached their understanding, and colored the views of the probation officer when he wrote the presentence report and recommendation.

Day by day, judges, prosecutors, defenders and probation officers encounter the same basic types of cases. Each brings to his work a blend of the conflicting ideas of justice held by important groups in the larger community. In time, courthouse workers develop a group sense of justice. They come to understand each other and learn to take each other's views into account. Each courthouse thus develops its own unique approach to dispensing justice. As a result, discussion of the details of each case is unnecessary. Each person knows what characteristics of an offender or his offense will mean guilt or innocence; they need only come to an understanding about the facts. In the course of their work, ultimately acted out in the courtroom ceremonies of justice, the officials develop and apply their sense of what is right in a way that enables the process to go forward in the face of irreconcilable community viewpoints. A closer look at the prosecutor in the Randolph case, Joe Carbo, shows how these crucial understandings are reached in the subculture of the courthouse.[1]

Assistant District Attorney Joe Carbo has always been systematic and in control of his affairs. In his two years as a prosecutor, he often has been annoyed at the way the office staff stuffs his in-basket with folders and papers. When he returns to his office after a long day in court, his desk is usually strewn with papers that snow down on him daily—police reports, presentence reports, copies of warrants, complaints, informations and so on. Every afternoon he must examine and initial these papers, marking them for insertion in the proper case folders. It is an unexpected part of his job, one he had not bargained for when he became a prosecutor.

Carbo looks the part he has chosen for himself—that of a goodlooking, bright and aggressive young lawyer of thirty-one, very much in command and on the rise. He did well in law school and after graduation took a job with a law firm. He sought experience that would lead him to an exciting career as a trial lawyer. However, he soon realized that clients did not come to the firm to have an apprentice try their cases. Usually, Joe was relegated to carrying the senior partner's briefcase or handling some of the less important matters, all in the name of gaining experience. He rarely saw a courtroom.

Soon Joe noticed that even the most experienced lawyers in the firm tried very few cases. They went to court on motions and preliminary matters but disposed of most cases by some kind of negotiation. It was too costly to do otherwise. When Joe finally progressed to what was called trial work, he found that it was mostly paperwork, often involving nothing more than the preparation and presentation of various forms and documents to the court clerk. The heart of the job and the key to success was maneuvering the opponent, usually an attorney for an insurance company, into a compromise. This was not to Joe's liking so, still seeking a career as a trial lawyer, he applied for a job with the district attorney.

Prosecutors' offices are always looking for clever young assistants like Joe Carbo. His kind is the cannon fodder upon which a good prosecutor's office is based. Most district attorneys are elected public officials; many of them, like Joe's boss, appoint most of their assistants on a merit basis. However, in some counties the hiring of an applicant depends more on his political connections than his skill as a lawyer.

The majority of prosecutors' offices give only on-the-job training to new staff. Thus Joe spent his first week on the job familiarizing himself with the courthouse operations and personnel. He dogged a senior prosecutor on his rounds. He learned all of the judges' names, the names of most of the prosecutors, and the names of a few public defenders. He watched preliminary hearings, arraignments and sentence hearings. He saw only one trial.

The following week, Joe was assigned four cases. He was delighted. By the end of the week, the four cases had grown to a dozen, and by the end of the month he was carrying a workload of about fifty files, most of them misdemeanor complaints and relatively petty charges. After another month, the fifty cases had multiplied and changed character. By then many of the misdemeanor complaints were handled by a new assistant district attorney. Joe was involved in screening and prosecutorial decisions, was dealing with the police on search and arrest warrants and was handling mostly felony cases.

Those early weeks were hectic. Despite his law firm experience, Joe was forced to learn a lot on the run. He often had to find out what he was supposed to do by asking an experienced police officer, a court clerk, or one of the secretaries in the office. Mostly he relied on his colleagues, all of whom had been in similar circumstances not long before. They encouraged him and seemed to expect that as a new man he would come to them for help. They also kidded him a lot, but tried to keep him out of serious trouble. "We're like doctors except that we don't have to bury our mistakes, they just go out and steal again," the man in the next office said. Several times during this period, Joe had to jump up in the middle of a phone call or an interview and hurry into the office next door to ask a more experienced man what to do. Gradually he became aware of the gap between "the way things are done around here" and the law as stated in the books. Without thinking much about it, Joe soon accepted the unwritten laws imparted to him by his colleagues as his guiding principles for handling cases.

It was imperative that Joe learn these unwritten laws well, because acceptance by the other members of the courthouse community was and is central to his whole reason for being in this job. He wants very much to succeed, to get promoted to greater responsibility and to be rewarded with a higher salary and position. But above all, he wants to earn a reputation as a trial lawyer. That is an asset, a commodity he can market in his pursuit of a career. Joe Carbo is a civil servant and a public administrator, but he regards himself primarily as a trial lawyer. Involvement with the criminal law is his job, but the job is merely a means to an end.

This professional viewpoint characterizes Joe's approach to his work with the police, whom he considers clients. Like any private attorney, Joe sits in his office waiting for clients who have legal burdens, in this instance arrest reports. His duty, he knows, is to prosecute these cases for the police just as a private lawyer works for his clients. But there is a difference. Much more frequently than a private lawyer, Joe must tell a client that he does not have a chance of winning—the evidence is no good, the witnesses are weak, the arrest was wrong.

This duty makes Joe an administrator of senior rank. Even police captains with twenty years' experience must come to him for decisions, and he usually has the last word. Joe's lawyer status makes him an expert who advises and counsels policemen in addition to serving them. Further, he sees the same policemen over and over. He comes to know and understand them, and they him. Like a corporation lawyer paid an annual salary to do legal work for a company, Joe is retained to do legal work for the police.

The professionalism that characterizes Joe's dealings with police detectives takes a slightly different form in his relations with other lawyers, particularly defense counsel and judges. The American prosecutor, unlike his European counterpart, is not part of a professional class that is distinct from or superior to the private attorney.[2] At most he is the equal of private lawyers of his age. American corporation lawyers, for example, tend to look down on Joe's line of work. For one thing, prosecutors and criminal defense lawyers do not make much money. For another, the ins and outs of criminal procedure are relatively simple when compared with the complex legal procedures involved in merging two corporations. The assistant district attorney is drawn from, and usually expects to return to, the ranks of the private bar. Its members are his colleagues, even if they are his opponents in particular cases.

Similarly, Joe does not see himself as a member of the judiciary or magistracy, as a French or a German prosecutor might. Many American judges, particularly those in the criminal courts, worked in their youth as prosecutors. As prosecutors they were advocates, subordinate to the judges and magistrates. Yet the relationship between prosecutor and judge is likely to be a special one, as is the relationship between prosecutor and police. Judges identify strongly with clever young prosecutors who follow career patterns similar to their own. Furthermore, the prosecutor is somewhat different from the other members of the bar, in that he is always in the courthouse and is likely to be assigned to a single courtroom on a continuing basis. Prosecutors come to know judges' quirks, and judges come to know theirs.

Joe identifies with courthouse personnel because he sees them as clients or fellow lawyers. He does not think of them, or of himself, as part of a larger system of criminal justice. In fact, he has rarely considered the purposes of criminal law. Nor has his legal training encouraged him to think in more abstract terms about why the system is as it is.

In his first year at law school, Joe was subjected to about fifty hours of class instruction in criminal law. The first half of the course dealt with the definitions of crimes—the differences between murder and manslaughter, burglary, theft and robbery—and with such mental elements as intent, responsibility and culpability. The second half centered on the study of criminal trial procedure, particularly the flowering body of doctrine embodied in the constitutional protections against illegal searches and seizures and self-incrimination, the rights to counsel and due process of law.

During the first weeks of school, when everything was still confusing and unclear, Joe's criminal law professor gave a dull and rambling lecture on retribution, deterrence, rehabilitation and isolation. As is typical of American legal training, these subjects were never discussed again during the next three years. Joe forgot about the lecture when he moved on to advanced courses in taxation, wills and trusts, corporations and bankruptcy. If his sense of criminal law as a program with a purpose and an aim is weak, Joe's exposure to the practical aspects of law enforcement outside the courtroom has been virtually nonexistent. He has never ridden in a police car, and none of his close friends are policemen. He has never visited a prison, or sat with a probation or parole officer as he interviewed a client or counselled a probation-er. Once, while an undergraduate in college, Joe and some of his friends had been arrested for being drunk and disorderly after a fraternity party. They had spent a few hours in a police lockup, but the charges were dropped early the next morning. Indeed, if Joe had been in serious trouble with the law, it is doubtful that he would have been hired as a prosecutor.

When he is off the job and relaxed, Joe Carbo will admit that he is not part of the cops and robbers aspect of the game. Nor does he see his job as a moral crusade (although one might get a different impression when watching him deliver his summation to a jury, his voice ringing with the tones of an avenging angel). His perception of what goes on around him tends to be technical and case-oriented. Like most of his colleagues, Joe has learned to see his effectiveness in terms of his capacity to handle the flow of work in a prompt and efficient manner, and above all, of his capacity to win cases, particularly trials. Little of his attention is directed toward policy. Unlike Judge Perkins, he rarely asks himself whether the system is working, and whether it is making wise choices in deciding who to charge and with what offense to convict them.

Dismissing Cases

Although Joe regards himself as primarily a trial lawyer, he has learned how rare jury trials are in the courthouse. It is only by disposing of at least ninety-five out of one hundred felony arrests that the courthouse can afford the time and energy necessary to bring the remaining cases to trial. Therefore, most of Joe's time and energy is spent in working to dispose of the majority of cases by dropping or reducing charges.

In each case, Joe Carbo's understanding of the facts is influenced by the courthouse environment in which he works. He decides his cases according to the customs of his courthouse—customs which have developed as his predecessors and contemporaries have tried to implement the demands made on them by community interest groups with varying conceptions of justice. They become policy, the criteria which everyone in the courthouse unofficially uses in assessing guilt and arranging punishments.

Even in the adversary world of law, men who work together and understand each other eventually develop shared conceptions of what are acceptable, right and just ways of dealing with specific kinds of offenses, suspects and defendants. These conceptions form the bases for understandings, agreements, working arrangements and cooperative attitudes. Norms and values grow and become a frame of reference which prosecutors, defense attorneys, judges and experienced offenders all use for deciding what is fair in each case. Over time, these shared patterns of belief develop the coherence of a distinct culture, a style of social expression peculiar to the particular courthouse. In performing his daily work, each prosecutor is indoctrinated into and becomes a contributing participant in the subculture of justice within the courthouse.[3]

This subculture is more than the collected chance views of the individuals working in a courthouse at any given time. Like a social class or an ethnic culture, it has a life and continuity of its own, a specialness of style into which new recruits are initiated and which they come to accept as their own. In part, the decisions made by courthouse officials like Joe Carbo and Judge Perkins reflect their individual senses of justice, and, in part, the interests and policies of the special organization (the judiciary or the prosecutor's office) in which they work. But, more important, these decisions also reflect the values shared by all the people who work in a particular courthouse.

These subcultures are not isolated from the outside world. Rather, they are responses to conflicts in the larger community. Courthouse personnel serve many masters. They must negotiate day-by-day procedures and policies that pacify the community groups who make contradictory demands on them. Political leaders who depend for reelection or reappointment on their ability to play on public fears and perceptions of crime press the courthouse to punish offenders severely. However, these same leaders also serve as the public's fiscal agents. By their budgetary decisions they force the courthouse to keep expenses down, to do less than may be thought necessary and to keep prisons from becoming overcrowded. The police, who are expected to keep the peace and at the same time vigorously enforce the law, demand that the courthouse back them up, accept their on-the-spot decisions, wink at any abuses of power, and react harshly to those who challenge their authority. Social workers and probation officers view the courthouse as the intake gate for their welfare and rehabilitation business. They ask the courthouse to be concerned with nonpunitive treatment of criminals rather than with punishment. Other segments of the community express their choices through interest groups that want prisons shut down, the judge replaced by a psychiatrist and the prosecutor replaced by a nurse. Finally, professional associations of lawyers and judges want courthouse operations to be a demonstration of their pristine ideals, unsullied by the sloppiness of compromise or the dirtiness of reality.[4]

These are only some of the interest groups who own the courthouse and who must be satisfied. Courthouse personnel must serve them all and avoid dissatisfying any of them. In doing this, they inevitably develop occupational and professional attitudes and procedures essential to getting the work done—just as do employees of factories, banks, business offices, government bureaus and other organizations.

The messages from the surrounding community received in one courthouse are likely to be different from those received in another. Accordingly, the group sense of justice in one courthouse might be quite different from that in a courthouse only a few miles away. For example, in one courthouse, burglars generally may be allowed to plead to a misdemeanor and receive probation on their first arrest, while in the next county, felony prison sentences may be common in such cases. Joe Carbo knows the customs of the courthouse in which he works, but he does not know if these ways of doing business and moving cases are used elsewhere. It is likely that he would be surprised at the variations in procedure and outcome that persist, even in nearby counties.

Prosecutors may not be aware of these differences, but private defense lawyers, who tend to get around more and who have clients spread over a broader geographic area, know that differences between courthouse cultures are important, even if subtle. Thus, practicing lawyers, no matter how competent, hesitate to take on a sensitive case in a town fifty miles away without bringing in a local lawyer to assist them. On Long Island, the law in action is not the same as the law in action in Brooklyn, despite the fact that the New York state statutes are supposed to govern both.

Because subcultures of justice are the outcome of bargaining and negotiating, there is little need for extensive day-to-day bargaining with respect to the settlement of individual cases. Once a set of courthouse practices has been negotiated with influential community interest groups, it becomes the law of that courthouse, no matter what the statutory law might be. As a result, everyone knows that cases with certain characteristics will be disposed of in certain ways, despite what the formal law says about how they should be handled. If prosecutor, defense attorney and judge all understand that labeling a particular man a burglar would be both unfair to the man and unnecessary for community safety, they are likely to search for a softer label—for example, trespass or unlawful entry—that will not have such unjust and useless consequences.

Except at times of crisis or scandal, the general public is indifferent to courthouse affairs, perhaps assuming that the criminal justice system mechanically operates as it is officially said to operate. It is the special interest groups that make their desires known. They have the influence, power and access to conduits of communications necessary for getting action. But it is obvious that these groups do not agree with each other about what should be done with, to and for accused persons. They send contradictory messages to courthouse workers.

It may well be that no community will ever gain widespread agreement on whether the objective of criminal law is to exact retribution, to deter, to isolate, to reform or rehabilitate, or on what combinations of these ends it wishes the machinery of justice to serve, and in which proportions. And as long as the community is torn by inconsistent aims, courthouse workers will be asked to serve more than one end. The American Bar Association's volume on *Standards Relating to the Prosecution Function and the Defense Function* puts the matter this way:

> The prosecutor has a dual role which reflects in a sense the ambivalence of public attitudes on law enforcement and is the source of some difficulties. On the one hand, the prosecutor is the leader of law enforcement in the community. He is expected to participate actively in marshaling society's resources against the threat of crime. . . . On the other hand, the office demands, and on sober thought the public expects, that the prosecutor will respect the rights of persons accused of crime. . . . The conflicting demands on a prosecutor may exert pressures on him which his sense of fairness as a lawyer rejects. Both his public responsibilities as well as his obligations as a member of the bar require that he be something more than a partisan advocate intent on winning cases.[5]

Clearly, however, when the attitudes of the professionals in the courthouse diverge too widely from those of strong groups in the community, problems arise. In matters of justice, as in all governmental activities, legitimacy depends on the consent of the governed. When there is broad disagreement about what should be done to criminals, that consent is threatened and the capacity of the courthouse to influence behavior and maintain respect is diminished. For example, in large cities, courthouse professionals become inured to much of the crime committed by young people who are not habitual criminals. Day after day they see these fruits of the community's larger ills: drug possession, car thefts, petty thefts, street fights. The events are so common that the officials do not regard the offender as someone dangerously abnormal who must be locked behind bars in a state prison. But a public aroused by a shocking case or fanned by demagoguery or police complaints often becomes outraged by what appears to be official softness on crime. Such consciousness may be created by the publicity surrounding a notorious case, as in the Watergate affair. Or it may be created by the inevitable accident which brings ignored practices to attention, or by the arrival in the courthouse of a new man—a judge, prosecutor or defender—who is not aware of and does not accept "how things are done around here."

Sometimes the divergence between the courthouse and the larger community arises because the justice professionals know that the legislature has embodied unwise policy in the law. Every prosecutor knows that politicians must be opposed to crime. In the heat of politics generally, or in the heat of political and press indignation about a particular kind of crime—for example, drug pushing or kidnapping—legislators set severe penalties. Their laws live on, but the penalties may not be proper at a later time in a changing community. They may even be improper at the time they are passed, considering the individual differences between offenses and offenders. For example the image of child molesting that the legislature has outlawed and the image of the child molester that the legislature has threatened with lengthy imprisonment and mandatory registration as a sex offender are not consistent with the courthouse subculture's typical experience of crime. Rather than encountering sex fiends or constitutional sexual psychopaths, prosecutors are likely to encounter inadequate old men who peek under little girls' skirts. When prosecutors choose not to prosecute such men for child molesting—as they frequently do—the decision is more than a bargained concession granted to the particular defendant or his lawyer. Rather it is the result of experts rightfully letting their expertise affect the way they do justice. The expertise, in turn, is knowledge based on past decisions that have developed into a common viewpoint, part of the subculture of justice.

Each subculture is thus a crystallized solution to the problems given courthouse workers by specific groups whose conflicting demands and conceptions of justice must all be somehow worked into the scheme of things. Each is a negotiated social order—a set of rules, understandings and customs—that has developed as courthouse workers have accommodated themselves to the demands of these various groups.[6]

When the influential public is aroused, powerful interest groups form coalitions to criticize and to focus resentment on the courthouse processes that are used to get rid of cases. A likely result of such public discontent is proposals such as those made by the Nixon Crime Commission which seek to abolish the negotiated guilty plea. These proposals ignore the underlying conflicts to which negotiation is a response. They assume that justice can be administered without confronting these differences. They seek an idealized criminal law that is clear and precise, and that does not have to accommodate messy disagreements and accidents. Such proposed cures are futile. In a free society, it is not wise to try for very long to administer the law in a manner insensitive to the community's whole range of legitimate and deeply held values and opinions. Such conflicts will not disappear simply because the courthouse mechanism for their adjustment is abolished. Among the virtues that would be lost in such "reform" is the remarkable self-adjusting capacity of the subculture of justice.

A Prosecutor's Discretion

Even before the prosecutor's initial screening, about one third of all felony cases are disposed of promptly after arrest by dismissal and release of the accused. No prosecutor sees any record of these arrests. The police sergeant in the stationhouse or the detective reviewing the matter concludes that a case is inadequate and does not even bother taking the papers to the courthouse. In an unknown percentage of these cases, prosecution was never seriously contemplated by the arresting officer. The arrest was made for other reasons. Perhaps when approached by an officer, a young man got smart and "flunked the attitude test."[7] He was handcuffed, searched and subjected to the other humiliations of arrest and booking before being released several hours later. Many arrests are made to get drunks off the street, where they are likely to get into trouble. Others are designed merely to separate fighting spouses or to harass prostitutes and drug addicts who congregate in public places.

Joe Carbo sees only those cases in which the police want to file a criminal complaint. He talks to the detective and reads the arrest reports. Although there may be cause for arrest in some cases, Joe dismisses them because he knows that conviction is unlikely in court, where guilt must be proved beyond a reasonable doubt. In some cases, witnesses are unavailable or are unwilling to testify.

Joe has learned to throw out most of the cases of assault among family members and friends. The argument may have been fierce the night before, and the next morning the victim may still be angry with the husband who beat her up, but it is most unlikely that she will still be angry and willing to testify a month later when the case finally comes to trial. In other cases there is evidence, but Joe either doubts the witnesses' truthfulness or doubts that a judge and jury will credit their story. Or the evidence of guilt may be clear but it was obtained by the police under circumstances that violated constitutional standards relating to searches, seizures, confessions or lineups and, therefore, is unlikely to be admissible in court.

Joe is occasionally involved in a decision not to prosecute because the accused could be useful to law enforcement. For example, "fences," persons who deal professionally in stolen property, are very difficult to catch and convict, but they are crucial to the careers of professional thieves. Accordingly, when the police catch a burglar who might be "turned around" to provide information and ultimately to testify against a fence, Joe is likely to agree to let the little fish go in hopes of hooking the bigger one. Similarly, small-time dope peddlers may be freed if they lead to big suppliers, and corrupt lower-level government officials may be given immunity from prosecution if they help to convict those higher-up. If the offer is accepted, however, the prosecutor faces the twin dangers that the informer will not deliver or that what he will provide is untruthful or useless. Many informants play a double game, providing enough information to maintain their credibility with the police and using their status as a license to steal without fear of prosecution. Joe Carbo views with skepticism all suggestions that he turn potential informers loose, but he also knows that, as a practical matter, informers provide the only effective way to catch the leaders of narcotics operations, corrupt officials and the bosses of organized and professional crime rings.

Finally, there is a substantial number of cases, perhaps as many as one in four, which are technically correct but which Joe would describe as "junky." These cases do not deserve felony prosecution because the punishment would be too severe. Perhaps a woman whose welfare check got lost in the computer stole some groceries, or a teenager who took a car drove it a few blocks and left it undamaged. Although technically these individuals are guilty of felonies, Joe has learned to divert such cases to dismissal or a filing on a minor charge. No plea bargaining is involved.

Joe considers the decisions made soon after arrest to be matters involving only him and the police. Unlike the charge decisions made later in the prosecution of felony cases, there is little internal office review of these decisions unless the police department complains. The judge and jury are not immediately relevant and only in rare cases is a defense counsel employed at this early stage.

But Joe Carbo's belief that these decisions are his alone to make is distorted. It understates the impact of the people he works with, the colleagues who helped him learn his trade. He knows what prosecutors, judges and even defense lawyers will think if he presses a charge. He also knows how the police view the situation. He can tell by gestures and clues whether the detective presenting a complaint is really anxious to prosecute the wrongdoer or whether he is not enthusiastic about the case and would be just as pleased if Joe took the responsibility for dropping it. In other words, Joe has learned how things are done in the courthouse in which he works. In large part, he bases his decisions on how he thinks other similar cases have been handled in the past. Cases which survive Joe's initial weeding out often are disposed of during negotiations with the police. The case of Ralph Childs is typical.

A week after Peter Randolph was arrested, Joe Carbo took his turn as complaint officer in the district attorney's office. A detective sergeant, Rudy Hernandez, brought in an arrest report on Ralph Childs and asked for a charge of burglary in the first degree. Carbo glanced at the report and turned to Hernandez for the details.

At 2:30 A.M. two officers, cruising in a patrol car, noticed an open window with the screen removed at the house of Alan Caldwell. As the driver slowed down, his partner saw someone walking around in the house with a flashlight. They parked their car down the street, stealthily approached the kitchen door, drew their guns, and burst in. They grabbed Childs, who was quite drunk and did not resist.

In many ways Ralph Childs resembles Peter Randolph. Both are young men. Neither has a prior record of conviction as an adult. They live not far from each other in rented rooms. Both are unskilled workers and both were drunk at the time of arrest. The major difference between the two cases, then, is not in the offenders. It is in the relationship between burglar and victim.

When Caldwell awoke and heard the commotion in his kitchen, he rushed downstairs to find the officers handcuffing his friend, Ralph Childs. He told the officers that he drove a truck, and that Childs worked for the same company as a loader. They had known each other for a few months. Childs had seemed lonely, and on a couple of Sundays Caldwell had invited him to his house to watch television.

A few nights before the arrest they had had a falling out over a poker game. The stakes were not high, but Childs had lost a few dollars and was out of money. He had said that he had a new electric drill and power saw in his room, so Caldwell had loaned him twenty dollars on an IOU for them. Childs had gotten back in the game and gambled away the money. Drunk, he had yelled that Caldwell had given him a fast shuffle. That had broken up the game. Caldwell and the others had written Childs off as a sore loser.

The next evening Caldwell had gone to Child's room to get either the money or the drill and saw. He had Child's IOU with him, and he demanded payment. Childs was furious. He argued that he would pay the twenty dollars the next week. But eventually he gave Caldwell the tools.

Childs admitted all that. He said that Caldwell had cheated him so he had gone to his house to take back the tools that were rightfully his.

When Hernandez had finished his report he asked for a felony burglary complaint. Joe said, "I don't see the intent." The policeman knew he meant something was missing: The fact that converts trespassing into burglary is the intent to steal on the premises. The detective was shocked, or feigned shock.

"What do you mean? He broke into this guy's house in the middle of the night. He jimmied the window like a pro. When we caught him he had the goods in his hands. So he lost the stuff in a poker game. He had no right to go breaking in for them."

Joe tried to joke these facts out of existence, "A friend does not a burglar make, even if he is a sore loser."

Sergeant Hernandez gave Carbo some more facts. "Well, in the first place he was no friend. Knowing somebody doesn't give you a license to steal from him. We've got the law . . . It's just lucky Caldwell didn't shoot the son of a bitch. The guy is a thief. Where did he get those tools in the first place? We both know he stole them. Or bought them for five dollars from somebody who did."

Joe stopped joking. "Look, Rudy, he has no record, nothing. He'd been drinking. Did he steal the tools? Do you know that?"

"He got that stuff someplace. And he broke in."

"So he broke in. We can make it a § 602 Trespass if you want. But it is hardly worth the paper and the effort—all the judge will do is fine him twenty-five bucks."

Hernandez would not give up. "Come on, this is clear burglary. The elements are there. Caldwell will testify."

"To what?"

"To burglary, for Christ's sake."

"This is just a social dispute. A civil matter. It's a fight over who owns some property. Look, it's not our policy to make arguments among friends into felony burglary. We can't win them."

"You can win this one—if you want to. Can you win a trespass?"

"If I want to. Do you really think this is a bad guy? No record. He just went in to get the tools. If we let him walk out of here, you guys won't see him again."

Now it was Hernandez' turn to joke. "OK, Joe. Paper the case. But you had better put up a big sign saying it's OK to steal as long as it's among friends."

The Ralph Childs case became a statistic. It was filed as trespassing. Childs pleaded guilty and was fined ten dollars. Caldwell was given back his tools. Later, perhaps, some crime commission would dig up both the record of the arrest—for burglary in the first degree—and the record of the trespassing disposition, and use the discrepancy as evidence that a felony complaint had been dropped in a plea bargain. But the subject of bargaining, if it may be called that, was the definition of burglary, and the facts as negotiated between Carbo and Hernandez did not support prosecution for that crime.

Long before Ralph Childs was arrested, someone in the district attorney's office had arrived at a policy to use a definition of burglary different from the one in the criminal code, one that excluded acts by social acquaintances. But that policy was not written down anywhere. Much depended on Joe Carbo's judgment about Child's intent and his ability to get Hernandez to accept that judgment. In Joe's particular courthouse, a case with facts like the one they negotiated is not burglary in the first degree. To dismiss the case outright, however, also would have violated informal rules, by failing to reward the police for their work. So the burglary was changed to trespassing. Everyone was relatively satisfied.

Negotiating the Facts

Joe Carbo's decisions do not end with the preliminary screening of arrest reports and complaints. Difficult decisions also must be made in the remaining cases, which will be filed as felonies. It is likely that a variety of charges are possible. For example, Joe Carbo had to decide whether to charge Peter Randolph with a single crime or a number of crimes, whether to charge aggravated burglary of a dwelling at night, or simple burglary, or perhaps only misdemeanor unlawful entry, or all of them. This decision would establish the setting in which later negotiations would occur, usually leading to a guilty plea.[8]

Often Joe is tempted to overcharge, to include the most serious offense he can imagine the evidence supporting. Overcharging is safe, it provides the prosecutor with a great deal of negotiating room, and it seems to furnish him with a threat to hold over the defendant's head in the form of heavy punishment. Sometimes young prosecutors become overzealous, but office policy is always set against overcharging. Charging every minor burglar as though he were a desperado reduces the credibility of the charges in genuinely serious cases. No one wants to go to trial with a weak case. By the same token, no prosecutor wants to set his charges so high that the defendant will not plead guilty. To ensure a degree of uniformity, Joe Carbo is required to submit all of his informations for approval by his boss and for weekly review at a meeting of the assistants. This kind of office review has become increasingly popular in recent years. It provides a good opportunity for all of the prosecutors to become familiar with what is going on in the office, to catch weaknesses in legal theory or proof and to avoid faulty prosecutions.

By now Joe Carbo knows pretty well how each of his colleagues is likely to see a particular case. Some of the prosecutors are tigers, always arguing to press the maximum charges to the hilt. Others tend to seek an easy way out by charging the mildest counts and letting the rest go. Some are sympathetic to young people on drug charges; others think the office should stay out of most sex cases. Some take the view that charges should be filed if there is legally sufficient credible proof to justify a conviction, while others insist that the correct standard requires that the district attorney not file unless the proof is such that he would vote to convict if he were on the jury.

Yet in all of this diversity there is unity, agreement, understanding. The tiger relaxes when the facts are right. The lamb becomes enraged when the offender is really bad. Young people on drug charges are one thing, but drug pushers are another, even if they are young men. Whether there is credible legal proof, or even proof beyond a reasonable doubt, depends on the definition of vague words like "credible" and "reasonable," and credibility and reasonableness are group definitions. That is, whether something is credible or reasonable to one person is closely related to whether it is credible or reasonable to another.

All such issues depend on facts. Yet Joe Carbo could not reconstruct Peter Randolph's activities the night he was arrested, and no one can project himself with certainty into the future to determine the impact of a given choice of punishment. In social life, unlike the physical and biological world, facts to a large extent must be negotiated matters. A description is found to be close enough to experienced reality, and the description is accepted as fact. The reality that is experienced is always more complex and ambiguous than the simple legal label with which the transaction ultimately is concluded.

It has been said that the pure and simple truth is rarely pure and never simple. Unlike the laws of physics, the facts in a case like Peter Randolph's can never be determined with certainty because they are largely a matter of the significance assigned to perceived events. One can imagine four very different headlines to the newspaper story describing Peter Randolph's presence in Mr. Simmons's garage:

a) Burglar Strikes at Night
b) Drunk Found in Garage
c) Man With Police Record Tries to Force His Way into Home
d) Unemployed Worker Gets into Trouble.

All are in their way accurate statements, yet each carries very different implications for how Joe Carbo had to respond to Peter Randolph.

If the prosecutors, defense counsel and judges who work in the courthouse were to spend their time trying to negotiate moral issues, they would never get their work done. Value judgments and conceptions of morality underlie the decision as to which version of the facts will prevail, but to concentrate on them to the exclusion of more pragmatic elements leads to paralysis, for agreement on such matters is impossible to reach. Procedurally, the officials' first task is to decide whether a defendant is guilty of a specific crime; if he is, the second task is to decide what, if anything, shall be done to him. To avoid becoming deadlocked in unanswerable questions, the professionals ask the second question first.

For example, the law states that any person who breaks into a dwelling intending to steal commits burglary. The law also says that he who commits burglary shall be imprisoned. One would expect the first question to be decided by the courthouse to be:

"Is this accused individual a person within the definition of burglary?" If he is, the officials must answer the second question, whether this person shall be imprisoned. Instead of following this logical order, officials making discretionary decisions often begin by first asking whether an accused person should be imprisoned. Then the prosecutor and other officials can decide whether he is guilty of burglary, of some other crime, or of no crime at all. "The facts," then, are not just evidence on one side or the other of the question, "Did he enter the house with intent to steal?" The process of finding facts on the question of whether a defendant is a bad person who should go to prison for burglary is a matter peculiarly subject to shading and negotiation.

The Prosecutors Confer

Joe Carbo was assigned to prosecute Peter Randolph on the day before the preliminary hearing. Looking back on the case from the day of sentencing, almost two months later, its petty character seemed obvious. But on the basis of the police report, the Randolph burglary did not look like an insignificant crime. A defendant with a prior arrest record was caught in an occupied house at night in the process of stealing. This is a serious offense; nighttime burglary causes great fear in its victims, and Mr. Simmons was thoroughly frightened. Many nighttime burglars are professionals who steal for a living. There is a large element of planning and choice in their crimes, so it is reasonable to believe that firm punishment will induce them to desist and, by example, will deter others from committing burglary.

Joe Carbo presented the Randolph case in these terms at the weekly office conference before filing an information. "Even if we only scare the burglar from burglarizing homes to stealing from stores and warehouses, we'll be increasing community security. People should be able to feel safe in their own beds at night," Joe concluded. Then he told his colleagues the case was clear-cut and unlikely to result in a trial. The charges probably would be reduced to a lesser degree of felony burglary and a guilty plea entered with the expectation of a prison sentence of two or three years.

Joe was surprised when one of the prosecutors doubted that the case was as strong as Joe suggested. "After all, he wasn't really in the house but only in the garage." Howard Sussman spoke up. "And nobody saw him touching that stuff that was piled up. How do you know he did it? The police didn't take fingerprints, and got no confession. In fact it sounds like he was so soused he was incapable of forming the intent to steal."

Carbo stared at his colleague. He considered Sussman an obnoxious nuisance, but did not underestimate his intelligence. His criticisms sounded unlikely, but one never could tell.

A senior prosecutor then volunteered some advice. "If this is going to turn out to be a weak case, don't push it too hard."

Joe knew what the man was driving at. The case might prove to be a loser at trial, and he could not afford to lose a burglary trial in which the defendant was caught in the house with the goods.

After some other prosecutors had made one point or another, the chief deputy summed up the group's assessment of the Randolph case: "It just isn't a case for five years to life, Joe. It doesn't look like burglary in the first degree. Go ahead and file it that way, but look into it and come down if you have to."

A Move Toward Consensus

Joe decided to ignore Howard Sussman's advice. He filed burglary in the first degree charges against Randolph. On the morning of the trial-setting conference Joe and Steve Ohler, the public defender, were chatting with Judge Perkins in the robing room behind the courtroom. Perkins looked over the morning's calendar and commented on its length: "We're getting swamped. We haven't been assigned any new judges, and the overload is killing us. Something's got to give."

Steve Ohler picked up the cue. Looking at Joe, he said, "If you pushed the serious cases harder and let some of the kids and drunks go we might be able to keep up."

Judge Perkins reinforced the point, saying to Joe, "A young fellow like you should be able to handle your caseload. I don't like to waste time with cases that should be disposed of."

There was not much Joe could say in response to the Judge's reprimand. He glared at Ohler who, obviously relishing the Judge's remarks, was nodding his head vigorously and grinning. But Joe knew the Judge was right. There were too many cases coming in. The outlook for a burglary conviction in the Randolph case became less rosy.

Randolph arrived, and when the case was called, Judge Perkins set it to be tried in a month. One afternoon about two weeks later, Carbo phoned Ohler and asked whether he had any idea about which of the cases coming up on the trial calendar were likely to be real trials and which ones might be disposed of. This kind of exchange of information is not unusual. Joe and Steve are adversaries, but they work together, and they share a concept of what constitutes just punishment. There is no need for either of them to go through the trouble of preparing a case for trial if the defendant is ready to plead guilty.

When the discussion reached the Randolph case, Steve told Joe he would go to trial. "You've got the facts wrong. This is a kid who drinks too much. No real record. I think the dummy just wandered into that garage looking for a place to pee. You'll look like a fool trying him for burglary in the first degree. There isn't a chance in a million that Perkins will send him to prison on a burglary rap. I'm not going to try to make a deal with you, old buddy. You don't have a case, and you can't play poker without chips, my friend."

Joe knew the public defender was trying to soften him up, and that when the bombardment stopped, he would make an offer. So he waited until Ohler had finished and then mildly asked him what he had in mind. The public defender suggested a plea to unlawful entry and a sentence of time already served in jail, plus probation. Joe was aware that he did not really know what Randolph was doing in Simmons's garage. Ohler might be right. Nevertheless, Joe rejected the offer. There was no need to agree to it because he could always get a similar deal later. "Talk about playing poker without chips!" he said to himself as he hung up the phone.

Overload, Weak Cases and Poker Games

The explanations prosecutors give for the informal procedures they use in their work tend to downplay the importance of what they are doing. These explanations make discretion appear mostly a matter of administrative overload and tactical maneuver. There are two principal variations on the theme of overload. One says that cases not prosecuted fully are weak ones in which evidence is lacking. The other says that the process of negotiation is adversary in nature and resembles war, poker or chess.

When asked why their courthouses are so dependent on arranged guilty pleas, prosecutors—as well as defense attorneys and judges—typically reply that they have no choice in the matter. They believe they are forced to negotiate and bargain to avoid trial because of the tremendous overload of cases. As one judge put it:

If all the defendants should combine to refuse to plead guilty, and should dare to hold out, they could break down the administration of criminal justice in any state in the Union. . . . The prosecutor is like a man armed with a revolver who is cornered by a mob. A concerted rush would overwhelm him. . . . The truth is that a criminal court can operate only by inducing the great mass of actually guilty defendants to plead guilty.[9]

There is some justification for this claim. A system which sends to trial less than five out of a hundred felony arrestees and which still lacks the capacity to give adequate time to investigate thoroughly even those cases which it does try, certainly seems overloaded. In metropolitan courthouses, there is simply not enough time to give each defendant all of the attention he wants, and probably needs. Most urban public services suffer from this overload problem—schools, hospitals, welfare offices and building inspectors.

Also, it is true that many weak cases come into the courthouse. As noted previously, the policeman's probable cause standard for arrest is by definition weaker than the beyond-a-reasonable-doubt standard that must be satisfied to justify conviction at trial.

Finally, it is true that the processes of trial and settlement of criminal cases do have strongly combative aspects superficially resembling a war or duel.[10] Undeniably, prosecutors and defenders sometimes use the adversary tactics of poker and chess in an attempt to win concessions from each other. On occasion, good defense lawyers do use strategy and tactics that threaten a prosecutor with the possibility that he will have to do what many citizens think he is supposed to do—give each case all the time and attention needed for maximizing punishment. Most commonly, they ask for jury trials when they neither want nor need them.

But in practice, most cases are disposed of in cooperative agreements reaching a consensus on facts and, therefore, on appropriate punishment. The watchwords are accommodation and compromise, not adversary combat. Incidents of genuine adversariness are rare in most courthouses, principally because the courthouse subculture itself represents a negotiated compromise position. Courthouse controversy is softened by a system that quietly balances conflicting community interests which, if pushed too blatantly, would lead to combat. Then it becomes a breach of etiquette for a lawyer to take a stance so adversary that it disturbs the conditions of peaceful coexistence.

The overload, weak case and poker attitudes about plea bargaining all imply that the prosecutor's role is totally adversary and that calendar problems, backlog, caseload, time pressures and similar indices of the burden of overwork are the evil roots of the problem. But it is simply not true that in an ideal criminal justice system every guilty offender would receive the full statutory penalty for the gravest crime that could be charged against him, and that only the burden of overwork forestalls this idyllic state. The idea that overwork forces the prosecutor to grant concessions to defendants in exchange for a bluffed out guilty plea all but ignores the prosecutor's concern for adjusting penalties to individual crimes and criminals in the interests of justice. It portrays the prosecutor both as a weakling and as an inhuman and unjust automaton who has been programmed to obtain the severest possible punishment for as many criminals as possible. Sadly enough, this damning but highly distorted portrait of the prosecutor is often painted by prosecutors themselves.

Here, culled from Albert Alschuler's interviews with courthouse workers all over the nation are some prosecutors' statements:

> We run a machine. We know we have to grind them out fast.
>
> I'll do anything I can to avoid adding to the backlog.
>
> We moved more than 2,000 cases through six courts during the past three months; clearly the most important part of our job is making defendants think they are getting a good deal.
>
> The first question I ask myself in deciding what to do for a defendant who might plead guilty is, 'How much time will I have to spend in the courtroom of this case?' The second question is, 'Can I prove the charge?'
>
> [A prosecutor suggested that he might say the following to a defense attorney] : Look, I'm awfully tired, and I have a bad calendar for tomorrow. Do you still want that deal you suggested?[11]

Each statement implies that only the prosecutor's burden of overwork causes him to offer deals or bargains too tempting to resist, and that attorneys for the defense, as agents of innocence, take whatever is offered them. But the statements rather unintentionally reveal, also, that so-called plea bargaining does not involve the adversary tactics of war and poker after all. By making such statements, prosecutors are necessarily revealing their strategy to the opposition. If prosecutors are interested only in maximizing punishment, why do they reveal weaknesses that can be exploited to decrease that misery?

These prosecutors, as well as others, seem to be advising the defense to slow down the machine, threaten trial, take up time and watch for a particularly clogged calendar. Even indifferent defense lawyers can deduce from such statements that—if the game is poker—they hold a number of wild cards and aces in every hand. A midwestern prosecutor told Newman, "All *any* lawyer has to do to get a reduced charge is demand a jury trial." But the matter is not so simple. First, defense lawyers who make such demands are merely exploiting the log jam in the courts, not creating it. Second, demanding a jury trial or otherwise threatening to take up time does not always bring a concession in the form of a reduced charge; this depends on the prosecutor's sense of justice, not merely his workload.

A California deputy district attorney told us, "I never take time into consideration in deciding whether to go to trial. If he [the defendant] should go to the penitentiary but won't plead, I'll go to trial no matter what the consequence, in terms of time, to me or the office. That's what I'm here for."

Like other prosecutors, this man settles most of his cases out of court. But his statement suggests that he is not in the adversary business of granting concessions to reduce his workload. Instead, he is in the business of judging the conditions under which it is right and just to send a criminal to the penitentiary. Left unspoken in his statement is the fact that men he believes should *not* go to the penitentiary are not going to go there, whether the defense uses delaying tactics or not.

Maybe the difference between this man and one who says he grants concessions because of his burden of overwork is a difference in the very conception of what plea bargaining is all about. Consider the way the assistant district attorneys in one California courthouse handle the cases of a private defense lawyer they believe to be incompetent. About one fourth of this attorney's clients plead guilty as originally charged. For the other three fourths, the lawyer always files for a jury trial. He may think he is threatening to increase the prosecutors' workload in order to win concessions, but he is not. All the assistant district attorneys in this county know that in the six years he has been practicing there *he has never once gone to trial.* He does not use the threat of trial to buy time on the street for his clients. He and his client always accept whatever disposition the prosecutor suggests whenever he suggests it; there is no bargaining.

If the district attorneys were only adversary machines of misery their question about this lawyer's tactics would contain its own answer: "Who does he think he is bluffing?" But in the real world, prosecutors are looking for justice rather than just for penitentiary time. They routinely grant so-called concessions to many of the lawyer's clients. They do so knowing full well that the attorney will not take up their time with a trial if they do not. "A defendant shouldn't be punished severely or treated unfairly just because he has a poor lawyer," one prosecutor said. "So we ignore the fact that this guy won't go to trial. We treat his clients just like those with good attorneys who might go to trial. Everybody might go to trial. That's not the problem. The problem is, is it worth it?"

If the guilty plea system were as adversary as the plea-bargaining and concessions language implies, prosecutors surely would use on defense attorneys every bluff and ploy said to be used against them. Attorneys for the defense rarely serve wealthy clients. Their overwork burden should make them just as interested as prosecutors in granting concessions. With both sides using poker tactics to gain advantages, the workday of the courthouse would be so crammed with bluffs, counter bluffs, and counter-counter bluffs, that there would be no time for dispositions.

When two combatants, playing by formal rules, encounter each other in the trial arena, there is little need for each to worry about the long-range effects his conduct is having on the other. Each battle is self-contained, and may the best man win. But in more informal relationships, a nasty adversary trick in one case is likely to have a bad effect on future cases. An Oakland, California, defense attorney illustrated this point by responding as follows when Alschuler asked him about protection of his clients' civil rights:

> I never use the Constitution. I bargain a case on the theory that it's a "cheap burglary," or a "cheap purse snatching," or a "cheap whatever." Sure, I could suddenly start to negotiate by saying, "Ha, ha! you goofed. You should have given the defendant a warning." And I'd do fine in that case, but my other clients would pay for this isolated success. The next time the district attorney had his foot on my throat, he'd push, too.[12]

This statement should not be taken literally. It is doubtful that the defense lawyer meant to say he unethically sacrifices one client in the interests of others. Rather, he seems to be saying that adversariness is avoided because it intrudes on the truth, understanding and goodwill so essential to prosecutors, defense lawyers and judges who must get the work done. In other words, it disturbs the subcultural conditions that make a crime "cheap" and courthouse life bearable.

If administrative crises and volume of work were the most important stimulants to developing and maintaining systems of arranged guilty pleas, prosecutors and judges should be expected to encourage defendants to plead guilty in direct proportion to the amount of overwork in their offices. There is no doubt that such encouragement occurs, as when on "bargain day" a prosecutor knocks down a whole host of cases that are awaiting trial, or when a presiding judge pleads with prosecutor and defense lawyer for settlement "because we have one judge sick and two on vacation this week." Yet it is significant that most suggestions of plea bargaining are made by defense lawyers, not by prosecutors or judges.

When Abraham Blumberg asked a large number of defendants to name the person who first suggested to them that they plead guilty, less than one in ten mentioned the district attorney.[13] More than one half named a defense lawyer. Other persons first suggesting a plea of guilty were psychiatrists, wives and other relatives, friends, policemen and fellow inmates. Consistently, when the same defendants were asked to name the person who most influenced the defendant in his final decision to plead guilty, 57 percent named defense counsel. District attorneys were named by only 16 percent.

Defense lawyers who persuade their clients to plead guilty to the crime originally charged or to a lesser offense are not merely lightening their own workload or helping prosecutors lighten their workload. Rather, they are participating in a justice subculture where everybody knows that justice could not be done if plea bargaining were abolished and a pure adversary system instituted, as advocated by both the Nixon Commission and New York Legislature. Defense attorneys often influence their clients to plead guilty because all of the so-called adversaries have tacitly agreed— usually without much conversation of any kind—that the defendant committed a crime, that his arrest was proper and legal, that the original charge was improper in view of the set of facts agreed upon and that the defendant should therefore be allowed to, and encouraged to, plead guilty to a crime punishable only by a fine, a few months in the county jail or probation.

The weak case explanation of the high incidence of arranged guilty pleas is similar to, and consistent with, the burden of overwork explanation. *The University of Pennsylvania Law Review* study allowed prosecutors to state more than one reason for their so-called bargaining.[14] Thirty-seven percent mentioned the volume of work, but 85 percent mentioned the strength of the state's case. Similarly, most of the prosecutors interviewed in Alschuler's study considered both "sympathy with the defendant" and their workload relevant to charge reduction, but *every* prosecutor said he considered strength of cases to be relevant. Two of them responded as follows:

> When we have a weak case for any reason, we'll reduce to almost anything rather than lose.
>
> We don't bargain for pleas here the way they do in Chicago. The only time we make a deal is when there is a weakness in the case.[15]

Both statements erroneously view the prosecutor as seeking whatever punishment he can get, demanding maximum punishment in every case but settling for less when that is unobtainable. Both suggest that the adversary relationship between prosecution and defense becomes manifest in prosecutorial bluffing and deceiving, designed to get some punishment for every defendant. This view of the prosecutor as a machine of maximum punishment rather than as a gentleman of justice has been explicitly voiced by a defense attorney:

> When a prosecutor has a dead-bang case, he is likely to come up with an impossible offer like thirty to fifty years. When the case has a hole in it, however, the prosecutor may scale the offer all the way down to probation. The prosecutors' goal is to get something from every defendant, and the correctional treatment the defendant may require is the last thing in their minds.[16]

There are two strange aspects to this statement. First, if the state's case "has a hole in it," why doesn't the defense attorney go to trial, rather than settling for probation? The very fact that a prosecutor makes some suggestion other than an "impossible" one should be the defense attorney's clue that the state's case is weak. Knowing or suspecting that a critical witness has disappeared or refused to testify, the defense has both a legal and a moral right to advise his client to plead not guilty, even if he believes him to be guilty.

Second, if it is assumed that prosecution and defense are locked in adversary combat, the weak case explanation of charge reductions casts doubt on the competence of defense lawyers. Were the system adversary, a public defender would exploit the prosecutors' statements about their weak cases, just as they would exploit their moanings about overwork. One prosecutor was amazed that anyone could view the strength or weakness of the state's case as the most important factor in the charge reducing process: "More than ninety percent of our felony cases end up in bargained pleas. I certainly hope they are not all weak cases."

The Prosecutor and the Public

One important question remains: If the burden of overwork and weak case explanations of charge reductions do not account for the practice of reducing serious original charges, or for the complaint officers' practice of avoiding serious charges, why do so many prosecutors voice them? Perhaps the answer rests in every prosecutor's need to pacify the conflicting groups pressing to have their interests implemented in the courthouse.

110

Attributing negotiated pleas to overwork is a political explanation of court practice. Voicing this explanation neutralizes important and powerful interest groups who say they want adversary procedures that would maximize the amount of punishment meted out to criminals. If the explanation is accepted, prosecutors can go about their plea-arranging way of doing justice without encountering too much damning criticism from community leaders who want them to be tough on criminals. They avoid losing elections or being fired.

The successful prosecutor blurs the competing conceptions of what his mission should be. One way to do this is to reduce adversariness in the interests of justice while at the same time arguing—loudly, clearly and publicly—that he engages in informal plea-bargaining practices because his office is overworked, despite careful fiscal management.

Lewis M. Steel, writing in a recent issue of *The New York Times*, made this point as follows:

> Fear of violent crime is rarely far removed from the consciousness of urbanites. Therefore, when it is reported that eight of ten city homicide cases have been resolved by plea-bargaining, with most sentences ranging from probation to a ten-year maximum, thoughts are stirred that the courts are releasing dangerous criminals to prey upon the populace.
>
> The implication is that if the courts were not so lenient the crime problem could be resolved. This implication is hammered home when district attorneys are quoted as saying they are forced into making these lenient plea-bargainings because they do not have enough money to try all the cases and that consequently "society is the loser."
>
> An analysis of the facts in most of these cases would indicate that the district attorney should have sought an indictment for a lesser crime, such as manslaughter. Therefore, what statistically appears to be a pattern of light sentences is grossly misleading. The reality is quite different. The system of plea-bargaining in homicide cases for lesser sentences results from a rigid policy of murder indictments in virtually every homicide. . . .
>
> It is therefore not surprising that district attorneys often agree to sentences that may appear lenient for the indicted crime of murder. They know many defendants plead guilty rather than risk the consequences of murder trials. If not for fear of the minimum sentence of 15 years to life, some would risk a trial, and a good percentage—perhaps one-third—would be acquitted. In addition, by the time a plea is agreed upon those accused have, in effect, already been sentenced to lengthy imprisonment. Extending their incarceration in a brutal and dehumanizing prison system only militates against rehabilitation. . . .
>
> Given these realities, it ill behooves a district attorney to complain about being forced to accept compromised pleas because of inade-

111

quate prosecutorial resources. Because of rigid over-indictment policies in homicides, plea-bargaining is inevitable and leads to sentences that as a general rule more than adequately exact punishment that fits the crime.[17]

Interest groups pressing for strict law enforcement can understand and accept the idea that tactical considerations, such as overload or a weak case, reduce penalties. On the other hand, a prosecutor who publicly admits that he is in sympathy with some defendants, or reduces charges because he believes the law too harsh, must do some fast talking. Similarly, proponents of adversariness on the part of defense lawyers can understand and accept tactical explanations for not fighting to the finish, but they are not likely to support an attorney who admits that his main job is to find some reasonable disposition of defendants he knows are guilty. It is therefore convenient, safe and reasonable for prosecutors and defense lawyers alike to attribute plea bargaining to mere defects in the warrior's armament—too much work and too many weak cases.

But the danger of such explanations of the guilty plea system is that they distort everyone's perception of what the courthouse is for. They create a reality which community leaders act upon but which is a misconception of what actually occurs. By decorating the courthouse to look like a slowed-down factory assembly line, they make people forget that it still bears some resemblance to a place of justice.

The overwork explanation implies that the function of the courthouse is to sentence guilty men to the punishments long ago stipulated by a legislature. If taxpayers would just pour enough financial support into the system, the idea goes, the county could hire the number of prosecutors and judges it would take to apply the rules rigidly to each case, and discretionary decision making would disappear.

The weak case explanation leads community leaders to believe that the prosecutor dismisses or reduces many charges on purely technical grounds. It misleads the public as to the prosecutors' real work, implying that if only the Supreme Court did not permit so many technical and frivolous defenses, the prosecutor would convict and punish all offenders.

The language of the poker game is highly inappropriate in a hall of justice. It implies that since trial is a risky course, the person holding a weak hand should cheat, lie and bluff to get the best possible deal. It assumes that the participants in the system practice trickery and deceit, and that they are not interested in the good of society or the good of the defendant. None of this is true, and prosecutors and defense lawyers, like judges, know it is not true. But it is politically expedient to talk about winning and losing cases as if they were poker hands, rather than talking about the process of doing justice.

In recent years, many people have become aware of the dangers created when coercive agencies, such as big-city police departments, win the power to determine their own size and methods. Such agencies can increase their personnel and gain acceptance of questionable procedures by encouraging public perception of something called "the crime problem," warning that the problem is growing at an alarming rate, and insisting that they need more support and more power to solve it. It is politically dangerous to permit officials to foster this public misconception. But the view of the courthouse, pushed by some officials, encourages similar misconceptions. The picture of the courthouse as an overburdened and slowed-down meat grinder both feeds upon and increases public demand for severity by creating an illusion—that the only business of criminal justice is to apply the narrow rules of the law strictly to all apprehended offenders and to punish them all as harshly as possible.

A more accurate and profitable way to look at the courthouse is to view it as a place where justice is done.

Offer and Acceptance

A few days before the Randolph trial was to begin, Joe Carbo started gathering his evidence and arguments. He wanted more information so he made a 4:00 P.M. appointment with the detective who had investigated the Randolph case initially. Then he went to work on his other cases.

When he went to court in the late afternoon for what he thought was going to be a straightfoward preliminary hearing of an assault with intent to commit murder, Judge Perkins reduced the charge to simple assault, and made some caustic remarks about the low standards used by the prosecutor's office to decide that they had proof beyond a reasonable doubt.

"Some zealous prosecutors seem to be pushing too hard," the Judge said in open court. Joe was the only prosecutor in the room; it was his case, and the barb found its mark.

Joe returned to his office late and tired, only to encounter a grumpy detective who had been waiting for over an hour to discuss the Randolph case. The detective let Joe know that he was prepared to work day and night to apprehend and assist in the prosecution of real criminals, but did not see why he should work day and night on a cheap burglary case like Randolph's.

When the detective had gone, Joe began the daily chore of neatly filing and sorting the papers in his in-basket. As he leafed through them, he considered the Randolph case. He needed more information, favorable or unfavorable, about Peter Randolph and his crime. However, he had no way to obtain this information. The detective had sarcastically told Joe what he already knew—that there was no missing evidence or missing witnesses to ask the prosecutor's investigators or the police to look for. There were no social workers or others to dig up employment records, school records or other social records. The probation department was forbidden by law from looking into the case because Randolph had not yet either pleaded guilty or been found guilty. Joe was even banned from talking with Randolph except in the presence of a public defender.

All he could do was to read the scant information that came across his desk on the case. A week ago the probation investigation report of Randolph's two-year-old joy riding conviction arrived in Joe's in-basket. It suggested that the crime could indeed be justified as joy riding and not car theft, even though it technically was car theft. Two weeks ago an aunt sent a letter saying Randolph had always been a good boy when he was little. It was headed "Dear Judge," but it somehow ended in Joe's basket. She wrote that Randolph's mother had done her best with the boy after his father had died, and that everything had been all right until he had gotten in with a bad bunch at school.

By the time Joe got down to the parking lot it was 10:00 P.M. and he was bone tired. He thought about the upcoming Randolph trial, about Judge Perkins and the detective and Steve Ohler and Howard Sussman's doubts. He went over his own doubts about what Randolph was doing at the kitchen door and what kind of a person he was.

As he drove home, Joe changed his mind. There was no point in being stubborn. Randolph did not seem like such a bad kid. The best solution was to treat his crime as a misdemeanor and to give him probation, plus time served.

The next morning Joe called Steve Ohler and accepted the terms he had proposed. He did not suggest that they check it out with Judge Perkins. "If you want insurance, you bring it up with

Perkins. I'll pass the word to Pollitzer. You call him too. I'll go along, but I'm not going to sell the deal."

"OK, counselor," Steve concluded. "I knew we'd play it through once you anted up and began to deal."

chapter six
Steve Ohler tangles with bureaucracy

In courthouses, as elsewhere, organization cannot be separated from policy.[1] The structure of courthouse work both reflects policy and is its source. We have stressed how values affect policy and organization. And we have seen how Peter Randolph saw the courthouse as a factory assembly line. He was treated as a case to be worked on rather than as a person to be worked for; no one cared who he was. To highlight the influence of organizational structure on policy, we now focus on the work of the courthouse officials who at first glance seem least bureaucratic and most independent—public defenders.[2]

The public defender's duty as an attorney is to represent his client to the best of his ability. But this duty is at variance with the need to dispose of cases expeditiously which is imposed by the defender's workload and the demands of the government bureau for which he works. Consequently, the public defender always balances his desire to ensure a just result for an individual client against his desire to please his superiors by moving the cases along.

Everything in Its Place

On the morning of Peter Randolph's guilty plea, Assistant Public Defender Steven Ohler parked his old VW at the rear of the parking lot behind the courthouse. As he walked across the deep lot he noted the parking arrangements. Although only the judges had reserved spaces, it appeared as if the public defenders were assigned parking spaces at the far end of the lot for their sorry collection of old cars and small imports. The assistant district attorneys usually parked their newer and sportier cars closer to the courhouse entrance. Most striking of all were the judges' Lincolns and Cadillacs which were parked close to the courthouse door, in a row of spaces reserved by name.

To Steve there is a striking similarity between the types of cars and the parking arrangements and life inside the courthouse. Public defenders are assigned to the losers in the system—persons charged with crime who are too poor to hire their own lawyer and who, by and large, are most severely punished. Perhaps that is why other courthouse workers as well as society tend to regard public defenders themselves as losers. Each courthouse bureaucracy rather grudgingly recognizes the rights of the impoverished defendants brought to it each morning. Practical action to provide these persons with lawyers has only recently been taken. Even now, Steve knows, the budget of the public defender's office is not comparable to that of the district attorney. Like the parking facilities, courthouse organization provides something less than equality for indigent defendants and their lawyers.[3]

The Making of a Defender

Steve Ohler is thirty-two years old and has been an assistant public defender since he graduated from law school seven years ago. He entered college during the early 1960s and was captivated by the social ferment and optimism of the period. The civil rights movement, the reform of police and court practices, the war on poverty—all of these promised social justice for the oppressed. The law and its courts were widely touted as effective instruments of change.

While still an undergraduate, Steve became increasingly aware of the fact that, in general, the poor suffer the most from injustice. He decided to do something about it. He enrolled in law school and specialized in criminal law. He received good grades in all his courses, and upon graduation received several offers of law firm jobs paying high salaries. He turned them down for a position as assistant public defender at nine thousand dollars a year.

Steve's three best friends at law school took jobs with service agencies funded by the Federal Office of Economic Opportunity. They represented the poor in disputes with their landlords, creditors and those who sold them defective goods. They helped poor women get divorces, enforced their rights to welfare, and helped them collect child support from absent fathers. They sued public housing authorities, welfare officials and hospital administrators, usually claiming that some administrative policy was depriving poor people of statutory or constitutional rights.

This was civil law, not criminal law, but Steve and his friends regarded their jobs as substantially the same—protecting poor people. As Robert Kennedy once said, "Too many people in our society know the law only as a stick with which they are beaten and not a shield that protects them."[4] Not only are the rules of society skewed against the poor, but the law is frequently used to do something bad to them.

Public defender's offices are mainly staffed by lawyers who, like Steve, once idealistically believed that they could improve the lot of poor people, rather than merely keeping the status quo. Without such idealism, the public defender system would collapse.

The defendant's right to a lawyer in all felony cases was recognized as a principle of constitutional law in 1962. In 1972, the same right was extended to misdemeanor cases in which a jail term is possible, but most communities had been furnishing legal services to at least some poor defendants for years. Most commonly, a judge simply assigned to a private attorney the duty of defending a person accused of crime. Unlike such assigned lawyers, public defenders work full time as government employees, just as prosecutors do. This system is common in some European countries. In the United States, it was first adopted in Los Angeles in 1913 and gradually spread to about one half of the states. In 1963 every state was required by court decision to provide public money for defense services for poor people accused of felonies, and the effect has been to create agencies which, whatever their name, tend to look like public defender's offices.[5] These agencies attract lawyers much more interested in doing justice than in processing legal cases.

Steve Ohler's first day on the job was remarkably similar to Joe Carbo's. He spent a few minutes meeting his new boss, the public defender, who wished him well. He took the oath, was assigned an office, and received his parking permit. After lunch, the chief deputy public defender explained the office setup and stressed the importance of protecting clients' rights and of ensuring that justice be done in every case, even at the expense of a trial. Steve suspected that the chief deputy had said these things many times before; nevertheless, he found in them a fresh confirmation of his idealism.

Steve discovered that his office had no formal training program or initiation process. During the first few days on the job, he was assigned to a senior colleague, who showed him around and answered most of his questions. After a few days of watching courtroom proceedings and learning the names of courthouse officials, Steve was assigned to a post of his own.

Unlike assistant district attorneys, public defenders ordinarily are assigned to a specific courtroom's cases, rather than being asked to process one case from start to finish. One defender tries to handle all initial appearances, another covers the courtroom where all preliminary hearings are held and still another handles arraignments. Once a case passes the arraignment stage, a presiding judge assigns it to a specific superior court judge, ostensibly for trial. Then the case becomes the responsibility of the defender in that particular courtroom.

There are organizational reasons for this zone defense arrangement in the public defender's office. First, it takes more of a defender's time to process a client's case from beginning to end. Time is lost going from place to place and waiting for cases to be called in court. The defender's office is chronically shorthanded; the work must be organized to make the most efficient use of scarce defenders rather than to provide the best service to clients.

Second, the public defenders in a courthouse cannot control the number of cases they will be assigned, nor may they decline to represent clients. In the prosecuting attorney's office, in contrast, a complaint assistant has broad discretion concerning which cases to prosecute, and on what charges. There is no complaint assistant to screen out cases for public defenders. They must take what comes, and it is quite impossible to predict what is coming on a given day. Accordingly, office manpower must be kept flexible, covering every courtroom.

Steve Ohler's first assignment, like that of most new public defenders, was to cover the courtroom in which initial appearances are held. The court clerk reads the complaint to the defendant, inquires whether the accused has a lawyer and, if not, whether he has money to hire one. In about three quarters of the cases the answers to both questions are in the negative. These defendants are routinely assigned by the judge to the public defender's office.

Steve quickly caught on to the routine. His job was to talk with each defendant, hoping to find a clue that would help the public defenders who would deal with the case as it moved through later stages. After the judge had set bail, the clerk would hand Steve a copy of the complaint and the police arrest report. If the client was free on bail, Steve would tell him to wait at the back of the courtroom. If the client was in jail, Steve would interview him briefly in the jury box while the court was hearing other matters or in the holding cell behind the courtroom during a recess. There was never enough time to explain very much to a client, or to gain much information from him. Within a few weeks Steve's interviews became routine. He asked about the accused's prior record, the details of the arrest, whether the police search had produced evidence or their questioning had gained a confession. Steve would jot down notes about each case, add them to the file, and pass the folder on to the lawyer handling preliminary hearings.

As he gained experience, Steve was moved from initial present-ment court to a preliminary hearing court and then to a felony trial courtroom. Each move brought him closer to a young lawyer's goal, the dramatic presentation of evidence and argu-ments to trial juries. Perhaps it was for this reason that each of Steve's moves was considered a promotion, despite the fact that pay raises did not necessarily accompany the new duties. In time and largely by chance, Ohler was assigned to Judge Perkins's courtroom.

For the last year Steve's primary responsibility has been to .epresent all of the indigent defendants assigned to Judge Perkins's court for trial. But because of the shortage of public defenders, particularly when some lawyers are ill, on vacation, tied up in a trial or swamped with other work, Steve occasionally must cover the sittings of another court judge in addition to his duties in Judge Perkins's court. At times, he also takes initial hearings or preliminary hearings for a few days, filling in where he is needed. He rarely handles a case from start to finish, and sometimes he finds it impossible even to follow a case through Judge Perkins's court. Instead, he receives. an armload of case folders in the morning, handles the pressing business of the moment, makes a few scribbled notes on the folder, and gives the file to another public defender, who may or may not handle the next stage in the matter.

To say the least, the zone defense system has severe conse-quences for the lawyer-client relationship. It is not unusual for an accused felon to have five or six different defense lawyers at one stage or another, each of whom can only make a quick attempt at doing justice. Public defenders have even fewer investigative resources than do district attorneys. They cannot call up a policeman or special investigator and ask him to interview a potential witness. Their basic source of information is not the client or his associates; it is the police arrest report and the file assembled by the prosecuting attorney's complaint officer. There is not enough time to become familiar with each case, not to mention with the client. The public defender tries to poke holes in the prosecutor's case, but he seldom is able to present witnesses and other affirmative proof of his own. Steve Ohler knows that this is not a good grade of service. Nor is it the kind of defense work he anticipated when he was in law school. He has long since come to realize that, like his friends who provide civil legal services to the poor, he is merely trying to prevent legal action against his clients. Rarely can he improve a poor defendant's situation. Nevertheless, he remains dedicated to the cause of indigent defendants. "Some protection is better than no protection," he often says. "Someone's got to be in court to answer when a case is called."

A Defender's Perspective

The very nature of the public defender's work isolates him psychologically from the persons around him. As an advocate in an adversary system, he cannot allow himself to be drawn too closely to judges and prosecutors, even though they are fellow lawyers. Nor can he allow himself to identify too closely with his clients, or even with the office in which he works. Often he finds himself in opposition to the criminal law itself, or at least to the aims of specific statutes. Yet like other public defenders, Steve Ohler is influenced by all of these factors in his daily work. There are strong pressures on him to cooperate, to identify, and his job is lonely because he considers these influences dangerous, even corrupting. He walks a tightrope, maintaining a balance between adversariness on the one hand and cooperation on the other. If he leans too far in either direction, he falls.

The sense of isolation that public defenders have from other courthouse workers, from policemen, and even from legislators, is matched by their isolation from defendants. Corporate lawyers tend to identify with corporation executives. Those who defend against personal injury claims begin thinking and acting like insurance company presidents. District attorneys come to identify with policemen and even to refer to themselves as law enforcement officers. But public defenders do not identify with criminals. Their clients are too unattractive.

All clients, including bank presidents, lie, cheat, stretch the truth and are hostile from time to time. But the public defender's clients possess these characteristics to a depressing degree. Most of them are guilty, but most believe, perhaps rightfully, that they are not as bad as the police and prosecutors say they are. Steve wants these clients to trust him, but he is seldom successful. For example, he rarely is able to overcome a client's stereotyped belief that prosecuting and defending is merely a battle of wits which the more clever man wins. Steve's clients, unable to hire brilliant attorneys, have been assigned a lawyer who seems uninterested in staging a dramatic trial that would establish their technical innocence. As a result, they are uncooperative or even hostile. They see the public defender as a government agent rather than as a lawyer.

In contrast, the clients represented by Steve's law school friends are also poor, but they and their lawyers like each other because both are fighting an unjust system. Moreover, the lawyers sometimes win their clients' cases. They not only avoid the disaster of eviction from a house or repossession of a car, but sometimes are awarded money damages or an injunction forbidding future abuse. The public defender is bound to lose most of the cases he is assigned. The majority of his clients ultimately will be convicted of some crime. Steve avoids judging his clients' guilt, but he is seldom persuaded of their innocence. Even when he successfully convinces a jury to acquit a client, he has mixed feelings. He recalls that line from the Gilbert and Sullivan operetta: "All thieves who could my fees afford relied on my orations, and many a burglar I've restored to his friends and his relations." If his client is a drug pusher, Steve occasionally wins by showing the judge that he must suppress evidence because it has been obtained illegally, thereby making it necessary for the judge to order the defendant released. Yet Steve feels that such winning is a form of losing— tomorrow the addict will either be back on the street dealing or be stealing to support his habit. The public defender must not let his own sense of justice intrude too far into his duty to protect ungrateful clients.

Steven feels particularly isolated from his boss and his fellow workers in the public defender's office because the allocation of work interferes with his relationships with defendants and routinizes interviews that he believes should be personal and professional. The need to cooperate, to keep his job, to get a raise, to win a promotion—all threaten to limit his independent judgment on what to do for a particular client. He knows that his boss not only wants him to be a good defense lawyer, but also wants him to keep the caseload moving.

Like a district attorney, the chief public defender can be a threat to his assistants, for he is under pressure to make the work of his office reflect attitudes prevalent in the political system of which he is a part. Most citizens do not know the name of their chief public defender, not to mention the name of his deputy or assistants. District attorneys are elected officials, but chief public defenders in most states are appointed by the county board of supervisors. The job is seldom a prestigious one, attractive to an ambitious man. Too often assistant public defenders are seen by the fiscal agents of government as lawyers paid to obstruct justice.

In Steve Ohler's county, one member of the county board of supervisors is especially sensitive to the law-and-order worries of the community. Once or twice a year he makes a speech criticizing the public defender's office for raising too many delaying technical motions and for what he regards as the lawyers' stubborn refusal to let guilty men plead guilty. His claim is that because they are paid by the county, they can afford to be as obstructionist as they want. After each such speech, Steve's boss explains the work of his office to the outside world; he also raises the official's point at the next staff meeting. He stresses the office's need to defend its clients and serve their interests, but he also points out the obvious need to keep abreast of the work. He tells the defenders that if there are too many trials, or even hearings on technical defense motions, the whole system will break down and they will lose the opportunity to give defendants any real help at all. The chief public defender's comments seem to have little effect on how cases actually are handled. Nevertheless, they remind Steve that he must isolate himself and be constantly on guard against the tendency to settle cases in the interests of office convenience.

Steve regards his job as holding the cruel aspects of the criminal law at bay. His duty, like that of other public defenders, is to challenge the actions of the district attorney—to get his man off, to get leniency, to get lighter punishment. He believes the stipulated punishments for most crimes are too severe, and he believes that the system puts tremendous pressure on defendants to acquiesce, to cooperate, to submit. His job is to find facts that will make severe punishments seem unreasonable, and to use constitutional law to prevent undue pressures.

Yet like most people, Steve does not favor crime or criminals. He is not opposed to the principle that people who commit crimes should be punished, educated, discouraged or isolated. But for each of his clients he must argue that *this* person is an exception to the general rule and, therefore, should not be punished as severely as the law allows. This perspective both isolates Steve from the general approach to law enforcement and sets him apart from other courthouse personnel. He often refers to judges and prosecutors as "them."

For Steve, the most frustrating sense of isolation comes when he represents a client whom he sincerely believes needs help. His initial duty is to assert his client's innocence. Therefore, he has few opportunities to advise clients about their real needs for assistance, and he has few personal counseling skills for inducing clients to accept his advice even when he does have an opportunity to give it. Worst of all, when Steve overcomes these hurdles and leads his client to plead guilty and to accept a so-called rehabilitative program—be it special treatment of drug addicts, psychotherapy for sex offenders, or vocational training for burglars—he frequently finds that the promise of help was a fake. The program does not exist, is all filled up, does not do what it claims to do, or is just a front for the same old punitive approach under a benevolent mask. To do his job each day, Steve must keep an isolating distance between himself and his hopes.

Competition and Accommodation

In law school Steve Ohler was taught that his job would be to oppose the prosecution. Consistently, the formal courthouse process is organized for individualistic competition between defenders and prosecutors, as though the law profession's and the public's stereotype of the defender's job were reality. No courthouse has an overall administrator or bureau to ensure that all personnel join hands in an effort to produce justice or, for that matter, to process cases. Instead, there is a productive bureau of prosecution and a counterproductive bureau of defense, both of which are mediated by a bureau of adjudication. It is no wonder public defenders and prosecutors think that they are fighting each other—they are officially organized to do so. Within the bureau of defense, too, the official stress is on case-by-case resistance to prosecutorial actions. Every public defender is supposed to give every assigned client all of the time and intelligence needed to show that his case is an exception.

But the unofficial structure of tasks and relationships in a public defender's office has more effect on the actual performance of individual defenders than the official structure does. Through experience the public defender learns to view most of his clients as wrongdoers who should be convicted of some crime and punished, rather than as presumably innocent men who should be defended. In the selective process occurring soon after arrest, the cases of obviously innocent men are dismissed by the prosecutor, as are the cases of men whose arrests were obviously illegal. The public defender's job, then, becomes more a matter of arranging pleas for the remaining guilty than of defending the innocent.

Experience also teaches the public defender that vigorously protecting each client from conviction and punishment will advance the criminal careers of some of them. He has trouble identifying with unattractive criminals of low social class. It is easy for him to identify more strongly with fellow lawyers—including judges and prosecutors—who symbolize law-abiding society. Moreover, he needs accolades from his fellow professionals more than he needs them from defendants. As time passes, he learns that he must be a good fellow, a moderate rather than an extremist, if he is to win these accolades. He might aspire to be either an adversary tiger or a man of justice—or some combination of both—but experience teaches him that his career will not be furthered by taking the most vigorous position in a case, especially if doing so means antagonizing the judge, the politically potent prosecutor, powerful law-and-order interest groups, or his boss.

Consistently, the public defender learns through experience that he has only transient contact with defendants but continuing and close professional, social and administrative relationships with other courthouse lawyers. No matter how strong his idealism, and no matter what the official claim about his relationship with clients, his actual perception of defendants is bound to be affected by the circumstances in which he encounters them, by the rush of business which forces him to be concerned with some things and prevents him from experiencing others. More specifically, the defender's view of his clients and the job he does for them is strongly influenced by staffing problems which decree that he has limited opportunities to know a client, that he must deal with only a segment of a case before passing it on to someone else and that he must depend on the files for information more than on what his client tells him.

Staffing problems ensure that neither lawyer nor client will see the other as an individual. Yet staffing problems currently are part of the informal organization of every public defender's office. The legal and public stereotypes of courthouse work, and the formal organization constructed to implement them, erroneously assume that defendants are rich men who can pay a lawyer for his personal services. Accordingly, if the lawyer is paid enough by a defendant, he is duty bound to drop all his other work and give his individual attention to that particular client. But of course the clients of public defenders are poor. They cannot buy a lawyer's exclusive services. Even defendants who are well off financially can seldom afford to buy all of the legal services that they think they need, and probably do need. Nor is the state going to buy individual legal services for all of its thousands of indigent defendants. To do so would be politically unthinkable and economically unfeasible. Until there is a change in courthouse goals, it seems inevitable that public defenders' offices will be unofficially organized to ensure that defense lawyers follow routine, accommodate, avoid disruption and pass the files down the conveyer belt to the next lawyer in line.

Transformation of Goals

The kinds of conflicts inherent in the public defender's job are likely to arise whenever an organization's goals are vague and its structure is loose. Measurement of success or failure then becomes impossible, and new, more quantifiable goals and tighter structure are likely to appear. The new organizational aims are likely to be more precise, and progress toward them can be set down in statistical tabulations.[6] For example, an organization dedicated to the imprecise goal of delinquency prevention is likely to transform its aims in such a way that progress can be suggested in annual reports revealing the number of children sent to summer camp, fitted with eye glasses, given extra help in school and so on. Similarly, a prison having rehabilitation as a goal is likely to compile statistics on the number of inmates enrolled in trade training and to remain silent about the number of prisoners repeating their crimes. And in courthouses, vague goals, such as enforcing the law or doing justice, are likely to be changed to goals worded in terms of the number of cases annually disposed of by dismissal, guilty plea or trial, the percentages of defendants placed on probation or sent to prison, or the averages of the length of prison and jail terms.

Courthouse subcultures of justice are transformed by concern for moving cases. Progress toward this unofficial goal is measur-

127

able—it is possible to compile statistics, to alter workloads, and to quantify budget requests. The inevitable effect of this transformation is that case decisions are based on what is good for court organizations as well as on what is good or just for society and individual defendants. When moving cases becomes a courthouse goal, justice decisions are compromised by bureaucratic needs.

From the standpoint of legislators and government executives, justice as a courthouse goal is not satisfactory because it is not measurable.[7] They need statistical evidence that the taxpayer's money is being well spent. One such measure of efficiency and effectiveness is the ratio of courthouse workers to the number of defendants processed each day, month or year. If it can be shown statistically, for example, that judges are overworked, new judgeships might be forthcoming. But if it is only vaguely asserted that justice might be better pursued if more judges were hired, new personnel are not likely to be added. For practical and bureaucratic reasons, then, the official courthouse goal of doing justice is melded with an unofficial goal—moving cases.

The practical effects of such goal transformation are evident in Steve Ohler's career. In his seven years as a public defender, Steve has not won promotions and pay raises solely because he pursues justice, although that is necessary. Neither has he advanced in rank and status solely because he occasionally challenges unconstitutional practices of police and prosecutors, although that also is necessary. He has won the accolades of his boss, even of Judge Perkins, primarily because he has an outstanding knack for processing the flood of cases that daily washes through the courthouse door. After seven years in his line of work, Steve, like other public defenders, regards himself as a specialist in constitutional law, insuring that his clients' rights are not and have not been abridged by police and prosecutors. He also sees his clients as persons in need of justice, leading him to refer to them as good guys, bad guys, helpless drunks, malicious killers or other kinds of people worthy of discretionary justice decisions. But on the other hand, he still views his cases as workload, as a personal burden to be lessened whenever it is ethically possible to do so, as a bunch of numbered papers he must rapidly and efficiently process like a clerk.

The Peter Randolph case came to Steve Ohler's desk in the same way that it came to Assistant District Attorney Joe Carbo's desk. A filing-room clerk dumped it in his in-basket, along with half a dozen other case folders. Like Randolph's, most of the cases were calendared for trial in Judge Perkins's court. The remainder were calendared for a hearing or trial in some other courtroom, where the assigned public defender was unable to handle them. Two men had resigned from the office within the previous two weeks, and one was occupied with a long murder trial. Their caseloads had to be divided up among the remaining public defenders, all of whom were already treading water trying to keep up with their own workloads. All of the cases were reassignments to Steve of work originated by another assistant public defender.

Steve thumbed through the Randolph file. It contained copies of the same papers included in Joe Carbo's file—the police report, the record of prior arrests, a transcript of the preliminary hearing and a copy of the newly filed information. Included also was a blank interview form with spaces where Steve was to record data such as the defendant's age, sex, race, occupation and his version of the incident. On the cover of the file jacket were scribbled notes made by the other public defenders who had handled the case thus far. The notes recorded what had happened to the Randolph case on a particular date and included a few cryptic words of advice to the next man down the line.

For example, on August 3, the day Randolph was first brought to the courthouse, an assistant public defender had scribbled the following:

Jail stuff. Not caught in house. Drinker dingbat?
No possibility of bail—no ties or money.

The case had passed to another assistant, who was handling preliminary hearings at the time, in addition to his regular work. He had scrawled an almost illegible paragraph which Steve deciphered as follows:

Dead bang burglary. Homeowner and police sold witnesses. What ties him to pile of property? No confession offered at prelim. Def. looks suspicious, confused. Probably lousy witness. Drinking man. No trial here. Try for misdemeanor and jail sentence.

A week before the trial setting conference, Steve went over to the jail for a talk with his new client. The five-minute interview confirmed the impressions he had gotten from reading the file. The arrest was not illegal; the police had warned Randolph of his right to remain silent and to have a lawyer; and the complaint assistant's charges were not outrageous. Randolph did not seem aware of what was going on and just wanted to ramble on in a vague fashion.

Charges of first-degree burglary can sometimes be beaten, even if the client was arrested in the house. It is a matter of creating doubt as to his intent to steal. If the defendant testifies that he was confused and thought it was a friend's house, or that he was just looking for a place to go to the bathroom, at least some jurors might buy the story. Even if only one juror accepted this version of the facts, it would be enough to prevent conviction. Unless the charge is a serious one, a hung jury—one unable to reach a unanimous verdict—is equal to a jury that unanimously acquits, because the prosecutor is unlikely to try the case a second time.

But to persuade even one juror that an accused burglar did not intend to steal is not easy. Among other things, it requires a defendant who is presentable, credible, sincere and articulate. Steve Ohler's defendants rarely have these characteristics. His short visit with Randolph had convinced him that Randolph did not have the image jurors like in a defendant either. To Steve, this meant that the case was not triable. Actually, Randolph appeared to be one of those defendants for whom a defense of confusion, ignorance or mistake would be quite reasonable. Ironically, such defendants are least able to establish at trial that they were confused at the time of the alleged crime. The ability to stand trial requires sterner and more cunning men than Peter Randolph.

To best serve all defendants, a public defender must very carefully select the few who will go to trial. One of his problems is time. If he does not dispose of a large percentage of cases almost immediately, he will be unable to give good service to any of his clients. Where constitutional rights have not been infringed and there is no credible chance of either a dismissal or an acquittal, it makes no sense to keep the case open. Another of the defender's problems is professional responsibility. In selecting the few cases on which he is going to focus his time and intelligence, he must carefully assess his clients' interests. If he selects incorrectly and ultimately loses, the defendant will suffer, receiving more punishment than he otherwise might. Every public defender also must consider his credibility as an adversary threat to the prosecutor. The ethics of his profession pit him against this opponent. If he does not dispose of open-and-shut cases, the prosecutor will not take him seriously as a lawyer—it would be too easy to bowl him over.

When Steve was first appointed a public defender his boss had warned him:

"Being a public defender is a tough job day in and day out," he said, "I hope you have the personality for it. Not everyone does. It's like being a doctor in an emergency hospital. It's no job for the squeamish. If you go to trial and make a mistake the client gets hurt, his family gets hurt, you get hurt. The hero who makes a constitutional case out of every cheap burglary that comes along hurts his clients in the long run. Few trials based only on constitutional issues work out to the defendant's advantage. Your job is to defend the person against the charge, not to reform the legal system. You take a hell of a risk if you insist on the fine points but don't win the argument. You're gambling with his life, because they will throw the book at him. Don't do it unless it's the only way out and the guy wants it."

Because Steve Ohler had been over these factors so many times, he did not have to weigh each of them carefully as he interviewed Randolph. He simply and almost immediately decided that this was a case to be disposed of by guilty plea. But making that decision did not end the matter. He had two more things to do. He had to persuade the prosecutor to agree with him on a proper sentence. It would be of no use to plead guilty unless there was some advantage for the client. Then he had to help Randolph see his position realistically. It would be useless to make a deal with the prosecutor if the client would not accept it.

The first task would be easy. Joe Carbo did not want to waste his time trying cheap cases any more than Steve did. Judge Perkins, who runs a tight courtroom, would expect Joe and Steve to keep the cases moving. Carbo probably already suspected that Randolph was not a bad kid. Convincing him would be simply a matter of mustering the right kind of facts.

As for Randolph, Steve was fairly certain that he would accept a plea that would get him only the time he had already spent in the county jail. He did not look like the type who was going to assert his innocence. By now the jail house lawyers would have advised him against going to trial. Nevertheless, he had to clinch a deal with Joe Carbo before talking to Randolph about pleading. Otherwise, he might set his hopes too high.

Measuring Efficiency

When Steve Ohler exercises his discretionary power to settle a case, no one is able to tell whether the settlement is made in the interests of justice rather than in the interests of bureaucratic efficiency. Even Steve himself is not certain. He knows that as he "plays it by ear" he does justice, meaning that he, as an expert, devises case dispositions that seem satisfactory. He also knows his boss will not rate him highly if he takes too much time with each case. Discretion exercised wisely in the interests of justice cannot

131

be readily distinguished from discretion exercised wisely in the interests of organizational convenience.[8]

There are a variety of ways for a public defender to excel. First, he can be a superior technician with unusual knowledge of criminal law and procedure, and outstanding ability to put that knowledge into practice. The defender uses such knowledge and skill as he asserts the innocence of defendants, formally challenging the prosecutor to prove beyond a reasonable doubt that all the elements of the alleged crime actually are present. He also calls upon all of his technical skills when he asks the judge for dismissal of a charge for some constitutional reason—the arrest was illegal, the confession was illegally obtained, the identification lineup was not properly conducted. This criterion of excellence is the one most commonly voiced by courthouse personnel as they rate each other. "He is a first-rate lawyer" means that he is better at the techniques of lawyering than some other public defenders are, no matter what the product of that skill may be.

Second, the lawyer's work is excellent if it creatively produces a desired end product—justice. As the work of a research chemist is, by definition, excellent if he makes important contributions to science, a public defender's work is, by definition, excellent if he contributes significantly to doing justice. As long as the defender is honest and ethical, it does not matter what techniques he uses to make this contribution or how many hours he spends in the courthouse. A defender may not be the cleverest legal mind, the most articulate advocate, or the greatest cross-examiner, but he will be respected if he has a knack for bringing cases to sensible results that are in his client's interests.

Finally, the work of the defender is excellent if he carries more than his share of his office's workload, whatever it may be. Processing a normal or usual or routine quota of cases is standard; doing it so rapidly that time is left over to process additional cases is excellent.

The last two measures of excellence are troublesome. No one quarrels with the idea that there are excellent lawyers and poor lawyers in courthouses, just as there are excellent auto mechanics and poor auto mechanics in repair shops. But measuring a man's excellence by trying to determine the quality of justice he does is an ambiguous exercise at best, while determining his contribution to the processing of cases is quite simple. There is a tendency, then, to fuse the two criteria of excellence—to measure a public defender's contribution to justice by counting the number of cases he handles. Courthouses and society have a handy slogan that makes such fusion of evaluation criteria seem quite reasonable: Justice delayed is justice denied. To receive high ratings, public defenders must possess sound discretionary judgment, but they must exercise it in such a way that justice is not delayed.

The shift in the measures of efficiency reflects the transformation of goals that has accompanied the development of courthouse organizations. In the language of the courthouse, phrases such as "administration of justice," "law enforcement," and "government by law" abound. These terms imply that the courthouse is a hierarchical bureaucracy in which each worker's duty is to follow strict rules set down by authorities above him. But courthouses are not, and probably never were, organized like armies in which a king or other authority passes orders down through the ranks. For centuries, courthouse work has been entrusted not to individuals or even to an organization, but to a set of organizations. First the judge, then the jury, and then the prosecutor and his staff appeared. Much later, accused persons were permitted to employ defense lawyers, and from this privilege grew the organization of the public defender and his staff. Judges were given small staffs as well, and to a limited degree, their work is now coordinated by a chief judge or presiding judge. Three separate bureaus developed—one to prosecute, another to defend, a third to adjudicate.

The consequences of this transformation for courthouse policy have been both drastic and dramatic. Everyone now has a bureau chief to whom he is responsible, and each worker draws his professional identity from the separate organization in which he works. If I am prosecuting, you are defending and he is judging, what are all of us doing collectively? The closest approximation of an answer is this: All of us are doing justice. The goal of mechanically enforcing the criminal law has been transformed into the goal of maximizing justice.

Yet this goal is as vague as the law enforcement goal it supplements. No one can state what ingredients must be mixed together to produce justice. Organizationally, this means that every imaginable kind of courthouse structure may be seen as devoting itself to doing justice or, at least, to administering it. There is no overall team to which all members subordinate their individual interests. On the contrary, the vagueness of ends and means makes it possible for each prosecutor, public defender and judge to believe that he is doing justice, even if his actions are on occasion upset by the actions of someone in another bureau. Justice can be said to be produced as I prosecute, you defend, and he judges, but if all three of us work twice as hard as we did last year, do we double the amount of justice? The answer, of course, is that no one knows. When each person does justice in his own way, guided by the rules of the bureau in which he works, overall courthouse progress toward the goal of maximizing justice can only be asserted, not measured.

The uncertainties about goals and measures are thus fed by the bureaucratic aspects of the organization of the defender's office. But these aspects are only part of the picture. Many of the individual defender's tasks cannot be set down in explicit sets of rules, enforced by a bureaucratic supervisor. Codes and handbooks prescribe official procedures for the clerical and housekeeping aspects of the job, but there can be no official rules telling public defenders how to maximize justice. Indeed, the very term "doing justice" implies an expert-oriented system in which each employee's duty is to use his own best judgment.[9] Assistants are expected to use discretion, initiative and ingenuity, rather than to comply with strict regulations from above. Their special knowledge of the law and their presumed knowledge of their clients makes each of them an expert on matters of individualized justice. Codes and handbooks cannot tell defenders how to move a caseload either. Because these lawyers are experts, they have great autonomy, a broad discretionary power to sort their cases as they see fit.[10] They cannot be instructed explicitly on how to dispose of these cases, any more than they can be instructed on how to do justice in each case. They are left pretty much on their own, guided only by unwritten policy and customs.

But at the end of the day, week or month, the reckoning comes. The supervisor allocating the cases to various assistants needs only the ability to count on his fingers and toes to determine whether each assistant has done a poor, standard or excellent job. If a backlog of cases is building up, he wants to know why. Subtly, and sometimes not so subtly, he reminds a negligent defender that the office is understaffed, that most defendants are guilty, that justice delayed is justice denied, that too many lawyers are trying to make big constitutional cases out of small-time burglaries, and so on. Such pressures are effective, primarily because they are rarely directed at an assistant's handling of individual cases. The assistant public defenders and their supervisor agree that justice must be done in each case and that severe punishments suggested by prosecutors must be turned aside in each case, but they also come to agree that there are organizational limits on how much justice can be done. Discretion to be exercised wisely in the interests of justice is measured as though it were discretion to be exercised wisely in the interests of organizational efficiency.

The tendency to equate efficiency with doing justice is demonstrated by the frequency with which the words "good deal" are used in busy courthouses. The phrase is everywhere. Public defenders typically urge their clients to plead guilty to a lesser offense because it is a good deal, and at lunchtime they are likely to tell each other of their recent successes in getting good deals for clients. Prosecutors also consider these arrangements good deals. The results seem just, even if it is never really clear in retrospect whether a particular defendant who pleaded guilty got a good deal or not.

Arranging good deals rewards both defender and prosecutor. More accurately, the good deals promote efficiency and at the same time contribute to high courthouse morale by ensuring that a prosecutor or defender can lose a case only if he goes to trial. This, too, is an organizational incentive to keep the caseload moving. The fusion of the two goals, doing justice and moving cases, helps make the public defender's life a rather pleasant one. Only a few men are excellent, but every competent lawyer who keeps his caseload moving may be perceived as doing justice and rated as a success. Accordingly, a public defender who expediently moves his cases is able to convince himself and his boss that he is administering justice and doing the best possible job of it, given the circumstances. And a public defender who is slow in processing his cases might claim as a professional that he must delay cases so that justice can be done for each of his clients. More realistically, he is able to claim adversary resistance in the form of hard bargaining by the district attorney whenever he is accused of bureaucratic inefficiency, even if there has been no bargaining at all.

Like public defenders, prosecutors obviously benefit from the fact that workload can be readily measured, while doing justice cannot. They too benefit from good deals that are perceived as just but which also move cases. No so obvious are the enormous benefits legislators receive from these good deals. By arranging to keep cases moving, no matter how trying the circumstances, public defenders let legislators rest. Legislators need not face the laborious task of determining what the aims of the criminal law are, or should be, and of revising it accordingly. The same arrangements allow legislators and other budget setters to avoid the difficulties of trying to measure the effects of their appropriations on the quality of justice. They are able to take the easy, clerical, bureaucratic route—measuring workload. Pressures for reform are dissipated. As time passes, the gap between what the people's representatives state as value and what is done in the courthouse widens, and more and more money, energy and personnel are needed just to keep the organization moving. In motion, the organization of the courthouse comes to resemble a Rube Goldberg contraption held together by Scotch tape, spit and baling wire, with amazing and ridiculous wheels and gears powering a useless assembly line.[11]

A Move Toward Consensus

When Steve Ohler first spoke to Joe Carbo about the Randolph case, Carbo seemed to hesitate. Then he took a tough stance. He did not say he would press the burglary in the first degree charge, but he made it clear that he wanted a felony conviction and some prison time. Steve made no proposal at all. He simply asked Joe if he thought Randolph's offense was worth all the trouble it would take to get a prison sentence. Carbo responded that there was no such thing as a cheap nighttime burglary of a home, that citizens were being frightened to death by men like Randolph.

Ohler did not press the matter. He knew that as the trial date drew closer, Joe would come to reason. They had been through the same thing hundreds of times before. The pressures in the prosecutor's office were almost as crushing as those in his own office. Eventually, Joe would recognize that professional burglars were one thing, and men like Peter Randolph quite another. Randolph was not so bad or dangerous that he had to be sent to the state prison. With luck and a little time, perhaps Judge Perkins would help Carbo see the light.

Fortunately for Steve, on the morning of Randolph's trial-setting conference, the bus carrying prisoners to the courthouse from jail was delayed. Judge Perkins, Joe Carbo and Steve chatted to pass the time while they waited, and Steve steered the conversation around to Randolph. He mentioned his client's immaturity, alcohol problem, fairly clean record and his apparent confusion at the time of the arrest. The Judge looked over the morning's calendar, sighed and mentioned the heavy overload. Steve then planted the idea that Randolph was just a confused young man with a drinking problem. Judge Perkins turned to Joe and told him frankly that he was wasting too much time on cases like Randolph's. Steve was so elated he could not help smiling. Joe glared at him, but Steve knew he considered pressure from Judge Perkins to be pressure for a reasonable and just disposition. He would come to his senses.

A few weeks before the Randolph trial date, Joe telephoned Steve to try to settle the cases scheduled for trial. They readily disposed of most of them, as they always did. But when they reached the Randolph case, Steve remembered the pressure Judge Perkins had put on Joe. He decided it was his turn to be tough. Sure of himself, he told Carbo he was going to trial, that he would accept no other form of settlement. Joe chuckled in response to this pressure and then invited Ohler to say what he really had in mind. Steve replied that Randolph had already spent enough time in jail and would plead guilty if the charge were reduced to unlawful entry and a sentence of time served. When Joe hesitated, Steve added that he also expected Randolph to be put on probation in order to get some help with his drinking problem. Then he closed the discussion by borrowing a phrase Carbo had often used when they were negotiating dispositions: "You can't play poker without chips, my friend."

Steve's stratagem worked. A few days before the trial date, Joe called him. Carbo said that he had discussed the case with his colleagues, studied the file, talked to the detective who originally investigated the case, and checked out Randolph's juvenile record. He also said that he had a homicide trial and two robbery trials coming up, and asked if Steve still wanted the deal he had proposed. Steve told him he did, and Joe then reminded him to tell Bob Pollitzer they had agreed on probation. One more case was on its way out the courthouse door. Steve's supervisor, Joe's supervisor and Judge Perkins all would be pleased.

Structural Coercion

An individual public defender may be firmly and unalterably convinced that he is an adversary defender of the poor and at the same time accommodate to the needs of an organization that requires him to persuade most defendants to plead guilty. He may consider himself an adversary lawyer who takes extreme positions which he might not personally agree with or think wise. He may think of himself as a wise and just legal counselor as well, advising his clients about their options and suggesting courses of action. But he gives little thought to the idea that he, a champion of individual clients, shares responsibility for a courthouse system that institutionally, organizationally, and tacitly coerces defendants into pleading guilty to something. Steve Ohler, like other public defenders, puts the matter this way:

> Overall, I don't get such bad results. I won about half my trials last year. Of all my clients, only about one in ten goes to prison. A lot more do jail time, but that means they aren't getting badly hurt. I can't keep them from getting wet, but I do hold back the tide. I bargain for leniency. In most of my cases I get a reduction in charge, which means a reduction in penalty. And whenever that happens I think I've done a good job.

But doing a good job of this kind is coercive, and the coerciveness has its roots in the legal profession. The primary mechanism for such coercion is the lawyer-client relationship and the complete dependence of the indigent criminal client on the lawyer's expertise.

As an expert bent on assisting each client as best he can, the public defender expects each client to consent to programs of action which he says are to the client's benefit, just as a medical patient consents to a painful surgical operation his doctor says will be to his benefit. As soon as a defendant agrees to be a lawyer's client, he submits himself to the authority of this expert. If the client cooperatively pleads guilty to whatever counsel proposed, the lawyer does not lose—his expert advice has been followed and the client has benefited. On the other hand, if the defendant stubbornly insists on going to trial against the advice of counsel, the attorney still cannot lose—he will either win the case or put responsibility for defeat on the client, who refused to accept the expert advice advanced in his interest. But if the lawyer advises a client to go to trial, and fails to prevent the prosecutor from proving guilt, he loses. His client goes to prison, which indicates that the lawyer either incompetently advised him to go to trial or incompetently prepared and presented his evidence and arguments. The message to the public defender is clear, even if rarely voiced: Do your clients and yourself a favor by advising them to plead guilty.

These pressures to be an expert legal counselor, rather than an advocate of men presumed to have done no wrong, are not evil in themselves. Few defendants insist that they are blameless, or even that they should be presumed blameless. What they want and need is an expert legal guide who will lead them through the courthouse maze, pay attention to them, help them with their legal and personal problems and demonstrate to a judge that they are not as bad as the bare facts of their crimes make them appear. The conception of the defense lawyer as an adviser who works on behalf of his clients promises all of these things. It also promises benefits to the state—defendants who are punished after receiving proper counseling will not be as alienated as defendants punished following a hostile and lonely procedure.

But the work of the courthouse, and particularly of the public defender's office, is as inadequately organized to keep these promises as it is to implement the presumption that all defendants are innocent. Defendants seldom have individual counselors to work on their behalf. The organization is arranged to shunt indigent defendants from station to station and to protect them from the grossest illegal procedures, not to give them the affirmative advice, help and counsel of experts.

We have already suggested the reason for this. It is because defendants are poor that they are made the clients of an organization rather than of men. Indigent defendants are perceived as welfare recipients, and guilty, undeserving ones at that, not as lawyers' clients. The organization supposedly serving them has neither the time nor the money to overcome the fact that defendants, because they are poor, are usually ignorant of the numerous technical defenses to criminal charges, and unusually ignorant of the discretionary range of punishments and dispositions available to prosecutors and judges alike. The organization neither defends nor counsels; it processes.

The attorney-client relationship between public defenders and indigent defendants is peculiar, if not unique.[12] Nowhere else in the legal system is the lawyer so restricted in his choice of clients. Nowhere else is the client so restricted in his choice of a lawyer. When a citizen selects and employs a lawyer to draw up a contract, collect a bill, initiate a damage suit or defend him in a criminal proceeding, he does not thereby give his attorney unlimited freedom to do anything he wants. The attorney is obligated by the rules of his profession and even by law to advise the client on his alternatives before he acts, and to let the client make the decisions. If the client does not like the lawyer's proposal he can reject it, and if the lawyer persists the client is free to dismiss him and get another counselor. At the same time, if the lawyer is convinced that his advice is sound, and the client will not take it or wants him to do something immoral or illegal, he can withdraw and invite the client to seek another attorney's services.

This standard conception of the lawyer-client relationship limits the actions of the expert. He can give all the advice in the world, but he cannot take actions that are outside the scope of the client's consent. A public defender would never plead a client guilty if the client did not agree to it, any more than a surgeon would perform an operation his patient had not consented to. Moreover, no boss, senior partner, supervisor or other person in authority can effectively command the lawyer to take actions his client has not consented to. The lawyer's duty is to do only what his client wants him to do, even if respecting the client's wishes brings disgrace, low status, poor pay and calumny to the lawyer. Chief public defenders, themselves lawyers, do not even entertain the idea of ordering an assistant to plead a client guilty, no matter how guilty the defendant appears, and no matter how heavy the burden of overwork.

But there are inherent problems with this concept. One is vagueness about what "consent" and "agree" mean. Another is the reality of structural coercion, despite the absence of personal orders and commands from above. A third is the assumption that lawyers and clients assigned to each other are free to dismiss one another if they cannot agree on a proper course of action.

In the final analysis, the clients of public defenders can only consent to let their lawyers do whatever the lawyers think best. They know nothing of their own courthouse organization, not to mention the mysteries of general criminal procedure. They must trust their lawyer, thereby giving him authority—as an expert—to do things they only vaguely understand. This is not a condition peculiar to public defenders' offices, of course. All experts must seek and obtain only general and quite vague permission, consent or agreement to take specific actions, ethical and professional codes notwithstanding. A medical expert, for example, can try to be specific, describing to his patient the costs, benefits and risks of an appendicitis operation, so the patient knows precisely what he is authorizing when he tells the doctor to operate. Alternatively, the expert can simply persuade the patient that "doctor knows best" and should be trusted, thus obtaining the patient's cooperation. Usually the medical expert chooses the second alternative. No matter how specific he tries to be, the fact is that he cannot communicate to a nonexpert everything he knows about the need for an operation. To be fully informed about what he is consenting to, the patient would have to be given a complete medical education and become an expert himself. There is not enough time, money, or skill available for that. Similarly, public defenders do not have enough time, money, or skills to make each client into a criminal lawyer. They must seek and obtain permission to take actions which clients only vaguely understand.

Each client's decision to plead guilty is in this sense an uninformed decision. The client depends on the lawyer to predict what his fate will be, but the defender does not, and cannot, describe all of the costs, benefits, and risks of the decision. Besides being limited by time and communication barriers, the defender is limited by his own uncertainty of what will happen to the client. Much depends upon "the facts," but definite facts are just not there for everyone to see.

The lawyer's advice to a client is also likely to be influenced by differences in his certainty about his client's ultimate fate in various circumstances. Significantly, he is much less certain about the consequences of a not guilty plea and a trial or even an unbargained for guilty plea than he is about the consequences of an arranged plea.[13] By arranging a plea, he can fix the outcome and limit the risks of following his advice. On the one hand, if the lawyer takes the champion-of-the innocent posture he must necessarily speak in vague generalities: "If you plead not guilty I will do my best to keep the prosecutor from proving that you are guilty." When pressed for an opinion as to the likely outcome, he is again restricted to vague probability statements: "I think we can win," "I think the prosecutor's evidence will be strong," "I think you are unlikely to be sent to the state penitentiary," and so on. And if pressed about the consequences of pleading guilty as charged, without negotiation, he can reduce the vagueness a bit but still must confess an inability to predict what will happen to the client: "I think you might be hurt less than you would if you pleaded not guilty," "The judge favors men who plead guilty," "The prosecutor says if you plead guilty he will put a word in with the judge," and so on.

On the other hand, if the public defender takes the counselor-serving-a-client posture, he is able to arrange a deal that he considers to be in the interests of the client and then present the client with the option of choosing between uncertainty and certainty. The presentation sounds something like this: "It is in your best interests to plead guilty to the lesser charge because if you do not, I am not sure what will happen to you [as above]; but if you plead guilty you will go to jail for ninety days." Now the lawyer's task is not merely one of estimating the chances of winning or losing; it is a matter of letting the client choose between certainty that he will be hurt a little and a possibility that he will be hurt a lot.

A client presented with such a choice is likely to plead guilty. However, he does not necessarily do so because he thinks the plea is in his best interest. He does not know what his best interest is. What the client does know is that it is better to limit his risks and accept a known amount of punishment than it is to risk an unknowable and potentially catastrophic amount of punishment. The client's decision to plead guilty is usually based on his preference for some degree of certainty as opposed to the risk of an unknown and possibly damaging outcome. He pleads guilty, then, because he has, like a medical patient, become convinced that "the doctor knows best."

The coercion of defendants is furthered by the practical difficulty for an indigent to dismiss his lawyer, and the rarity of a public defender deliberately withdrawing from a case. There are disadvantages for the defendant if either action occurs. Except in notorious cases, public defender services are provided, for the most part, on a take-it-or-leave it basis. A defendant who dismisses a public defender is likely to find himself with no legal assistance at all. Some defendants, especially those who have been through the courthouse many times, choose to act as their own lawyers, and consider their own skills better than those of public defenders. But unsophisticated defendants have few grounds on which to judge the quality of the legal advice given them, and they have no real opportunity to test a lawyer's judgment by dismissing him and becoming the client of another. Consequently, if a public defender advises a defendant to plead guilty, that is the only advice he is going to hear.

Moreover, a public defender cannot ethically withdraw formally from his status as a particular defendant's lawyer. To do so would almost certainly put the man in jeopardy. A public defender who cannot make a defendant see the fallacy of going to trial on an open-and-shut felony charge can scarcely withdraw, but he can nevertheless shift from defender to counselor and in the counselor role convince the defendant that his interests will best be served if he pleads guilty. He thereby protects his credibility as an adversary who really means it when he tells the prosecutor some other case is triable. The interests of an unsavory defendant are sacrificed to the interests of other defendants, present and future.

All of these characteristics of the lawyer-client relationship in public defender offices are part of an organization which collectively sends the same order to most defendants: Plead guilty to something and get out of here, or you will wish you had. Individual public defenders are not at fault. We have never met a public defender who even remotely hinted that he advised clients to plead guilty unless it was in the client's best interest to do so. To admit soliciting guilty pleas for reasons of personal gain, or organizational convenience would be to confess to unprofessional practice. In our experience, individual defenders are not lazy, incompetent, unethical or dishonest. Their consciences are clear. They are the honest and hard-working watchdogs of the police and prosecutorial systems, and, as courthouses are now arranged, they really should not be expected to do much more than keep those systems reasonably honest.

Offer and Acceptance

On the morning the prosecutor finally telephoned and agreed to a misdemeanor-and-time-served compromise, Steve Ohler had a few minutes to spare after his discussion with Joe Carbo. He went directly to the county jail to talk with Randolph. He knew what he was going to do and say. The Randolph file told him what to expect, and the way his work was structured and organized ensured that he would find just what he had been led to expect. Because of the zone defense system, his view of himself as adversary lawyer, the limited opportunities to know and serve clients, the pressures from Judge Perkins and others to dispose of his bloated caseload, and the necessity that he fulfill his obligations to the public defender's office, Steve's perception of the case was firmly set. Other realities could scarcely intrude.

When Randolph came into the lawyers' room at the jail, Ohler did not recognize him at first. There were too many faces, familiar and unfamiliar, in his life. Steve acknowledged the presence of his client only when the guard called out his name. He motioned Randolph to a chair beside a vacant desk, and once this formality was over he immediately went to work.

The conversation was short and to the point. The public defender informed the defendant that the district attorney had agreed to take a misdemeanor plea for time served and probation. There was no mention of any options open to Randolph beyond Steve's bare statement of the truth: "You can insist on a trial if you want to, but that will keep you in jail longer." Randolph wanted to get out of jail and seemed prepared to do whatever would produce that result most quickly. He agreed to plead guilty to unlawful entry.

Steve never did hear Randolph's disjointed story about what he was doing in Simmons's garage. Nor did he stop to explore what was going to happen to Randolph after he left the courthouse or what should happen to him. There was no time and no point in doing so. Steve had obtained a good result. His client's constitutional rights had not been infringed. His client was not sent to jail or labeled a felon. He had moved a case. That was all he was expected to do, and that was all the structure of the courthouse gave him the opportunity to do.

chapter seven
Acquiescence and severity

Peter Randolph's experience dramatizes the remarkable emphasis American criminal justice places on gaining guilty pleas and the remarkable extent to which the threat of severe punishment is used to gain these pleas.[1] Perhaps the strangest aspect of the situation is this: Neither the emphasis on gaining acquiescence nor the emphasis on severity is necessary. It would not have been difficult for Joe Carbo to prove Randolph guilty at trial of one or more of the felony counts. It was not necessary to keep Randolph locked in a cell for two months awaiting judgment of his fate. He could have been released safely, pending trial, without much danger that he would have run away. If he had been released before trial, he would have presented no greater danger to the community than he did when released after sentence. Neither was it necessary for Steve Ohler to lure Randolph with that extraordinarily tantalizing piece of bait—the fresh air of freedom. And it was bizarre, not to mention unnecessary, to threaten a man like Peter Randolph with conviction of an offense carrying a possible maximum sentence of life imprisonment. While it seemed eminently right to make Peter Randolph's behavior punishable by law, surely a smaller club would have sufficed. In the present system of criminal justice, however, harsh penalties are essential, because it is through threats of severe punishment that acquiescence is obtained.

There are, of course, defendants who, having committed crimes, are prepared, even eager, to confess and accept responsibility for them. Others seem to recognize no guilt or responsibility, but nonetheless plead guilty. Professional thieves and burglars, for instance, may consider punishment merely a cost of doing business. They want to keep this cost down, yet they recognize that occasionally the price must be paid. When it is their turn, they may as well pay with a minimum of fuss.

In a third category are those who say that they engaged in criminal behavior, but that, to a degree, their crime was justified. Even when they plead guilty, these people do not truly consent or confess in the sense of freely admitting guilt.

Finally, there is the huge majority of defendants—men like Peter Randolph, who submit to the painful consequences of conviction but do not know for certain whether they committed any of the crimes of which they are accused. Such defendants are so unschooled in law that they form no firm opinion about their technical innocence or guilt. Neither do they actually agree or disagree that it is just to punish them. They do not know enough about themselves to tell the lawyers what to do.

For all but that small number of defendants for whom confession is positively motivated, it is incorrect to say that the accused sincerely agrees that he is guilty as charged, or even that he feels guilty of what he pleads to. Neither do most defendants think the punishment they receive is fair and just. It is more accurate to say that the criminal defendant "goes along." He "plays it by ear," just as others do, and fits his tune with theirs. He does not repent. He acquiesces, allowing his conviction to occur unchallenged, because he fears the consequences of doing otherwise. Later, most defendants, particularly those like Peter Randolph, feel they were victimized; that they pleaded guilty without really knowing what they were doing:

> In a Wisconsin case ... a woman charged with murder in the second degree admitted guilt at arraignment and, in response to inquiry by the judge, said she did not want an attorney even at state expense. She said, "I am guilty but I didn't plan or intend to kill anybody." After some discussion with her, the judge refused the plea, assigned counsel, and rescheduled arraignment. At the second arraignment the judge asked the defense attorney if he had conferred with his client and discussed the case with her. The attorney replied in the affirmative, stating that

the defendant's recollection of what happened was vague, and in fact she could not remember any significant details. The judge then asked the defendant, "Do you wish to continue your plea of guilty?" The defendant answered, "Yes. I will plead guilty to get this over with. The suspense of not knowing what I have done is driving me crazy."[2]

Acquiescence

If many defendants who plead guilty do so without understanding why, and in the end feel cheated, it is logical to ask why they acquiesce. While there are numerous reasons, hopes and fears that motivate a defendant to plead guilty, the basic motivation is fear of punishment. Everyone who has ever worked in a criminal courthouse knows that the main issue in discretionary decision making is the kind and amount of punishment the defendant is to receive. Defendants overwhelmingly plead guilty not because they repent, but to avoid or limit pain. Some judges claim that pleading guilty is a sign of contrition and mature acceptance of responsibility. Defendants who confess, they say, are further along the path of reformation than those who do not repent. This is true in some cases. But if only one half of the felons pleading guilty in the courts were truly repentant and prepared to repudiate their criminal sins, there would be no need for harsh penal laws, extraordinarily long prison sentences, fortresslike prisons or the degradation of status that attends the label "felon." Much of the money spent on "rehabilitation" programs could be given to the poor. America would not be plagued by its high rate of repeated crime. In an ideal world, the criminal justice process—or some similar process—would produce a high incidence of guilty pleas that represented more than mere acquiescence. That world has not yet arrived.

The requirement that a wrongdoer somehow acknowledge his guilt is not new. Confession as a virtue reflects an older system in which punishment was consciously used for sacramental expiation of sin, as well as the temporal punishment of the wrongdoer. Physical torture is no longer permitted as a means for obtaining a guilty plea in place of a genuine confession, nor is abject and full confession demanded in many cases. But very strong psychological and organizational pressures to "go along" are tolerated, as well as a number of face-saving techniques that enable an accused to acquiesce without formally confessing. Some of these techniques are given obscure Latin names, such as *nolo contendere* or *non vult*, but the net effect of the formal word game is that the accused allows punishment to be imposed without either trial or explicit confession.

147

The Supreme Court, speaking through Justice Byron White, recently said:

An individual accused of crime may voluntarily, knowingly and understandingly consent to the imposition of a prison sentence even if he is unwilling or unable to admit his participation in the acts constituting the crime. . . .[3]

It is no accident, then, that the American criminal justice system insists on acquiescence. The acquiescence is valuable because there is something abhorrent about punishing a man who claims he was not responsible for the crime of which he has been found guilty. Punishment seems less offensive if he claims only technical innocence, admitting that he violated the law but successfully arguing that the state cannot prove it beyond a reasonable doubt. If, however, the defendant confesses, saying that it is all right to punish him, all reservations disappear. Even an insincere guilty plea reduces the concern the state feels for punishing men who claim innocence. Therefore it is essential that such pleas be forthcoming. If a defendant "goes along," as most defendants do, government officials and the rest of society assume, happily but erroneously, that by so doing he has both confessed and assumed responsibility for his crime.

Despite its synthetic quality, the acquiescence of the accused remains extraordinarily important to officials. With it, the criminal justice process operates economically, promptly, smoothly and without the disruption caused by challenge. It is even said that acquiescence and cooperation are necessary prerequisites for effective therapeutic treatment. Some authorities claim that acquiescence, by insuring rapid processing of an individual's case, makes punishment more effective. If criminals are to be conditioned against crime by painful punishment, and if this pain is to be effective it should be inflicted as soon after the crime as possible. Lengthy trial procedures widen the time gap between the crime and its punishment; acquiescence by a guilty plea narrows it.

Acquiescence also eases any doubts about whether a defendant is guilty, and about whether his sentence is just. Even if there were enough money and personnel to give a full and speedy trial to every defendant, it is likely that officials would still seek acknowledgment from the accused that they were doing the right thing in condemning and punishing him. The constitutional rule is that punishment should be imposed only when there is a high degree of certainty as to an individual's guilt. Such assurance is usually lacking, for the facts in criminal cases often are indeterminate and cannot be reconstructed with certainty. Human events simply do not come in neat packages. Observers, including judges, are occasionally quite unsure whether the proof presented at trial has demonstrated guilt beyond a reasonable doubt, even if a jury says it has. The best way to mollify such uneasiness is to avoid trial altogether by securing a confession or acquiescence in a guilty plea.

Imagine a case in which the defendant has without doubt committed the crime charged, but in which he nonetheless sincerely insists upon his innocence and contests the legitimacy of his condemnation. One might think that such a defendant is mad or psychopathic, but this is not always so. In a political trial, for instance, the accused may see his behavior as morally justified or even demanded by higher values. Recent examples are the trials of Father Berrigan, Daniel Ellsberg, and the Black Panthers. In each case the defendants claimed that their behavior was morally legitimate, and whatever its formal legality, not appropriately punishable.[4]

The entire nation heard and read transcripts of tapes in which the President of the United States and his aides proclaimed their own guilt, yet the continued insistence of Messrs. Haldeman, Ehrlichman and Mitchell that they were innocent, and the failure of President Nixon to acknowledge his guilt left many people disquieted. Without acquiescence in such cases, society is left in doubt as to its moral judgment and is uncertain whether condemnation and punishment serve to cast out devils or contribute to the passion of martyrs.

Acquiescence thus has an intrinsic value. We have stated this value in moral and legal terms, but it can be stated in a variety of other ways. In political science terms, the consent of the governed legitimates the governors' exercise of authority. Consent of the punished validates the actions of those who punish.

In psychological terms, the exercise of punitive authority, with its attendant aggression, domination and destructiveness, generates guilt and anxiety in the official. The official gets greatest relief from this anxiety not through the dispassionate approval of his colleagues, nor from the law, but from the acceptance of the punishing act by its victim. It also helps if the punishing act is called something it is not—treatment, therapy, rehabilitation.

In sociological terms, the accused's acquiescence justifies the official's softening of the formal requirements of law. In the adversary view of criminal proceedings, the prosecutor is expected to demand that the resisting defendant be hurt as much as the law allows. This polarization of position is dissolved by the accused's acquiescence and abandonment of a hostile posture. Like the submission ceremony in barnyard behavior, the defendant's acknowledgment of his subordinate position allows the official, whose dominance is confirmed, to be tolerant, and even benign, rather than aggressively hostile.

It is correct to say, then, that the contemporary guilty plea system does much more than merely keep courthouse budgets low and help get cases settled quickly. Guilty plea procedures have important control functions and, at the same time, great psychological value. It is no wonder that over the years very severe punishments have been legislated and administered in an apparent design to maximize the frequency of acquiescence among persons accused of crimes.

Severity

The severe physical brutality characteristic of past criminal legal systems has been replaced by the psychological pain inflicted as the state restricts the liberty of criminals by confining them in dismal cages within the walls of state and federal prisons. It would be erroneous, however, to believe that this pain is carefully reserved for those who have been convicted and sent to prison. The American criminal justice system makes life painfully unpleasant for a person arrested on a serious criminal charge long before it convicts him. He is abruptly separated from his home, his family and his work, and jailed until and unless he can buy his way out of the cell by posting bail. Local jails, notoriously the most degrading kind of penal institutions, are a national disgrace. They are old, filthy, and understaffed. Most are packed with several times the number of inmates they were built to contain. In effect, many are run by trustees and other old cons among the sentenced prisoners, the sharks of the criminal culture. In this setting, ironically, the unsentenced and presumably innocent prisoner gets the worst of two worlds. Because officials do not know him, he is subjected to more stringent regimentation than sentenced prisoners. Because inmates do not know him, he is scarcely able to escape the harassment and abuse of his more experienced and powerful cellmates, who know each other.

If the arrestee does not get out on bail within a few days, he is likely to learn that his job is gone, his personal property has disappeared or is in danger of repossession by the landlord or finance company, and that his friends are less friendly. In short, he is soon alone and stripped of all he might possess:

Viewed from the perspective of maintaining the plea-bargaining system, pretrial detention and demoralizing conditions in jails are highly functional. They discourage the defendant from bargaining too hard; they place a high price upon filing motions or demanding a trial; they encourage him to rat on his friends in order to end his own ordeal. This is not to argue that those in authority consciously plan rotten jails; clearly most are concerned about jail conditions. But it is to suggest that such conditions are functional, do serve the needs of the production ethic that dominates our criminal justice system.[5]

The court system facilitates this engine of misery which makes the arrestee a nonperson. His case, which is supremely important to him, does not seem important to anyone else. It is shuffled along, pushed through routines that winnow out the men to be subjected to all the punishment the law allows. The defendant's contact with counsel is likely to be brief and unsatisfactory, and his appearances in court dominated by mysterious procedures, with lawyers speaking a strange jargon which is foreign to him. He is required to endure all this, although he has not yet been convicted of breaking any law. If he is ultimately acquitted he will be set free, but he will not be compensated for the deprivations he has suffered, the expenses he has incurred, or the opportunities he has lost.

However, the psychological severity of jails and courts seems mild in comparison to the punishment and deprivation of opportunity that accompany felony conviction. Prisons are isolated both by their walls and by their location far from the community of the offender. The prison's depersonalizing routine deliberately attacks and often destroys the inmate's dignity and individuality. That is what inflicting psychological pain means, and that is what is intended by imprisonment. In many states, prison conditions can only be described as inhumane. Indeed, a federal judge recently found that the entire Arkansas prison system constituted cruel and unusual punishment; the system, as well as specific practices within it, was declared unconstitutional. But even the best prisons are degrading, terrible places. As the Director of the California Department of Corrections recently said:

Some people have gotten the mistaken idea that prison is a "good place." No prison is a good place to be because human beings are locked up, controlled, deprived of personal freedom and forced as a matter of necessity to give up many of the rewards of individuality.

Any prison, no matter how modern, is a punishing place. Further, prisons do not rehabilitate; they merely offer opportunities for rehabilitation in a strange and artificial atmosphere. It is the individual in those cases who motivates and rehabilitates himself.

California, probably more than most states, invests much taxpayer money for the purpose of rehabilitation. We've education from literacy training to junior college, teach 43 trades, conduct wide-ranging counseling and therapy programs, and offer an immense variety of work experiences. Despite this investment, prison is not and never will be the ideal underlying setting for rehabilitation—because of the circumstances which cause persons to enter prisons and require them to stay there. This is especially true of mammoth institutions where personalized programs are close to impossible. To illustrate, if you have a friend or a family member who has some kind of personal adjustment problems, you would not send him to San Quentin for a couple of months to get rehabilitated.[6]

The severity of imprisonment is accentuated by the uniquely long sentences imposed under American law. Sentences of twenty-five to forty years are ordered for a variety of offenses, some of which involve neither violence nor direct threat of it.[7] Actual periods of confinement typically are shorter than the sentences imposed, for most prisoners are released before the end of the maximum term allowed by law. Parole, good time allowances, and other forms of remission have been invented to soften the pains of lengthy incarceration. Nevertheless, in the United States the average amount of prison time actually served for various offenses is very long in comparison to other civilized nations.

Experience indicates that the long maximum terms provided by statute are too often used merely to maintain behavioral controls within American prisons. All prisoners know that the consequence of failure to adjust in prison is more imprisonment. Thus the severity made possible by statute serves as a measure of the time a prisoner can be deprived of his freedom if he fails to comply with prison rules, not as a measure of the pain he should suffer because he has violated the law. Tragically enough, most long-term prisoners eventually adjust to their prison.[8] They find a home there and are uncomfortable in the demanding outside world. When released they are likely to soon crumble under the pressures of freedom and commit another offense, which brings them back to the courthouse and ultimately returns them to an existence in which they can survive. Other prisoners are state-raised youths who have lived in institutions of one kind or another virtually since school age. They, too, have found a home behind bars, perhaps the only secure home they have ever known. The criminal justice system with all its severity is doing nothing to help them. On the contrary, it reserves its severest penalties for them.

The length of imprisonment is aggravated by the idleness that typifies most prisoners' days. With the exception of a few relatively backward states in which convict labor still makes the prison system a profit-making organization, most prisoners spend as many as twenty hours a day in idleness:

The public image of state prisons as beehives of productive activity, with "cons" working long hours manufacturing auto tags, road signs, brooms, and clothing, is largely erroneous. Even the few so employed seldom work more than six hours a day. The rest are subjected to the demoralizing and wasteful assignment of trying to appear to be busy at housekeeping tasks, most of which can be completed easily in the first hour or two of the work period. . . .[9]

Nor does punishment end upon release from a penal institution. When the inmate leaves the prison, he is likely to be released on parole. As a parolee he remains subject to supervision and control, may be arbitrarily arrested and searched and is limited in his movements and associations. His social and economic opportunities are limited. He can find a job only by lying about where he has been for the past few years. Most well-paying occupations are closed to him, and he is likely to find himself stuck in a dreary progression of dead-end jobs. The stigma of felon status is lifelong and rarely can be eradicated. This punishment is severe in the most absolute sense, for a felony conviction may mean condemnation to an underclass. It is not surprising that accused persons and defendants go along with courthouse routines enabling them to avoid felon status.

These are some of the absolute connotations of severity, but harshness is a relative word and includes a sense of the proportionality of punishment to crime. When a man intentionally kills or maims another, it seems more fitting to cage him in prison for a long time than it does when his offense is nonviolent and involves only the taking of another's property, or when it is not clear that his offense hurts anyone but himself. If one is concerned with the proportionality of crime and punishment, it is difficult to accept the fact that a man may be sentenced to ten years imprisonment if he, for example, steals fifty dollars worth of apples or the carcass of a jackass, or forges a federal income tax refund check for $2.98.[10] This is harshness. In more or less dramatic form, this harshness permeates American criminal codes and significantly deadens society's sense of proportionality.

Harshness breeds harshness as everyone involved, including the potential criminal, becomes accustomed to the idea that a crime is punishable by a ridiculously long prison term. Penalties escalate as sensibilities to the consequences become deadened. Proposals to reduce penalties across the board to a more reasonable level are seen as depriving the punishment of any impact. Yet it is only because society, like drug addicts, has built up high tolerance through habitual overdose, that it needs such increasingly massive injections to get the desired jolt.

The American criminal justice system actually imprisons only a small proportion of the population, but the proportion is higher than it is in European nations. Worse, the proportion of citizens that the system directly threatens with lengthy imprisonment is staggering. If everyone arrested were pushed through the system, the United States would be a nation of convicts. Each year there are over nine million arrests for offenses other than traffic violations, of which approximately three million are for felonies. Of course, an unknown number of persons are arrested more than once each year, but if this complication is ignored, the statistics show about one arrest annually for every eight persons between ages eighteen and thirty-nine. Certainly a society that places so many people in jeopardy has a very severe criminal law.

The potential harshness of the system makes acquiescence of the accused vital not only to the accused himself, but to officials as well. The dire possibility of a nation of convicts is avoided by sending only a few of those arrested to prison. Too often, however, there is no clear difference between the behavior of those who are flushed out of the system without any punishment and the few who are sent to prison for many years. Accidents, tactical considerations, indifference of prosecutors, and the hunches of judges and defense lawyers sometimes make the difference between a very harsh sentence and quick release with no punishment.

Defendants use the plea of guilty to a knocked down offense as a means of reducing the likelihood of disasterous punishment. The individual official, be he policeman, prosecutor, defense lawyer, or judge, also uses the arranged guilty plea to avoid the unacceptably rigorous application of the letter of the law. Without opportunities for a way out in compelling cases, conscientious men would hesitate to participate in the enforcement of the criminal law. As an experienced and compassionate judge has written, "If every policeman, every prosecutor, every court and every postsentence agency performed his or its responsibility in strict accordance with rules of law, precisely and narrowly laid down, the criminal law would be ordered but intolerable."[11]

Discretion is needed, and is present, in every criminal justice system to deal with the unusual case. But contemporary American law is so harsh that its full application in all but an occasional aggravated case would be unthinkably cruel, expensive and socially

154

destructive. Discretionary adjustment is needed in most cases, not just in unusual ones. Amelioration of the rigors of the written law is the norm, not the exception, in current practice. Virtually everyone who comes to official attention on a charge of crime, whether or not he is arrested and prosecuted, is its beneficiary to some degree. Full application of the law is both morally repugnant and economically unthinkable.

It is when the punishments are most brutal that people justifiably look to the formal legal system for help in controlling those in power. Arbitrary power is dangerous under any circumstances, but it becomes oppressive as the severity of the sanctions it may impose increases. People may well accept a quick, simple and somewhat arbitrary system for deciding whether a motorist must pay a ten dollar parking fine, but they recoil from the use of the same process to decide whether the same citizen shall be imprisoned for fifteen years. Judicial sentencing discretion would not be so embarrassing if the range of potential idiosyncracy were not so wide. Similarly, the discretion of parole boards and other correctional authorities would be easier to accept if their casual and overambitious judgments did not spell the difference between one year and life in custody.

But it is often true that before an official can soften the harsh punishment called for by the criminal code, he must persuade the accused to acquiesce, and to agree that he deserves some punishment, no matter how mild. Unfortunately it is also often true that officials use means that would not conceivably be possible except in a system designed to be brutal. Both the police power of pretrial detention and the prosecutor's power to overcharge illustrate this. If the police are able to jail a man before conviction for a period equal to or greater than any sentence that is likely to be imposed, the accused might just as well plead guilty; it costs no more. Similarly, if a prosecutor is able to charge a man with attempted murder when he wants him convicted of disturbing the peace, the accused had better plead guilty to disturbing the peace lest the book be thrown at him.

When the system is severe, the accused is justifiably afraid to plead guilty to the crime charged. However tempted he may be to pay the ten dollar fine and go home, the path of acquiescence becomes less tempting as the alternative penalty increases. No one casually pleads guilty to robbery when the likely punishment is twenty years in prison. Conversely, only a man very confident of his ultimate vindication will chance capital punishment rather than plead guilty to murder. From the perspective of both the official and the accused, it is the unacceptable severity of the formal system that makes the demands for discretionary ways out so urgent, just as it is the compelling demand to get rid of cases by the guilty plea that leads to undue harshness for those who resist. The two aspects of the problem are inextricable.

Legislature v. Courthouse

An ironic result of overreliance on the guilty plea is that however compassionate its intent may be, it leads to severe harshness in some cases. The guilty plea system tends to become not the extension of leniency to those who acquiesce, but the meting out of crushing pain to those who insist on their innocence or otherwise resist. If, for example, a courthouse subculture has established about sixty days in jail as the proper punishment for first offenders who have committed minor burglaries, in that courthouse sixty days in jail is the legal norm, no matter what the statutes might stipulate as a proper punishment for burglary. Any jail term in excess of sixty days, then, is severe punishment, and a prison term of two, five, or ten years—as called for by statutory law—is very severe punishment indeed. In other words, when the law in action sets a certain punishment as usual and just for defendants of certain kinds, invoking the penalties provided by statutory law constitutes severity.

Imposing this form of severity is an everyday occurrence in courthouses throughout the nation. The need to gain the acquiescence of most accused persons leads officials to place a heavy price in the form of enhanced severity—authorized by statute—on those who insist on a formal trial but who are found guilty. An example occasionally must be made of the uncooperative defendant who contests his case unsuccessfully. Similarly, when opportunities to avoid or delay punishment are introduced by procedural and constitutional reforms ordered by the Supreme Court, as has been done in recent years, there is a reciprocal tendency of officials to evoke the severe statutory law and to forget the less severe "courthouse law" when dealing with defendants who have unsuccessfully used the new legal tactics. Thus the winnowing effect of discretionary practices in the courthouse can be, and is, manipulated to sort out for severe pain the defendants who do not acquiesce. As Professor Kenneth Culp Davis has put it, "The discretionary power to be lenient is an impossibility without a concomitant discretionary power not to be lenient, and injustice from the discretionary power not to be lenient is especially frequent; the power to be lenient is the power to discriminate."[12]

This tension between discretion and the rule of law also stimulates legislators to enact more severe penalties for crimes which are special targets of community outrage, for example, selling narcotics. As they do so, they increase the pain of those defendants who do not acquiesce, but their legislation makes little difference to those who do because they are permitted to avoid conviction on these minor offenses by pleading guilty to a lesser offense. To a considerable degree, the legislature becomes an agency of harshness and the courts become agencies for protecting citizens from this harshness. The net effect between the legislature and the courthouse is a rather steady increase in statutory severity for certain crimes. Such legislative action follows an established pattern:

Step I. Laws calling for severe punishments are passed by legislatures on the assumption that fear of great pain will terrorize the citizenry into conformity.

Step II. Criminal justice personnel soften these severe penalties for most offenders (a) in the interests of justice, (b) in the interests of bureaucracy, and (c) in the interests of gaining acquiescence.

Step III. The few defendants who then insist on a trial and are found guilty, or who in other ways refuse to cooperate, are punished more severely than those who acquiesce.

Step IV. Legislatures, noting that most criminals by acquiescing avoid "the punishment prescribed by law," (a) increase the prescribed punishments and (b) try to limit the range of discretionary decision making used to soften the harsh penalties.

Step V. The more severe punishments introduced in the preceding step are again softened for most offenders, as in Step II, with the result that the defendants not acquiescing are punished even more severely than they were at Step III.

Step VI. The severity-softening-severity process is repeated.[13]

Several social trends suggest that it is legislators rather than court personnel who are out of step with the times. The severe pain and misery now stipulated in criminal statutes are no longer in accord with other forms of social behavior. Punishments deemed appropriate in the past, when all life was more restricted and painful than now, are no longer needed. Even the tortures used in early prisons merely increased the level of physical pain experienced in everyday life by slaves, serfs and working-class persons everywhere. But physical suffering has been reduced in America, and in most parts of the world. In the last few generations punishment as a means of social control has dramatically declined in the home, the school and the church. Parents, husbands, teachers and schoolmasters are less free to use physical violence to enforce their will. The terror of eternal punishment in hell is a less important element in religion. It is reasonable for legislators to reduce criminal penalties accordingly, bringing them in line with these improvements.

Because the quality of life has improved, even those statutory penalties which have not escalated, and the majority have not, now seem more severe than when they were enacted. In general, Americans place a greater value on freedom now than in the past. Because of this trend, confinement in a prison for five years is a much more severe penalty than it was only a few years ago, even though prisons have been made into cleaner and physically more comfortable places for doing time. To leave old statutes untouched is to threaten criminals with increasing psychological pain—the pain stemming from loss of liberty. This disparity between stipulated punishments and social expectations is fundamental to the widespread tendency in courthouses—and in police departments, prison departments and parole departments as well—to soften the severe punishments officially set down in statutes. The development of local subcultures of justice and their discretionary processing of criminal cases seem to be responses to the need to bring actual punishments back in line.

Further, the more brutal punishments and long prison terms were invented at a time when class distinctions between the punishers and the punished were clearly defined and carefully observed. The reduction of social distances has accompanied the development of democracy and the invention of new means of communication. A larger proportion of the population now appreciates the situation of those who commit crimes. Imposing the pain of a long prison term is no longer viewed indifferently as the caging of an animal or a savage creature from another planet. This keener sympathy for criminals, if greater social integration may be called that, is still restricted by prejudice against blacks, against the "poor ways" or poor people and against ethnic cultures. But even such blind bigotry seems to be diminishing. As social distance between criminal and citizen has diminished, severe punishment of criminals has become less acceptable, making it necessary for courthouse workers to soften legislative severity.

Trends in the labor market and conditions of work also are relevant to statutory severity. Imprisonment, the primary method for hurting criminals now specified in statutes, developed at about the time the slave labor system was beginning to wane. Despite the revolutionary stress on painful deprivation of liberty when imprisonment was first invented, the modern form of imprisonment took shape when state officials learned how to use convict labor in the production of wealth. But today prisoners are not overworked; on the contrary, as pointed out earlier, prison officials and inmates alike deplore the characteristic idleness in prisons. Now that the business community has no need for convict labor—and in fact has effectively outlawed productive prison labor in the United States—it is no longer economically reasonable to commit men to institutions designed to use their labor. For that matter, it is hardly reasonable to act on the assumption that criminals being punished in prisons are also being held in check while they learn to be "productive members of society." Owing to improved technology and increasing automation, society needs far fewer productive members than it once did, and before long it will need even fewer. Any economic need for lengthy prison terms has long since disappeared, and discretionary courthouse practices accordingly adjust downward the severity stipulated in statutes.

A desire for acquiescence, and the genuine acquiescence that occurs when a criminal accepts responsibility for his crime, are basic aspects of criminal justice. But acquiescence is deprived of meaning when it is gained by coercion, no matter how indirect or subtle. The harshness of the severe penalties stipulated in statutes serves the officials' need to witness acquiescence, but prevents criminals from agreeing that the penalties imposed on them are just. It has become essential that courthouse subcultures of justice mitigate the severity set by legislatures. Even as they do this, however, courthouse personnel use the potential severity of the criminal law to motivate a perfunctory acquiescence that can be seen in many pleas of guilty. The quality of justice will improve if potential severity is reduced and courthouse personnel find procedures to secure genuine acquiescence.

chapter eight
The path
to reform

The experience of Peter Randolph suggests that the American courthouse is in disarray. Victims of crime, as well as defendants charged with crimes, too often feel mistreated. They as well as judges, prosecutors and defense lawyers too often feel trapped by the demands of the system, doubting that they are producing the best brand of justice, but unable to improve it. Lawyers and social scientists who have studied courthouse operations too often come away uncertain and disillusioned, concluding that the processes have little significance either for understanding crime or for reducing its incidence. The public too often finds the courthouse a seamy place and is dissatisfied with the way it deals with criminals.

Despite these widespread tendencies to view courthouse practices critically, the outlook for basic reform is not cheering. Efforts to eliminate discretionary decisions or to limit them substantially seem bound to fail because there must be a place in the courthouse both for the rule of law and for discretion. Nor is the tendency to bureaucratize officialdom likely to disappear. The sense of community that once characterized rural villages is no longer characteristic of the United States, particularly its urban areas, and it cannot be relied upon to support better courthouse operations. The American faith in severe punishment seems too deep to permit significant reductions in statutory severity in the near future.

This situation in the courthouse is too distressing to ignore, even if no simple solutions are apparent. It demands a further examination of the proposals for change that have been put forward. The plans for improving the quality of criminal justice range in scope from basic restructuring of the courthouse process to rather minor cosmetic and technical changes. Some suggest that the nation completely eliminate all discretionary decision making, abolish guilty plea negotiations or regularize the guilty plea process and bring it out in the open.

We shall consider each of these proposals in turn, starting with what appears to be the most sweeping plan for reforming the criminal law, the elimination of discretion, and moving to more modest changes in guilty plea procedures. We believe that none of them is likely to change effectively the way the courthouse operates. Real reform will come only when our country confronts the more farreaching aspects of bureaucratic organization, the political relationship of the courthouse to the community and the severity of the punishment provided in the law for criminals.[1] We do not have any satisfying, detailed program for solving the courthouse's difficulties. But we are confident that greater attention to the more profound aspects of the problem is essential to change in wise directions. It is clear that the ultimate goal of reform should be a courthouse setting in which rules and individuality can be balanced, not settings which exalt one of these values and deny the other. It also is clear that if such reform were achieved, courthouse processes would much more accurately reflect the community's sense of justice.

Eliminate Discretion

The most radical approach to reform is typified by the recommendation of President Nixon's National Advisory Commission on Criminal Justice Standards and Goals. This organization proposed the following as a "national priority":

> As soon as possible, but in no event later than 1978, negotiations between prosecutors and defendants—either personally or through their attorneys—concerning concessions to be made in return for guilty pleas should be prohibited. . . .

162

We have already commented on this extreme recommendation in several different contexts. Detailed evaluation is difficult because the Commission does not discuss the basis of its proposal, nor does it indicate how its goals might be accomplished, or what the effects of such change might be.

The Commission's proposal can be read as calling solely for a ban on negotiations for or the elimination of guilty pleas. But the Commission's characterization of the subject matter of negotiations as "concessions" rather than "adjustments" suggests a more farreaching proposal: that discretionary decision making be banned from the entire criminal law process, not just from the courthouse. The Commission implies that the severe punishments stipulated by legislators are appropriate and normal, that statutes are clear, and that all criminal laws should be enforced with vigor. Any deviation from these impeccable legislative rules is a concession to criminals and is to be avoided.

The misleading assumption here is that criminal laws can be stated precisely and their enforcement made automatic—little or no human element is necessary to justice.[2] According to this argument, the job of the police is to make an arrest in every case in which there is evidence that a crime has been committed. To do otherwise is to grant "concessions." Judges, prosecutors and even jurors are assumed to have comparable obligations to enforce the law automatically, in strict compliance with clear rules stated in statutes. Justice is achieved by administration—a great machine grinds out punishments for the guilty, and each official serves as a cog in the driving wheel. All the gears are closely meshed. No one has freedom to make the machine go faster or slower, or in a direction incompatible with that taken by the others.

Associated with this mechanistic view of the way the system should operate is a similar mechanical view of the impact that punishing criminals has on the larger community. The idea is that crime and punishment are finely balanced; thus, adding to the pain imposed on criminals is bound to have a significant and perceptible impact not only on the behavior of offenders, but also on that of citizens at large.[3] For example, it is commonly assumed that people refrain from armed robbery merely out of fear, and that if the penalty for armed robbery were raised from ten to twenty years in prison, the fear would increase and the armed robbery rate would decline. In such a view, the calculus of deterrence is the basis of the criminal law; therefore, the lawmaker only need do his sums carefully in order to insure that appropriate amounts of pain are inflicted on wrongdoers, thus terrorizing the citizenry into conformity.

We have already discussed the fallacy of this mechanistic view. It is difficult to take seriously the suggestion that criminal justice personnel should merely enforce the criminal law as written, making no modifications appropriate to the circumstances of the offense and the background of the offender. There is a great difference between administering the law and doing justice. The first is "law enforcement" in the strict sense, and that term suggests an organization based on rank in which each worker's duty is to follow strict rules set down by his commanders. Among policemen, this version of duty is reflected in the saying, "I didn't make the law; I just enforce it." A defender, prosecutor or judge guided exclusively by this conception of duty would make no "concessions"; he would be a robot, an automaton, a nonthinking clerk. On the other hand, the very term "doing justice" implies an expert-oriented organization in which each employee's duty is to use his own best judgment. Policemen do not grant concessions when they use their common sense to keep the peace without enforcing the law. Instead, they do justice. Similarly, courthouse personnel do not grant concessions when they modify severe statutory laws in light of the facts of individual cases.

As long as the prosecutor retains discretion to charge various offense, and the judge has power to impose various sentences, negotiation in some form seems inevitable. When room to maneuver is built into the administration of criminal law, as it must be if justice is to be done, it is unrealistic to expect that people will not seize the opportunity to use it.

Admittedly, there is a political problem: The American criminal justice system does not work the way many citizens have been led to believe it does or should. By and large, Americans have been taught to expect mechanical uniformity; they are increasingly discovering the variations stemming from discretionary flexibility. One tempting response to this observed departure from expectations is to try to get tough, to propose as the Nixon Commission did that flexibility be abolished and the criminal justice system returned to the practices of idealized good old days. A more difficult, but more effective solution would be to tackle and modify the unrealistic expectations.

Surely the American people can be taught that flexible decisions are essential to "liberty and justice for all." Furthermore, they surely can be made to understand that discretionary handling of criminal cases is a lubricant that in a complex society promotes social peace among groups with strong, but nevertheless conflicting, interests in what should be done to, with and for criminals.

164

The outcome in the Peter Randolph case makes sense, even though it was reached by a strange path. If there were no room for flexibility in the law, Randolph might well have been convicted of burglary in the first degree and sent to prison for life. Thoughtful people can see that this would have been a bad result and recognize the need to make distinctions among burglars that demand different penalties for the same crime.

Abolish Plea Bargaining

A narrower interpretation of the Nixon Commission's proposal suggests that it refers to courthouse operations only. All guilty pleas would be abolished, and all cases given full trial. This is the approach taken in the Netherlands, the Soviet Union and other European countries where a trial is held and evidence presented, even if the accused admits his guilt. Such a system is likely to lose the advantage that is now gained from weeding out the cut-and-dried clear cases and holding trials only in the truly contested ones. When a trial is held now, it is usually a careful and deliberate proceeding in which the presumption of innocence has meaning because, in fact, a substantial percentage of the trials are decided in the defendant's favor. But if a full trial were to be held in every case, including those in which the defendant virtually admits guilt, the proceedings would likely degenerate as officials looked for shortcuts to avoid the interminable demonstration of the obvious. The presumption of innocence would be modified by experience to a presumption of guilt. The general quality of all trials would suffer, and the tendency toward ceremony without substance would be accelerated, even in cases deserving painstaking consideration.

At the very least, the Nixon Commission proposal certainly would abolish negotiations between prosecutors and defenders because it asks for rigid courthouse settings in which defendants simply choose between pleading guilty and not guilty. But men who are going to prison for fifteen years, whether they plead guilty or not, are likely to demand their right to a trial. The effect would be an enormous increase in full trials, requiring massive legislative appropriations of money and manpower.

Such a system was adopted on a limited scale by the New York State Legislature, at the urging of Governor Rockefeller, when it increased the penalties for serious drug offenses and then removed the possibility of a guilty plea to a lesser offense. It is too soon to judge the impact of these laws definitely. However, the legislature later modified and softened these provisions, probably because indications suggested that the laws operated precisely the way any careful observer of criminal justice processes would expect them to operate. Thus, arrests and charges for the stipulated offenses went down, presumably because police and prosecutors were reluctant to participate in the injustice of dealing with small-time offenders, who make up most of the cases, under the harsh laws. Predictably, the number of trials and the time delay to trial increased. Equally predictably, arrested persons who might be charged with nonnegotiable crimes were booked for lesser offenses, to which they pleaded guilty. Instead of abolishing discretion, the New York law seems only to have shunted it into a different arena.[4]

It is not reasonable to believe that legislatures will provide the resources necessary for full trials of even one half of the cases now coming into courthouses. For financial reasons, if for no others, adoption of a no-plea-agreement system surely would stimulate some abbreviated form of trial or other simple procedure for the disposition of cases that are not seriously contested. The likely net effect of the proposed reform, then, would be merely a change of the subject of negotiations from the guilty plea to negotiation about the disposition to be made if the defendant agrees to an abbreviated trial rather than demanding his right to a full one. From the perspective of either the defendant or the community, the change will not be significant.

This kind of negotiation is already common in the Los Angeles Superior Court, where about one third of the felony defendants receive a perfunctory trial known as a "trial on the transcript of the preliminary hearing." Courthouse personnel refer to this procedure as a "slow plea" (of guilty) because about 80 percent of the defendants are found guilty, mostly by prearrangement. The California Supreme Court has recognized that the trial on the transcript and the guilty plea are functionally identical, and has imposed the same procedural safeguards on both.[5]

Ironically, several of President Nixon's top aides and Cabinet members, charged with offenses related to the Watergate scandals, were saved from prison by the very process the Nixon Commission seeks to abolish. Few of these men pleaded not guilty and went to trial; all but one of those who did were found guilty. At least eight men who could have been charged with serious crimes pleaded guilty to minor offenses. For example, President Nixon's personal lawyer Herbert Kalmbach could have been charged with crimes ranging from extortion to misuse of public funds, but he pleaded guilty to only two minor breaches—setting up an improper campaign committee and promising a man an ambassadorship in exchange for a large campaign contribution. Jeb Stuart MacGruder could have been charged with perjury before both a grand jury and a petit jury, but he pleaded guilty to lying to an FBI agent. Former Attorney General Richard Kleindeinst, who lied under oath to a congressional committee, also could have been charged with perjury; he pleaded guilty to the strange charge that he "did refuse and fail to answer accurately and fully" the questions asked by a committee member. It is said that these and similar arrangements were made in exchange for information about crimes among "higher ups" in the Nixon administration, but there is no doubt that potentially severe penalties were also reduced in the interests of justice and through a process of "negotiations between prosecutors and defendants."

The Nixon Commission proposal certainly was not based on even a perfunctory examination of courthouse organization. It unwisely suggests that command-and-obey procedures be substituted for the expertise of judges, prosecutors and defenders. Overlooked are the drastic organizational changes that would be necessary if courthouse experts were forced literally to administer the law. Workers would have to be organized into a more rigidly hierarchical structure than now, each with a commander responsible to a central courthouse authority who would in turn be responsible to the legislatures making the laws. Individual judgments regarding the rightness or justness of an action would be forbidden. In organizations based on rank, worrying about such things is the job of the commanding officer. Such obsession with law enforcement, rather than justice, is unrealistic. There is and can be no rigid chain of command in the courthouse; no one is clearly the boss, the chief, or even the foreman or the section head. Instead, as we have seen, the judges, the prosecutors and the public defenders must belong to three quite different, and in many respects uncoordinated, organizations.

Regulate Guilty Plea Procedures

Long before the Nixon Commission presented its proposal to the nation, President Johnson's National Crime Commission suggested that plea negotiations should be acknowledged as legitimate, brought out into the open, and regulated by judges:

The negotiations should be freed from their present irregular status so that the participants can frankly acknowledge the negotiations and their agreements can be reviewed by the judge and made a matter of record. Upon the plea of guilty in open court the terms of the agreement should be fully stated on the record and, at least in serious or complicated cases, reduced to writing. If there is a written memorandum, it should contain an agreed statement of the facts of the offense, the opening positions of the parties, the terms of the agreement, background information relevant to the correctional disposition, and an explanation of why the negotiated disposition is appropriate. This material should be probed by judicial questioning.[6]

These suggestions, aimed principally at increased protection of defendants, have been taken seriously by courts and legislatures. New rules of criminal procedure announced by the Supreme Court of the United States for federal courts, and by the high courts of several states, are consistent with them, as are new statutes passed by several state legislatures. The new procedural rules and regulatory statutes have recognized the reality and legitimacy of plea negotiations, and prosecutors and defenders find it less necessary to negotiate covertly, fearful that they are engaged in an impropriety. Defendants can, therefore, be more fully informed of the consequences of their pleas. Agreements are stated in open court and recorded for future reference, thus reducing opportunities for misunderstanding and failure to keep promises. The judge's position is enhanced because he is able to rule on the propriety of an explicit dispositional agreement made by prosecution and defense, and he is not limited to going along with sentencing arrangements whose justification he really does not understand. The defendant is not assured that if he agrees to a certain sentence he will receive that sentence. But if the judge decides not to approve the prosecutor's and defender's written agreement as to charge, plea and disposition, the defendant has the right to withdraw his guilty plea and start negotiating anew. The substance of the law is left untouched by such reform, but its operations are exposed to view, perhaps stimulating pressure on the legislature for change.

These proposals proceed on the assumption that a crucial fault with existing practice is the irregular, informal and invisible status of guilty plea negotiations. The aim is to move the guilty plea into the courtroom. The assumption is that if the process is subjected to procedural restraints, made visible to all, and made a regular and binding part of the court process, its vices can be controlled or eliminated.

The Johnson Commission proposals exemplify the lawyer's approach to reform, which typically is to reform procedure. If decisions are being made badly, the lawyer's solution is to create a better procedural structure in which the decision will be made.[7] He assumes that the quality of the result will then be ensured. The lawyer's favorite procedural model is the judicial one, in which decision is based on specific evidence presented to the decision maker by trained advocates proceeding according to specific rules. Most criminal law reforms over the past generation have embodied this faith in the judicial model. The remedies proposed by lawyers for malfunctions in the criminal law process—from arrest to parole—have been routinely similar: Replace the questionable practice with a formal judicial hearing, or at least with something resembling a hearing. Sadly, most of these reforms have been disappointingly ineffective.

Appellate court judges, being familiar with this model, have reacted to the justice system's ills in their constitutional decisions somewhat like a doctor with but one bottle of pills in his little black bag: If interrogation or lineup identification procedures in police stations are unfair, treat these problems like courtroom problems by giving notice to the accused, providing counsel to challenge the officials, making the proceedings adversary. If presentence reports are prepared in a slipshod manner, disclose the report to defense counsel and subject the report writer to adversary cross-examination. If prison disciplinary practices are questionable, transform each disciplinary hearing into a miniature trial, complete with the right to confront witnesses, to cross-examine, to challenge legality of evidence. If parole revocation procedures are unsatisfactory, change them into something similar to a judicial trial. If juvenile courts are hurting children they are trying to help, move lawyers into the hearing room, judicialize the whole affair.

It is time to recognize that problems of justice cannot be solved merely by imposing an adversary system model on every facet of the criminal justic system.[8] Judicialization cannot eliminate the causes of police unfairness or probation officers' incompetence. It cannot make prison officers less interested in expediency and more concerned with fairness. The introduction of an attorney into juvenile court proceedings will not eliminate the overcrowding of juvenile facilities or eliminate the tragic fact that many good intentioned juvenile programs hurt the young people they are trying to help and protect. The judicial call for adversary resistance to officials ignores the causes of the conduct that is to be resisted.

Further, it is a lawyer's conceit that if a formal and public judicial process is established, that is where the decisions will be made. Every corporation executive and business manager knows better. The inevitable result of trying to make a discretionary decision-making process into a judicial hearing, without changing anything else, has been the creation of a new discretionary process elsewhere. The exercise of discretion is a response to a fundamental need for flexibility, for procedures that are fair because they avoid formal rules. Consequently, the criminal justice system has a remarkable capacity to accommodate itself to lawyers' efforts to structure it rigidly. Like a closed tube of toothpaste, if squeezed in one spot it merely pops out in another. Efforts to formalize the police procedures used when suspects are informed of their rights result in "Miranda mumbles." Efforts to formalize probation reports result in reports that elegantly say nothing. Efforts to formalize prison-disciplinary procedures lead to punishments informally administered by individual guards. Efforts to formalize the juvenile court lead to an increased tendency to deal with juveniles outside the courtroom. And efforts to formalize courtroom plea bargaining predictably result in prosecutorial screening conducted somewhere else. Too often, overreliance on the judicial model places the protections of a hearing and a lawyer in an empty room; the work gets done elsewhere.

Judicialization also makes the process slower, more expensive and, ultimately, less certain. The model called for seems unrealistic and unworkable. Indeed, the shortcomings of the judicial model have been a major cause of the very processes it is now called upon to cure. Procedural preoccupation reduces the capacity to deal with the caseload and increases the incentive for officials to dispose of cases by negotiated means. In this way, exclusive reliance on procedural safeguards may tend to increase, rather than reduce, the ambit of discretion, as officials seek some way to get their jobs done.

Thus, proposals to legalize and regularize the guilty plea process are of real, but limited, use. It makes sense to insist that hidden negotiations be forced into the open, that dispositional agreements arrived at through negotiation be kept and that the opportunity to negotiate be more equally available to all defendants. Ideally, making plea negotiations clearly legitimate will encourage prosecutors and defense lawyers alike to gather, present and discuss before a judge the kinds of information now gathered by probation departments for presentence reports, thus individualizing the punishment accorded each defendant. These proposals deserve adoption as a means of reducing the venality and potential corruption that accompany the secret negotiation.

It would be a mistake, however, to think that the root of the problems with the guilty plea will be cut out by so mechanical a solution. Judicialization does nothing to protect defendants from tacit negotiations, structural coercion and the purchased plea. Informal plea negotiations and agreements will not go away just because new rules say they should. Unless judicialization is accompanied by more fundamental changes, informal plea negotiations will remain unchanged, but they will be sanctified by a new veneer of perfunctory judicial ceremony. Mere procedural reform is likely to magnify, not decrease, the duplicity of the ritual guilty plea in open court. Even now, perfunctory answers are given to hollow questions, fulfilling formal legal demands but violating the demands of justice.

The unlikelihood that procedural reforms alone will penetrate to the heart of the problem can be seen in the experience of the Los Angeles Superior Court—the largest felony trial court in the nation. California has taken three significant steps toward regularizing the plea negotiation process: (1) plea negotiations have been legitimated, and they are conducted openly; (2) a statute mandates that the agreed-upon arrangement must be stated and recorded in open court before the plea is offered and that a defendant can withdraw his plea if the judge does not go along with the agreement; and (3) in Los Angeles County, as described earlier, an abbreviated trial based on the transcript of the preliminary hearing has been introduced as a compromise between the arranged plea and full court trial. Lynn Mather's recent study of this court suggests that the effect has been to increase rather than to decrease informal plea negotiations. Moreover, the agreements and dispositions continue to revolve around assessment of "what the case is worth," and worth continues to be determined by perfunctory negotiations about the facts of the defendant's prior record and current offense. One public defender, for example, said that 90 percent of the time he and a district attorney agreed on "appropriate dispositions," but he told of a "very serious," and "very dead bang case" where a difference of opinion centered on evaluation of the defendant's character—if he was a "professional burglar" as the district attorney claimed, he should go to state prison; but if he was "just an old drunk" as his attorney argued, county jail would be appropriate:

> The guy was caught drilling a hole in the wall next to a safe in a store. There's no defense at all. And he's got five prior burglary convictions— and they're all good priors. I wanted to go to Greene [a judge holding short trials on the basis of the transcript of the preliminary hearing] and plead him. Maybe we could keep him out of state prison then. In any other court it's prison for sure. The guy's just an old drunk. But [the district attorney in the case] wouldn't agreed to going to Greene.

171

And the D.A. has to consent to [going to a short trial on the basis of the transcript.] He figures with five priors and drilling a hole in the wall by the safe, the guy's not just an old drunk. That he's a professional burglar. I don't think so, though.[9]

Judicialization, in Los Angeles or elsewhere, should be recognized for what it is: an attempt to reduce the welshing and potential corruption that accompany secret negotiation. It would be a mistake to believe that it will eliminate these completely or that it will materially reduce structural coercion, indifference and other vices stemming from the perceived need to settle cases quickly and cheaply. It ensures that defendants are not openly told lies about the consequences of a guilty plea, but it does not ensure that the punishments they receive are either appropriate or fair.

Therefore, we turn our attention to the needs for more basic reform: the need to reduce the tendency of bureaucracy to treat people routinely; the need to bring the courthouse into a closer political relation to its community; and the need to reduce the severity of punishment. We are not talking about simplistic proposals to sweep away what is without suggesting what might be. Nor are we dealing with technical procedural changes which can be carefully engineered. At best what we are able to suggest are promising directions for reform. What follows is not a detailed legislative program but a suggestion of what should be on the agenda for reform.

Break Up Bureaucracy

It is essential that the routine handling of persons be reduced to achieve a balance between the rule of law and individuality. As long as decisions are the results of formulas for processing cases rather than of informed human judgments, justice will not be done. But in a mass society, it is unreasonable to ask for a return to the courthouse practices of a less complex world. There is no practical way to return to the simpler rural communities and urban groups of the past. Further, there are no tried and tested techniques to humanize bureaucracies, to arrest the tendency of bureaucracy to outgrow its usefulness and to become an impersonal machine. Therefore, it makes no sense simply to plead that existing courthouse bureaucracies should somehow surmount the tendencies of all large organizations to serve themselves and use assembly-line techniques in human affairs. Nevertheless, there are several points at which the impersonality of courthouse bureaucracies could readily be lessened.

One obvious example is the zone defense system of the public defender's office. From the defendant's perspective, the current system is a nightmare. In each court appearance, he is confronted by a new set of faces. Except for him, every actor in the drama knows the script. Each time he appears he has a mysterious encounter with an attorney who is concerned only with the particular segment of the matter to be dealt with that day, and who never is able to take time to see the defendant as a real, live human client. As Mather has flatly stated, "Although defendants provide the reason for the court's existence, they do not share directly in the culture of the court." Surely if each defendant had a lawyer he could identify as his own, he could play a greater part in the proceedings, even if his lawyer did not have time to give him all the attention he should have.

Another need is to modify what might be called the "committee on criminal justice" system that goes into operation in many courthouses once a defendant's case has been set for trial. In that system, a single judge, prosecutor and public defender serve the same courtroom, collectively processing all the felony cases coming into it. The three members of the committee work with each other daily, face-to-face, sometimes for years. These justice committees, like all committees, develop stereotyped routines which get cases processed but which give only passing individual attention to each. Moreover, even when individual attention materializes, it is attention to a defendant's case, not to the person of the defendant himself.

But an easy solution in the form of breaking up the justice committees will not significantly loosen the restrictions on courthouse consideration of individuality. Even those prosecutors, judges and defenders who only occasionally find themselves dealing with each other on some aspect of a case also develop routines which can all but ignore the human attributes of defendants. A broader approach to the problem would seek ways to enlarge committee membership to include the defendant himself. The mere presence of a defendant at sessions "in chambers" or at the bench when his fate is decided by a trio of lawyers would make a difference. However, experience with parole board hearings has demonstrated that mere presence is not enough. A committee can ignore a person even when he is sitting in the room. If justice is to be done, the subject of a committee hearing, even an informal and unofficial one, must somehow be treated as a genuine member of the committee.

Certainly this is difficult to do when the subject of discussion among the professionals is a technical one and the defendant is obtuse, naive or obstreperous. Certainly this is uncomfortable to do when the subject of the discussion is "How shall this person be hurt?" and the person to be hurt is staring the other committee members in the eye. However difficult and uncomfortable it may be to engineer the specifics of defendant participation, the costs of perpetuating his exclusion from the process are so high that the effort must be undertaken. If the defendant is given a more prominent place in the proceedings, officials will be led to explain what is going on in terms that he can understand. Hopefully, this will lead to greater acceptance of the outcome, thus decreasing the frequency of perfunctory acquiescence and increasing the proportion of defendants who genuinely agree that the sentences imposed are just.

The excessively routine treatment of people in courthouses could also be mitigated by giving the victim of crime a place in the process. Current courtroom procedures for determining guilt or innocence restrict the participation of the victim to testifying as an ordinary witness to the occurrence of the alleged criminal event, not as a person damaged by it, and with a special interest in the outcome of the proceedings. The victim is not asked what he thinks should happen to the accused person, nor is he able to make a claim for damages in the criminal court. Punishment of criminals must of course remain a concern of the state rather than becoming a matter of retaliation by individual victims.[10] Creating too prominent a place for victims might lead some people to take the role of avenger. But officials could no longer depend on mechanical routines if they were confronted more directly with the need to persuade the victim to recognize the offender as another human being and the offender to recognize the humanity of the victim he has wronged.

These proposals are scarcely definitive or exhaustive, but they do suggest directions for reform. They also suggest the irony of contemporary courthouse practice: Discretionary decision making practices concerning plea and sentence arose as a counterbalance to mechanical and routine procedures for enforcing the law, but later these practices became mechanized themselves. Instead of becoming increasingly sensitive to individual differences and individual needs, the procedures for arranging penalties through guilty plea negotiations have become bureaucratically routinized. The potential for individualization must once again be introduced.

For routine to be entrenched there must be a large number of cases that can be handled as if they were all alike and have interchangeable parts. An important step toward reintroducing the potential for individualization, therefore, is to break up the huge downtown courthouses.[11] In many nonmetropolitan courthouses, standards of performance demand an individualized approach to justice, and in every courthouse there are some responsive and sensitive officials who are able to personalize justice despite the way their work is structured. They manage to disrupt the flow of cases to provide a better brand of justice. It seems reasonable to assist them by dividing large metropolitan court systems into smaller districts, locating small-volume courthouses closer to the homes of the people brought into them, thus making them accessible to witnesses, victims and observers.

The oversized, remote, impersonal downtown courthouse is a threatening place for most people who come into it and is desirable only for the convenience of the professionals—lawyers, judges and clerks—to whom it is useful to have one place where all their business is conducted. The local community court can serve as a nucleus around which a number of new community-centered institutions can grow. But this proposal presents substantial risks as well as opportunities. Fragmented local courthouses can become entrenched political fiefdoms, hostile to the immediate community and more susceptible to boss-rule and corruption; the unhappy experience with decentralized local courts in such cities as Philadelphia, New York and Baltimore should make us cautious. Finally, a small-scale community court is likely to be manned by a single judge and a small group of prosecutors and defenders, spawning a new form of the justice committee problem. On balance, however, we prefer to take the risks associated with decentralization, largely because we think that for most large cities the process of downtown centralization has gone too far. Courthouses have reached a size that effectively precludes either efficiency or humanity.

The Courthouse and the Community

The courthouse is a political unit. The entire criminal law process—from passing laws to punishing men for violating them—is a political process basic to the fabric of society. In the past, there were signs of participatory democracy in courthouse operations. The politics of the community entered the courthouse through citizen participation in grand juries and trial juries, through reliance on private complaints as the basis for prosecution, through delegation of judicial responsibility to local community leaders serving as lay magistrates and justices of the peace.[12] But these mechanisms for making the courthouse responsive to broad segments of a community, rather than to just narrow portions of it, have atrophied. Ordinary citizens have been increasingly overlooked, with the result that courthouse officials now seem more responsive to voices within the courthouse than to the broader body politic.

The American system is notable among civilized nations for the relatively limited role it assigns to ordinary citizens in the fixing of guilt and punishment for crime. Laymen get into courthouses as jurors, to be sure, but juries see less than one case in twenty and their role has been greatly limited. Instead of judgment by a jury of peers who know the defendant and understand what he did, the law now insists on judgment by a jury of strangers who must know nothing about the case, do not read the newspapers and are without a viewpoint. Moreover, in all but a few states the jury plays no significant part in fixing punishments. It is limited to listening passively to technical presentations of legally circumscribed evidence and returning a yes-or-no verdict on the issue of guilt.

As long as the work of the courthouse is primarily the responsibility of professional specialists, as it now is, procedures and decisions will reflect the interests and perceptions of these specialists. There is nothing wrong with that, providing the values of the professionals do not deviate too far from the values held by a cross-section of the people in the larger community. A problem arises when the courthouse professionals become more responsive to internal needs and customs than to the views of the taxpayers they are supposed to serve. The problem becomes critical when the professionals give their viewpoints a distinct political identity, and try to persuade the taxpayers that the professionals' perceptions are reality.

American experience is replete with instances of such tail-wagging-the-dog politics in criminal justice affairs. In recent years, for example, police and prosecutors have been seen catering to repressive law-and-order interests and exploiting fears of a crime wave and terror of the criminal-as-violent-predator in order to gain budgetary support, reelection and immunity from outside legal interference with their activities. The statistical reports of crime have been shaped to serve these political interests and distorted to present a misleading picture of what professionals know most of their work to be. The FBI and various state and local agencies issue periodic statistical reports inevitably indicating a rise in the crime rate. But these statistics usually do not measure the number of people convicted or otherwise found by a court to have committed particular offenses. Rather, they are based either on crimes reported and recorded by the police or on arrests made. Incidents are grouped in broad categories, and no allowance is made for the majority of cases in which it later is decided that no crime was committed or in which what originally was recorded as a burglary, theft or assault later was reduced to a much less serious descriptive category.[13]

The artificial nature of these statistics became evident when the federal government modified its law enforcement grant policy, which had been to give financial aid to cities with high crime rates. The new policy gave large grants in proportion to the reduction of the crime rate in target cities. A city no longer would receive extra money because its crime rate was high, but if the rate went down, it would be granted more money for police equipment and services. This amounted to thinly concealed bribery of police departments to make "the crime problem" go away statistically, and impressive results were obtained. The crime wave magically receded, apparently in large part because policemen simply threw crime reports in the wastebasket. Certainly there is a better answer than this. Free government will not survive indefinitely a situation in which public employees have such effective power to manipulate their employer's perceptions, and even their own perceptions, of what criminal justice work entails.

The courthouse, like other criminal justice agencies, has become something of a private club from which both legislators and ordinary citizens are excluded. The isolation of courthouse workers enables them to place odd, if not incorrect, labels on their activities, deluding the public and themselves. For example, they speak of the burden of overwork, weak cases, and granting concessions even as they do justice; they speak of administering justice while engaged in coercion; they speak of rehabilitation and treatment while imposing punishments; they speak of serving criminals while merely protecting them from illegal procedures; they speak of individualization while bureaucratically processing cases in ways that dehumanize the criminal and ignore his victim.

One corrective measure for bureaucratic shortsightedness and delusion is to break up the private club and get the people involved more directly, to open up the courthouse and encourage laymen to come in. In Norway and other nations a three-person panel of judges formally sets the sentences of convicted felons. One of the judges is a layman. In the United States, the need is not so much for lay judges as for citizen participation in the informal procedures by which charges, pleas and dispositions are arranged. Perhaps if every courthouse had "public members"—some assigned to prosecutors, some to public defenders, some to judges—these procedures would, more frequently than now, be concerned with furthering social order rather than with reinforcing false notions of what courthouse work is all about. Intelligent men and women, perhaps selected in the same manner as jurors but for longer terms, would bring to the courthouse the wisdom as well as the politics of the home, the street, the factory. We are not persuaded that the decisions on what shall be done to offenders now being made by prosecutors and public defenders fresh out of law school are any more just than they would be if they were made by persons with more worldly experience but less legal training. Public participation might be a first step toward creating community consensus about crime, punishment and justice.

Among the oldest systems of public order is one in which each clan, village or neighborhood is responsible for the behavior of its members. Widespread conformity is gained as each member grows from childhood to adulthood and is given an increasing stake in the social, economic and political affairs of the group. When a member misbehaves, his conformity is regained through nonviolent assistance by such persons as family, friends, or neighbors who are close to him in social status. It is unrealistic to believe that urban America could return to such an effective system of supervision and control. The society is too large, too differentiated, too complex, too mobile. Ultimately, however, America must find better procedures than it now has for inspiring conformity to criminal laws, and better procedures for restoring the conformity of those who violate them. It is not enough to keep asserting that it is possible to frighten citizens into conformity and criminals into not repeating their offenses. A sense of community is needed. A courthouse more open to the laymen it serves would not necessarily produce this sense, but it would steer the community in the right direction.

If the courthouse were moved closer to the people, as we proposed earlier, the lay persons participating in the proceedings could be neighbors, friends, even relatives of the defendants. The dispositions they advised might actually be more severe than current dispositions. There is no guarantee that neighbors are more sympathetic than strangers; they may be harsher in evaluating behavior that threatens them directly than a dispassionate stranger might be. The difference would be this: The neighborhood proceedings would be less likely to be so impersonal that everyone involved in them would be alienated from the political order represented by the criminal law—the offender, his friends and family, his victims, the witnesses to his bad conduct and even the decision makers themselves. Sitting face-to-face in the courthouse, neighborhood criminals and neighborhood noncriminals would gradually learn that both crime and punishment are best viewed as very personal and undesirable hurts, inflicted on people by people. And it might be possible that this increased consensus about the undesirability of both crime and punishment would eventually extend to the area around the courthouse.

More positively, these changes in the courthouse would inevitably lead to some increase, however small, in the sense of community among the people living in the courthouse district. As things now stand, life in the central areas of large American cities is not community life. On the contrary, it is characterized by weak social ties, conflicting values, few legitimate opportunities, and indifference to crime. Rudiments of the "we" and "us" concepts characterizing true communities are present, but they refer mostly to the idea that "we" are residents while police and courthouse personnel are outside agents of oppression and coercion. And, of course, in many inner city neighborhoods, the law enforcement apparatus is in fact an outside force of repression. Because there is so little sense of neighborhood in ghetto areas, widespread conformity to criminal laws cannot be effectively inspired by local residents. And because crime rates are therefore high, the state tries harder than it does in other areas to control by deterrence, fear, terror. The cycle must be broken. One way to break it is to encourage neighborliness by moving courthouses into residential areas and encouraging local citizens to share the decision-making processes of their courthouse.

In the final analysis, the key to low crime rates lies in group relationships, in the recognition and reward secured by lawful conduct. The effective deterrent is the fear of loss of group status, not fear of legal penalties. For most citizens, robbing a liquor store or stealing a neighbor's television set is unthinkable, no matter what the probabilities of arrest. They have a personal stake in conformity to a group standard. The long-range solution to high crime rates is first to create more local groups that reward lawful conduct, thus giving more and more citizens a stake in conformity, and then to cement these groups into larger and larger units—first communities and then a society.

We doubt that this dream of a single societywide morality will ever come true. There is even good reason to doubt that a community can ever be *a* community so far as consensus about crime, punishment and justice is concerned. But we do believe that greater citizen participation in the justice processes within the community will help fuse residential areas into groups in which crime is unthinkable behavior.

Decriminalize the Law

It is hardly novel or revolutionary to propose reducing the punishments for crime. The recent literature of the criminal law has seen a number of powerful proposals that victimless crimes such as sex between consenting adults, prostitution, some drug offenses and gambling be altogether eliminated from the penal code. The dangers of overcriminalization have been noted not only by legal scholars and sociologists.[14] They have also been discussed by the Federal Bureau of Investigation, the National Crime Commission and British Royal Commissions. As the FBI reported to the National Crime Commission:

> The criminal code of any jurisdiction tends to make a crime of everything that people are against without regard to enforceability, changing social concepts, etc. The result is that the criminal code would become society's trashbin. The police have to rummage around in this material and are expected to prevent everything that is unlawful. They cannot do so because many of the things prohibited are simply beyond enforcement both because of human inability to enforce the law and because, as in the case of prohibition, society legislates one way and acts another way. If we would restrict our definition of criminal offenses in many areas, we would get the criminal codes back to the point where they prohibit specific, carefully defined, and serious conduct, and the police could then concentrate on enforcing the law in that context and would not waste its officers by trying to enforce the unenforceable as is now done.[15]

This statement makes the typical proposal that certain offenses be eliminated from the code, partly on grounds that enforcement of these cases entails heavy costs in terms of the use of professional manpower. Certainly such a process would eliminate a large number of provisions from existing penal codes. However, it is not clear that such reforms would result in a substantial change in the day-to-day operations of the felony courts. Many of the likely casualties of proposed code reforms are similar to "blue laws"; they remain on the books but are seldom invoked and are certainly not a large part of the court or correctional workload. Major exceptions to this are criminal laws dealing with the abuse of alcohol and the use of drugs. Here public attitudes are changing rapidly, and if in the near future much of this behavior ceases to be criminal, a very substantial part of the work of the criminal courts and of the prisons will have been eliminated.

In California in recent year, narcotics cases have accounted for over 40 percent of the felony cases and about 15 percent of the prison population; moreover, drunkenness and drug-related offenses account for most of the misdemeanor offenses, and it is on such charges that most of the occupants of local and county jails are confined. One county jail warden told us that 80 percent of his prisoners are there on drug-related offenses. Unfortunately, however, the decriminalization of narcotics and alcohol offenses would not eliminate the problems of this or any warden, or of court and prison officials. This action would merely transfer social concern from locking men up in order to punish them, to locking them up for some other reason, such as treatment. This might have some advantages, but it would not necessarily result in fewer persons being confined, although the sign swinging on the steel gates of the locked institution would bear the name "Hospital," "Drug Abuse Prevention Center," or "Detoxification Facility," rather than "Prison," or "Jail."[16]

The elimination of the offenses that are usually cited on the agenda for decriminalization would reduce the number of occasions in which police and prosecutors now exercise their discretion not to prosecute. It would not reduce the felony court caseload or the prison population by very much. Virtually all of the violent and property crimes and commercial hard-drug trafficking that are the everyday business of the felony courts are offenses which most citizens believe should and must be punishable. Realistically, these kinds of behavior will not be deleted from criminal codes until there is a radical change in public perceptions. Therefore, code reform, which reduces the number of acts which are now defined as criminal, is an important but only a partial solution to the troubles. It may be desirable for many reasons to eliminate whole classes of conduct from criminal prohibitions. But to control the vices present in the operation of discretion and the guilty plea it is more important that the state threaten with less severe punishment those persons it chooses to continue to define as criminals.

Reduce Severity

We are seeking courthouse settings where the social need for government by law is carefully balanced with the social need for individuality. A basic factor blocking achievement of such balance is statutory severity. If legislatures would reduce the statutory maximum punishments for crimes, the extensive unofficial modification of the statutory law we have been describing would be unnecessary. Discretionary decision making could then be restricted to cases in which the punishment must be adjusted to the circumstances of individual offenders in the interests of justice, rather than being used to soften the punishment of almost every criminal brought into the courthouse.

Severe punishment is widely believed to have a great capacity both to modify the behavior patterns of offenders and to discourage criminality by the general public. However, the best scientific evidence seems to show that severity is only one of many factors which affect the efficiency of punishment.[17] Among the conditions that may have greater effectiveness are certainty and immediacy of punishment, the availability of secondary reinforcements after punishment to remind the offender and to strengthen the deterrent effect, and the availability of rewarding alternatives to the punishable behavior.

A proposal to limit the severity of punishment in America is only a suggestion that we bring our practice more in line with the penal policies of virtually every other civilized nation in the world. Other countries, including those with rather rigid, conformist and moralistic atmospheres, maintain an even higher degree of public acceptance of the administration of justice with a markedly lower incidence of severity threatened against or actually inflicted on offenders.

It is highly unlikely that people would suddenly turn to crime even if the potential penalties now specified in statutes were greatly reduced. Certainly the fear of being caught and sent to prison for ten years discourages some men from engaging in holdups. But just as certainly, some men are not discouraged and will commit armed robbery no matter how high the penalty is set. The question really is: How many men and what kind of men are discouraged by one level of punishment but not discouraged by a substantially less severe one? Who would argue that the number of individuals discouraged from bank robbery by a statutory threat of ten years in prison is significantly greater than that of persons who would be discouraged by a statutory threat of five years? It seems likely that legislatures could diminish the potential penalties of existing laws several times before there would be a substantial change in deterrent effect.

Reducing statutory penalties does not mean abandoning the need to protect society against the truly dangerous criminal. There *are* men who must remain in prison a long time and some who must spend virtually their entire lives in custody. A few men belong in prison because their potential for aggressive, violent and seriously predatory behavior has been demonstrated repeatedly. Some of them are mentally disordered. Some present no clinical picture of insanity but are deeply committed to a dangerously criminal way of life. We are not convinced that dangerousness can be predicted by psychiatrists or anyone else. It can be objectively observed, however, that some offenders have proven their dangerousness. The professional thief, the Cosa Nostra murderer, the persistent robber, the flagrantly corrupt public official, the habitual white-collar thief—all of these people are frightening, and legislators are justified in demanding that they be isolated for substantial periods of time.

However, a penal code containing long potential prison terms neither effectively identifies the appropriate recipients of such harsh punishment nor specifies alternatives by which society can reach these men. The most severe terrors of the criminal law may be intended for the most dangerous offenders only, but in practice, they are reserved for the poorest, the weakest and the blackest. The needs for social defense could be met more equitably if the basic punishments for crimes were very substantially reduced, and special provisions were included in the code to deal with the specific situations of men with intolerably bad records of crimes.

Aligning statutes with contemporary conditions of American life will not destroy or tarnish the hallowed character of the criminal law. In contemporary urban courthouses, the severity threatened in statutes is seldom imposed, but such reduced severity does not disrupt the cherished belief that criminals should be brought to the dock, condemned, degraded, and the majesty of the law made incarnate in their downfall. The symbolic role of dramatic courthouse ceremonies is retained, even if used ineffectively. Further, the agencies of hostility and condemnation retain their visible symbols—uniforms, robes, guns, cages. There is no reason to believe that these ceremonies and symbols—and the social attitudes behind them—would disappear if legislators officially decreased the severity of punishments. Indeed, if severity were decreased, the ceremonies and symbols used in courthouses could again take on the dramatic meanings they once had.

If severity were reduced, the unreliability of acquiescence gained through threat would be reduced also, and the value of the accused person's acceptance of responsibility for his crime would be enhanced. In the first place, a society threatening a criminal with a year in prison is not as much in need of discretionary softening devices as is a society threatening the same criminal with ten years in prison. Imposing a mild punishment is not as unthinkable as imposing an unreasonably severe one. In the second place, the criminal threatened with a year rather than ten years in prison is more likely to agree, really and sincerely, that the society of which he is a part has an acceptable interest in doing things to, with and for him. But as long as legislators insist on severe statutes, they will be stuck with a control system that is officially harsh but not rationally related either to restoring the criminal, helping his victim or lowering the crime rate. A less severe system could legitimately claim to pursue a vision of justice, a vision that includes sanctions for misbehavior that operate within the community, that effectively motivate behavior changes, that reinforce the offender's social commitment but do not permanently isolate or stigmatize him.[18]

Legislative Restraint

When we propose that the routine of bureaucracy be limited, that there be more citizen participation in courthouse affairs and that statutory severity be reduced, we are asking only that fundamental democratic principles be recognized as relevant to dealing with criminals: Government should interfere in people's lives as little as possible, and when it must interfere, it should hurt the citizens as little as possible. We recognize that this suggestion lacks the immediate appeal that the promise of a simple cure might have, but we think it is more realistic than overblown illusory promises of technical solutions.

Americans are prone to believe that there are engineering solutions to all problems. When they are doing something badly, they are inclined to think that the solution lies in the direction of investing money and talent to learn how to do the same thing more efficiently. For example, many persons, lawmakers among them, nourish the idea that a bad criminal justice system will be improved by technological breakthroughs designed to make the system work more efficiently. Americans insist on this engineering approach to justice largely through ignorance; they do not know what else to do. But technological efficiency is not the same as doing justice. Before the United States pours more millions into studies of court administration, systems analyses, improved detection technology and computerized record keeping, it ought to decide what it is trying to do. When a programmatic goal is clear, a technological approach is reasonable. Years ago, for instance, America wanted to electrify rural farmhouses, and later to put a man on the moon, so it hired technical experts and gave them enough money to complete the task. But the path to achieving the social goal of justice is not so clear. Because no one knows how to engineer justice, it might well be that doing something to engineer change is worse than doing nothing.

Controlling human conduct is not like controlling chemical reactions or the tensile strength of metals. Human engineering is unreal engineering. If a person is engineered the way a concrete highway is engineered, he ceases to be a person. Moreover, in governmental affairs Americans settle for sloppy inefficiency by choice, knowing that in inefficient government there is freedom. They bridle at programs to tinker with souls, even when the souls belong to criminals. The problems of contemporary courthouses are not engineering problems, and the solutions therefore cannot be engineering solutions.

In the juvenile justice system, in fact, workers are increasingly discovering that doing nothing to a delinquent or predelinquent youth is less harmful to both the delinquent and the community, in a large percentage of cases, than doing something. When doing something stigmatizes the youngster out of proportion to his offense, be it skipping school or stealing a car, it is better to do nothing than to devise processes that would stigmatize him more. And so it is in the criminal courts. Hiring more and more courthouse professionals, including judges, so that something harsh can be done to more and more criminals is futile. Yet this is the approach being taken by the federal government as it annually pours one billion dollars into anticrime programs designed to punish more criminals more systematically, more efficiently and more severely. In the long run, this repressive policy might be more harmful to the nation than the disjointed, relatively humane, and discretionary system of criminal justice the programs are trying to replace.[19] There is a genuine risk that the criminal law will become an engine of oppression and coercion, further isolating and driving into rebellion the millions of people it unnecessarily hurts.

In the end we return to the basic relationship between law and discretion. We have repeatedly suggested that the great strength of allowing officials to exercise discretion is that it provides a flexible means by which they can decide how to act in a particular case in the face of a variety of circumstances. Discretion provides a context for affirmative action when the people, acting through their representatives, are unable to tell government officials precisely what they want them to do or how they are to do it. Citizens do know that they want judges, police, prosecutors and other courthouse officials to act with caution and restraint and this knowledge defines the role of law. For law is admirably suited as a tool for imposing restraint and caution. Its rules are more useful for prohibiting forbidden action than they are at providing the affirmative impetus for desired action.

Our legal system has been at its best when it serves as a limit on government, checking official power to act coercively against individuals and groups. Our Constitution, for instance, is much clearer in forbidding governmental racial or religious discrimination, abridgment of freedom of speech or cruel and unusual punishment than it is in giving content to the President's duty to take care that the laws be faithfully executed. Similarly, the statutory provision of a punishment for an offense is best viewed as a statement of the limit beyond which officials cannot go. Even the biblical measure of "an eye for an eye" is not to be understood to recommend that criminals' eyes be gouged out; it is a legislative stipulation limiting the point beyond which punishments may not be imposed on criminals. It is time we ask legislators to once again be agents of official restraint, setting limits on action, rather than the overambitious crime curers they have ineffectively tried to be in recent times.

If legislators and other lawmakers doubled their efforts to keep officials from unnecessarily damaging criminals, and halved their efforts to make criminals and potential criminals fearful of severe punishment, the split between the law and discretion would be reconcilable, even if persistent. No law, no rule, no command can provide an exclusive standard for courthouse officials to make decisions about punishments. Nor can it prescribe what should be done to or for a particular criminal. What lawmakers can do effectively is set strict limits on the kinds and amounts of pain officials can impose on criminals, leaving to courthouse officials the choice of the level of punishment actually to be imposed within these limits. Reduced potential severity in statutes would thus facilitate a more flexible system that could be adjusted to reflect the unique character of individual criminals, while remaining subservient to the rule of law. The outcome would be more justice in the criminal justice process.

The problem of preventing crime is principally one of giving more citizens a stake in conformity. The effective strategy is to make crime unthinkable, not to devise more efficient ways to repress it. The courthouse procedures and ceremonies can both stimulate and reinforce people's willingness to conform. By increasing concern for the individual, by connecting the courthouse's work more closely to the community and by reducing the severity of the punishments inflicted, the legislature can help the courthouse make a virtue of adherence to the prohibitions of the criminal law. In acting out ceremonies of justice, the courthouse can help the community reconcile its rules to its sense of justice and deflect its hostility and rage toward criminals in less harmful directions. When all is said and done, the search is one for justice, and justice is not found primarily by reading books or penal codes. It is acted out daily in the way people like Peter Randolph are treated. How that activity is carried out in the courthouse will determine whether justice lives.

bibliographic notes

Chapter 1: The Troubled Courthouse
1. The term discretion is used by lawyers in a variety of ways. Frequently it means normlessness, the absence of controlling rules. Sometimes it describes the procedural context of a decision that is reached informally and is not subject to review.

   For example, Congress from time to time has delegated to the President broad power to control the economy, set quotas on imports and even freeze wages and prices. Few rules govern the President's use of this discretionary power; he is to act as he thinks best when he decides that the national interest requires it, subject only to Congress's power to rescind the delegation by law and the electorate's ultimate power to remove President and Congressmen at the next election. The private and informal atmosphere in which juries deliberate, and the insistence by law that there shall be virtually no review of the correctness of jury decisions gives every jury broad discretion to acquit the accused in a criminal case. Yet juries do not operate in a normless situation. On the contrary, the judge is likely to instruct the jury at great length on the law it is supposed to apply.

   The two aspects of discretion are usually found together.

When there is no announced norm to govern decisions, it is hard to know what evidence is relevant and what procedure is appropriate. When there is no defined process for making decisions, it is difficult to discern what standards are being used. Rules and norms soon become little more than suggestions to the decision maker. When a policeman decides not to make an arrest, or a prosecutor declines to file a charge against a person accused of crime, the official is on his own, because there is not likely to be a formal hearing or other procedure. In these situations there are few determinative legal criteria to effectively bind the official because his decision is not subject to review. On the other hand judicial sentencing occurs in a formal procedural setting, marked by written probation reports, a hearing in open court at which counsel, the defendant and sometimes witnesses may testify and argue, and perhaps even review of the sentencing decision by an appeals court or judge's sentencing council. Nevertheless, sentencing is largely discretionary because of the range of choices usually open to the judge and the paucity of criteria to guide his exercise of authority.

Two helpful examinations of the complexities of discretion are Kenneth Culp Davis, *Discretionary Justice* (Baton Rouge, La.: Louisiana State University Press, 1969) and Mortimer Kadish and Sanford Kadish, *Discretion to Disobey* (Stanford, Calif.: Stanford University Press, 1973). Both books use discretion in criminal justice settings as an illustration of a broader set of problems involving the legal control of administrative officials. More generally, "Discretion and Its Exercise, Chapter 9 in James D. Thompson, *Organizations in Action* (New York: McGraw-Hill, 1967) considers where discretion lies in complex organizations, the motivations for exercising it and some of the consequences.

2. The complex negotiations leading to the entry of a *nolo contendere* plea by Vice President Spiro Agnew is described in Richard M. Cohen and Jules Witcover, *A Heartbeat Away* (New York: The Viking Press, 1974), especially Chapters 11–16. See also Jack Koen and Donald J. Newman, "Two Perspectives on the Agnew Plea Bargain" 10 *Criminal Law Bulletin* 80 (1974).

3. The general report of the National Advisory Commission on Criminal Justice Standards and Goals is entitled *A National Strategy to Reduce Crime* (Washington, D.C.: U.S. Government Printing Office, 1973). The discussion of plea bargaining

is found in a specialized report entitled *Courts* (Washington, D.C.: U.S. Government Printing Office, 1973). The recommendation regarding abolition of plea negotiations is:

As soon as possible, but in no event later than 1978, negotiations between prosecutors and defendants—either personally or through their attorneys—concerning concessions to be made in return for guilty pleas should be prohibited. In the event that the prosecution makes a recommendation as to sentence, it should not be affected by the willingness of the defendant to plead guilty to some or all of the offenses with which he is charged. A plea of guilty should not be considered by the court in determining the sentence to be imposed. (*Courts,* p. 46)

The discussion of this proposal notes that the Commission's position is not the one recommended by its own Court's Task Force and that it is contrary to that of the National Crime Commission and the American Bar Association. Moreover, the report candidly says that the proposal "does not address itself to mechanisms for enforcement of the proposed ban on plea negotiations," and suggests that implementation would depend on "voluntary compliance." (*Courts,* p. 48)

The Nixon Commission is the most recent of numerous crime commissions in this country. In 1920 civic groups in Cleveland sponsored a commission to study their local crime problem, led by the distinguished scholars Roscoe Pound and Felix Frankfurter. The Chicago Crime Commission was established at about the same time and it is still in operation. New York City had its Seabury Commission in the early 1930s. State crime commissions were active, too. The most notable of these were the Missouri Crime Survey (1926), the Illinois Crime Survey (1929) and the Oregon Crime Survey (1932).

On the federal level, the National Commission on Law Observance and Enforcement was established in 1929. Known as the Wickersham Commission, it fulfilled President Herbert Hoover's campaign promise to study enforcement of the prohibition laws. The Commission's report, published in 1931, ran to fifteen volumes, covering crimimal courts, criminal procedure, prisons and other topics, as well as enforcement of prohibition laws.

During the 1964 Presidential campaign, "crime in the streets" produced strong political pressures which were channelled by the Johnson administration into creation in 1965 of the President's Commission on Law Enforcement and Administration of Justice, frequently referred to as the National Crime Commission. The Commission's general report, *The*

Challenge of Crime in a Free Society (Washington, D.C.: U.S. Printing Office, 1967), was the work of nineteen commissioners, sixty-three staff members, one hundred and seventy-five consultants and hundreds of advisors. It made about two hundred specific recommendations. The Commission also published ten specialized reports and several dozen research studies and consultant's papers.

In the spring of 1968 the nation was shocked by the assassinations of Martin Luther King and Robert Kennedy. In response, President Johnson appointed the National Commission on the Causes and Prevention of Violence under the chairmanship of Milton Eisenhower. The staff reports of this Commission extend over fifteen volumes. One of these, *Law and Order Reconsidered* (Washington, D.C.: U.S. Government Printing Office, 1969), is an excellent overview of the general shortcomings of the American legal system.

On the general problems and limitations of presidential commissions, see Virgil Peterson, *Crime Commissions in the United States* (Chicago: Chicago Crime Commission, 1945); Anthony Platt, editor, *The Politics of Riot Commissions* (New York: Macmillan, 1971); and Richard Quinney, *Criminology* (Boston: Little, Brown, 1975), pp. 265–268.

4. These new laws amend a number of provisions of the New York Penal Law and Criminal Procedure Law. The amendments are found in Laws of New York 1973, Ch. 276, 277 and 278. Governor Rockefeller's program is outlined in his annual messages to the legislature reprinted in 2 *McKinney's 1973 Session Laws of New York* 2309, 2317–2320. These laws were further amended in July of 1975 to permit plea bargaining by most narcotics offenders. *New York Times,* July 12, 1975, p. 1, col. 1.

5. The new Los Angeles plea-bargaining rules announced by the late District Attorney Busch are described in the *Los Angeles Daily Journal,* January 22, 1974, p. 1. The text of a parallel set of rules announced by then District Attorney Richard H. Kuh of New York County on August 14, 1974 is reprinted as "Plea Bargaining: Guidelines for the Manhattan District Attorney's Office," 11 *Criminal Law Bulletin* 48 (1975).

6. The proposed Federal Rules of Criminal Procedure dealing with plea bargaining were announced by Chief Justice Warren Burger and transmitted to the Congress on April 22, 1974. In most major respects the proposed rules are similar to those recommended by the American Bar Association's Project on

Minimum Standards for Criminal Justice, *Standards Relating to Pleas of Guilty* (New York: Institute of Judicial Administration, 1968), the American Law Institute's *Model Code of Pre-Arraignment Procedure*, § § 350.1–350.9, and the California Penal Code, § 1192.5. Congress suspended the effectiveness of the proposed rules to August 1, 1975 pending further study. P.L. 93–361, 88 Stat., 397. They are now scheduled to go into effect in amended form on December 1, 1975. Federal Rules of Criminal Procedures Amendments Act of 1975. P.L. 94–64, 89 Stat. 380 (July 31, 1975).

Chapter 2: The Odyssey of Peter Randolph
1. The arrest data are derived from statistics submitted to the FBI by local police departments, *Crime in the United States, 1973* (Washington, D.C.: U.S. Government Printing Office, 1973), Table 24. The population between the ages of eighteen and thirty-nine was approximately sixty-five million in 1973. There were about nine million nontraffic arrests in the United States that year. Of these arrests, at least five million were for drunkenness, vagrancy, loitering, disorderly conduct, driving under the influence, marijuana possession and similar charges. Alternative ways of dealing with homeless men and skid-row residents are discussed in Raymond Nimmer, *Two Million Unnecessary Arrests* (Chicago: American Bar Foundation, 1971).

   Over 75 percent of the persons arrested for the seven most serious crimes reported by the FBI, the so-called index crimes, were under the age of twenty-five. Index crimes are murder, forcible rape, robbery, aggravated assault, burglary, larceny over fifty dollars, and automobile theft. Persons under the age of eighteen account for 50 percent of the property crime offenses in the index. Males arrested outnumber females by six to one. Slightly over one-third of all persons arrested for index offenses are black, as are a majority of all those arrested for violent crimes.

2. The arrest distribution statistics are drawn from *Crime and Delinquency in California, 1973* (Sacramento, Calif.: Bureau of Criminal Statistics, 1974), Table 13. California is the largest state, and its statistical reports permit analysis that is not possible with the FBI national statistics or those of most other states.

   There are several important limits on all of these statistics.

At most, they record official police responses to crime; they should not be understood as indicating what crimes are committed or who commits them. Much crime is unreported, and in many cases of reported crime no official action is taken or no arrest is made. Moreover, even as descriptions of the official processing of cases after arrest, the statistics available are incomplete and subject to various criticisms. On the limitations of crime statistics see Thorsten Sellin, "The Significance of Records of Crime," 67 *Law Quarterly Review* 489 (1951); Marvin E. Wolfgang, "Uniform Crime Reports: A Critical Appraisal," 111 *University of Pennsylvania Law Review* 708 (1963); and Donald J. Black, "Production of Crime Rates," 35 *American Sociological Review* 733 (1970).

3. Of the 239,395 reported adult felony arrests in California in 1973, 62,844 (26 percent) resulted in conviction of some crime, but only one-half of these (31,000) were ultimately sentenced as felons. Of the 176,551 arrests for which there was no conviction, most were eliminated from the system at the early stages of police, prosecutorial and judicial screening. For instance, on a statewide basis, police released without charges 19 percent of all felony arrestees. The great local variation can be seen by comparing the Sheriff's Office of Los Angeles County, which released 32 percent of all felony adult arrestees, with the Sheriffs' Offices in neighboring Ventura County, which released 3 percent, and San Bernardino, which released 5 percent.

   The Chicago experience is similar in outcome. The American Bar Foundation's Supervisor of Research reports that the Chicago police release few felony arrestees, but that 80 percent of all such persons are disposed of by a lower court judge presiding at a preliminary hearing: Donald M. McIntyre, Jr., "A Study of Judicial Dominance of the Charging Process," 59 *Journal of Criminal Law, Criminology and Police Science* 463 (1968). For a comparison of release processes in New York and California, see Floyd F. Feeney and James P. Woods, "A Comparative Description of the New York & California Criminal Justic Systems: Arrest through Arraignment," 26 *Vanderbilt Law Review* 973 (1973). The National Crime Commission's *Task Force Report: The Courts* (Washington, D.C.: U.S. Government Printing Office, 1967) contains as appendices surveys of the process in Detroit and Baltimore.

4. The suspect who pays a bail bondsman his premium does not get his money back when he appears for the hearing, even if

the case against him is dismissed. The bail bond system thus gives the arresting policeman effective power to impose a fine on the indigent persons he arrests, whether they are ultimately found innocent or guilty. It also gives the policeman effective power to punish by confinement in jail those suspects who cannot raise enough money for a bail bondsman's premium.

During the past decade several attempts have been made to reform the bail system in a number of states. The effort has been to eliminate the bail bondsman, to insure that release is equally available to rich and poor defendants, and that freedom is granted for reasons related to whether the defendant will appear for a trial. Few of these reforms have fulfilled their promise. America's jails remain glutted with unconvicted persons held only because they lack bail money.

The problems presented by the bail system are attacked in Daniel Freed and Patricia Wald, *Bail in the United States* (Washington, D.C.: U.S. Department of Justice and Vera Foundation, 1964); the American Bar Association Project on Minimum Standards for Criminal Justice, *Standards Relating to Pretrial Release* (New York: Institute of Judicial Administration, 1968); and Ronald Goldfarb, *Ransom: A Critique of the American Bail System* (New York: Harper & Row, 1968).

Several studies indicate that the arrested person denied release on bail is more likely to be convicted and punished severely: Anne Rankin, "The Effect of Pretrial Detention," 39 *New York University Law Review* 641 (1964); and New York Legal Aid Society, "The Unconstitutional Administration of Bail," 8 *Criminal Law Bulletin* 459 (1972).

The limited impact of bail reform is documented in Paul Wice and Rita James Simon, "Pretrial Release: A Survey of Alternative Practices," 34 *Federal Probation* 60 (1970); and Paul Wice, "Bail Reform in American Cities," 9 *Criminal Law Bulletin* 770 (1973).

5. The conversation between Randolph and Public Defender Vincent Long is based on the report by Glen Wilkerson, "Public Defenders as Their Clients See Them," 1 *American Journal of Criminal Law* 141 (1972); and David Sudnow, "Normal Crimes: Sociological Features of the Penal Code in a Public Defender's Office," 12 *Social Problems* 225, 267–268 (1965).

6. In "A Study of Judicial Dominance of the Charging Process," *op. cit.* McIntyre reports that in those communities in which the lower court judge dominates the early screening process, the preliminary hearing is likely to remain a very important

part of the system, disposing of 80 percent of the felony arrests. In Los Angeles, the preliminary hearing is less important to screen charges, but the transcript made at the hearing is used as the crucial statement of facts upon which most cases are tried. Kenneth Graham and Leon Letwin, "The Preliminary Hearing in Los Angeles," 18 *UCLA Law Review* 635, 916 (1971). See, in general, Frank W. Miller and Frank J. Remington, "Procedures Before Trial," 339 *Annals of the American Academy of Political and Social Science* 111 (1962).

7. There are almost 17,000 state and local courts and 90 federal district courts with jurisdiction to try criminal cases in the United States. There are great variations in the structure of court organization, and a confusing variety of names have been given to particular kinds of courts. What all state systems have in common is a set of lower courts which try minor offenses (misdemeanors) and also deal with the early stages of serious offenses, and another set of courts of general jurisdiction which have power to try serious offenses (felonies). The lower court goes by such names as justice of the peace court, magistrate's court, municipal or city court, district court, parish court and county court. The court of general jurisdiction may be called the circuit court, the superior court, the district court or the supreme court (New York only).

8. See George F. Cole, "The Decision to Prosecute," 4 *Law and Society Review* 331 (1970).

9. The right to grand jury indictment in felony cases was included in the federal Bill of Rights and in the constitutions of many states because it was considered important that the bringing of serious charges reflect the judgment of a representative body of the local community. In most cities, however, the grand jury lacks the means to review independently the vast number of serious charges presented to it. Grand jury proceedings are secret, witnesses are not permitted to have a lawyer present to advise them and the accused generally has no notice of the proceedings, nor is he entitled to appear and tell his side of the story.

The grand jury has become largely subservient to the prosecutor, who decides what matters will be presented and what witnesses heard. The prosecutor's legal judgments as to what accusations should be made are inevitably accepted by the laymen grand jurors. In most states the law provides very limited opportunities for legal challenge of the grand jury's actions. For these reasons, most states have abolished the requirement of grand jury action in all felony cases, and in routine cases permit the formal accusation to be drawn up by the prosecutor, acting alone. This precise statement of the charge or charges is called an information. In such states grand jury indictments are rarely used except in notorious and politically hot cases.

A critical and historical review of the grand jury, with proposals for reform, is found in Leroy D. Clark, *The Grand Jury: The Use and Abuse of Political Power* (Chicago: Quadrangle Books, 1975).

10. The problem of delay in the administration of justice, both civil and criminal, is pandemic. The problem is the central theme of a general review of American criminal justice process, Lewis R. Katz, *Justice is the Crime: Pretrial Delay in Felony Cases* (Cleveland, Ohio: The Press of Case Western Reserve University, 1972); Anthony Amsterdam, "Speedy Criminal Trial: Rights and Remedies," 27 *Stanford Law Review* 525 (1975). Jerome Skolnick has likened the prosecutor to the guardian of a funnel, whose major task is to make certain that the funnel is not blocked. Skolnick, "Social Control in the Adversary System," 11 *Journal of Conflict Resolution* 52 (1967).

11. The studies referred to include Rankin, "The Effects of Pretrial Detention," *op. cit.,* and New York Legal Aid Society, "The Unconstitutional Administration of Bail," *op. cit.*

12. Jails are county or municipal institutions used both to house detained persons accused, but not convicted, of crimes and to incarcerate persons serving relatively short sentences after conviction of misdemeanors. Prisons are state institutions which hold long-term prisoners, generally those convicted of felonies and sentenced to serve one year or more. There are over 4,000 jails in the country holding persons for more than 48 hours, and on any given day they hold more than 160,000 persons. In addition, there are tens of thousands of police station lockups and other facilities for short-term confinements. A recent federal survey indicates that about 90 percent of these jails have no facilities for exercise, recreation or education, almost half have no medical facilities and a quarter have no visiting facilities. The situation is described in detail in Ronald Goldfarb, *Jails: The Ultimate Ghetto* (Garden City, N.Y.: Anchor Press, 1975). The basic statisti-

cal study is the 1970 National Jail Census published as U.S. Department of Justice, *Local Jails* (Washington, D.C.: U.S. Government Printing Office, 1973).

13. The description of Randolph's jail experience is based on Hans W. Mattick and Alexander B. Aikman, "The Cloacal Region of American Corrections," 381 *Annals of the American Academy of Political and Social Science* 109 (1969); and Gerald G. O'Connor, "The Impact of Initial Detention upon Male Delinquents," 18 *Social Problems* 194 (1970).

14. The questions asked by the judge in this fictitious ceremony are consistent with constitutional requirements regarding the judge's duty to ascertain that every guilty plea is both voluntary and informed. These requirements are discussed on pp. 147–150.

15. The study referred to is Abraham Blumberg, "The Practice of Law as a Confidence Game: Organizational Cooptation of a Profession," 1 *Law and Society Review* 15 (1967). See also Blumberg, *Criminal Justice* (Chicago: Quadrangle Books, 1967), Chapters 4 and 5.

16. The classic study on the use of legal torture is D. Jardine, *Use of Torture in the Criminal Law of England* (London: Baldwin & Cradock, 1837). While official legal torture disappeared in England at the end of the seventeenth century, it persisted in France until 1789 and was not formally abolished in parts of Germany until 1831. See, in general, John Langbein, *Prosecuting Crime in the Renaissance* (Cambridge, Mass.: Harvard University Press, 1974).

17. The first state conviction reversed on grounds that a coerced confession ("third degree") deprived the accused of due process of law was *Brown* v. *Mississippi,* 297 U.S. 278 (1936).

18. Lytton Strachey, *Elizabeth and Essex* (New York: Harcourt Brace, 1928), p. 80.

19. Under the California statute the charge could be reduced to a misdemeanor only with the consent of the District Attorney, and the policy of the Los Angeles District Attorney then was to grant this consent only when the defendant agreed to plead guilty to the reduced charge. The California Supreme Court declared the provision requiring the district attorney's consent to the charge reduction unconstitutional in *Esteybar* v. *Municipal Court,* 5 Cal. 3d 119, 485 Pac. 2d 1140 (1971). (See especially footnote 2.)

20. The case referred to is *Parker* v. *North Carolina,* 397 U.S. 790 (1970). See page 60.

21. Statutes or court rules make a presentence report mandatory for certain classes of offenses in about one-fourth of the states. In many states and the federal system, a presentence report is discretionary with the judge, although in some of these states he may not grant probation unless there has been a presentence report. A study of the relation between presentence reports and dispositions showed that most judges follow the recommendations of the probation department. Robert M. Carter and Leslie T. Wilkins, "Some Factors in Sentencing Policy," 58 *Journal of Criminal Law, Criminology and Police Science* 503 (1967); and Robert M. Carter, "The Presentence Report and the Decision-making Process," 4 *Journal of Research on Crime and Delinquency* 203 (1967).

22. In most states the judge is the central authority fixing sentences. In about one-fourth of the states, the jury has some role in fixing the length of sentences in some cases. In several western states, notably California, the judge is limited to deciding whether a convicted felon is to be imprisoned; the term of imprisonment within statutory limits is fixed by an administrative board.

   In the majority of states in which the judge sets the term of imprisonment a variety of statutory systems are used. The judge may sentence to a definite term or he may fix a minimum and maximum term. The paroling authority may have power to release the prisoner after serving a fraction of the fixed term or after the minimum fixed by the judge. The best short but comprehensive treatment of the issues is Prof. Peter Low's "Preliminary Memorandum on Sentencing Structure" in II *Working Papers of the National Commission on Reform of the Federal Criminal Laws* (Washington, D.C.: U.S. Government Printing Office, 1970). See also Lloyd E. Ohlin and Frank J. Remington, "Sentencing Structure: Its Effect upon Systems for Administration," 23 *Law and Contemporary Problems* 495 (1958). Note, "Statutory Structures for Sentencing Felons to Prison," 60 *Columbia Law Review* 1134 (1960); American Bar Association's Project on Minimum Standards for Criminal Justice, *Standards Relating to Sentencing Alternatives and Procedures* (New York: Institute of Judicial Administration, Justice Project, 1968); Robert O. Dawson, *Sentencing: The Decision as to Type, Length and Conditions of Sentence* (Boston: Little, Brown, 1969); and Sol Rubin, *Law of Criminal Correction,* second ed. (St. Paul, Minn.: West Publishing Co., 1973), Chapter 4.

23. Although defense attorneys in the United States commonly address the court at sentencing time, this practice is rare among prosecutors. In Canada, similarly, "The prosecutor's reluctance to speak to sentence unless requested to by the judge seems general." Brian A. Grosman, *The Prosecutor: An Inquiry Into the Exercise of Discretion* (Toronto: University of Toronto Press, 1969), p. 54.

24. The statistics are from *Crime and Delinquency in California, op. cit.,* Table 17, p. 58.

25. The kinds of circumstances in which police exercise their discretion to arrest are analyzed in Wayne R. LaFave, *Arrest: The Decision to Take a Suspect into Custody* (Boston: Little, Brown, 1965). Our conclusion that the police are not doing a shockingly bad job should not be taken as blanket approval for the way police discretion to arrest is exercised. On occasion, police officers misuse power in repressive, racist and corrupt discretionary choices. Our point is merely that the major vice is not that policemen are prone to arrest without complying with legal standards of evidence. For analyses of police practices and problems see Jerome Skolnick, *Justice Without Trial: Law Enforcement in Democratic Society* (New York: John Wiley & Sons, 1966); Arthur Niederhoffer, *Behind the Shield: The Police in Urban Society* (Garden City, N.Y.: Doubleday, 1967); James Q. Wilson, *Varieties of Police Behavior* (New York: Atheneum, 1968); Paul Chevigny, *Police Power: Police Abuses in New York City* (New York: Random House, 1969); Egon Bittner, *The Functions of Police in Modern Society* (Rockville, Md.: National Institute of Mental Health, 1970); Albert Reiss, *The Police and the Public* (New Haven, Conn.: Yale University Press, 1971); American Bar Association's Project on Minimum Standards for Criminal Justice, *Standards Relating to the Urban Police Function* (New York: Institute of Judicial Administration, 1973); and Maureen E. Cain, *Society and the Policeman's Role* (London: Routledge and Kegan Paul, 1973).

26. The President's Commisson on Law Enforcement and Administration of Justice, *The Challenge of Crime in a Free Society* (Washington, D.C.: U.S. Government Printing Office, 1967) p. 176.

27. Frank W. Miller, *Prosecution: The Decision to Charge a Suspect with a Crime* (Boston: Little, Brown, 1969), pp. 161–162.

28. The rule for automobile accidents described in the text is

based on the legal doctrine of contributory negligence. This doctrine is being replaced in an increasing number of states by a rule of comparative negligence in which liability is assessed in proportion to the relative fault of the parties. Victor E. Schwartz, *Comparative Negligence* (Indianapolis, Ind.-Allen Smith, 1974). On March 31, 1975, the Supreme Court of California adopted a form of comparative negligence. *Li v. Yellow Cab Co.*, 13 Cal. 3d 804 (1975).

29. Gilbert N. Lewis, *The Anatomy of Science* (New Haven: Yale University Press, 1926) p. 9.

30. A number of published studies describe the operation of the criminal courts in specific American jurisdictions:

    a) The American Bar Foundation conducted a monumental study of the criminal justice process in Kansas, Wisconsin and Michigan about twenty years ago. The results are reported in five volumes: Wayne R. LaFave, *Arrest: The Decision to Take A Suspect into Custody* (Boston: Little, Brown, 1965); Donald J. Newman, *Conviction: The Determination of Guilt or Innocence Without Trial* (Boston: Little, Brown, 1966); Lawrence P. Tiffany, Donald M. McIntyre, Jr., and Daniel Rotenberg, *Detection of Crime: Stopping and Questioning, Search and Seizure, Encouragement and Entrapment* (Boston: Little, Brown, 1967); Robert O. Dawson, *Sentencing: The Decision as to Type, Length and Conditions of Sentence* (Boston: Little, Brown, 1969); Frank W. Miller, *Prosecution: The Decision to Charge a Suspect with a Crime* (Boston: Little, Brown, 1970).

       The American Bar Foundation also sponsored a study of the criminal justice system in Detroit—Donald M. McIntyre, Jr., ed., *Law Enforcement in the Metropolis* (Chicago: American Bar Foundation, 1967).

    b) The President's Commisson on Law Enforcement and Administration of Justice sponsored two small but pungent studies of the criminal lower courts in Baltimore and Detroit. *Task Force Report: The Courts* (Washington, D.C.: U.S. Government Printing Office, 1967), Appendix B.

    c) Harry I. Subin of the U.S. Department of Justice, Office of Criminal Justice, published an influential and shocking study of the Washington, D.C. Court of General Sessions, *Criminal Justice in a Metropolitan Court* (Washington, D.C.: U.S. Government Printing Office, 1966). This study was extended in the *Report of the President's Commis-*

sion on Crime in the District of Columbia (Washington, D.C.: U.S. Government Printing Office, 1966).

d) The status of the lower criminal courts of metropolitan Boston are described in Stephen R. Bing and S. Stephen Rosenfeld, *The Quality of Justice* (New York: Lawyer's Committee for Civil Rights Under Law, 1970). The workings of the same courts are described in two articles by Richard Harris, "Annals of Law: In Criminal Court," *The New Yorker,* April 14, 1973, p. 45–88; April 21, 1973, p. 44–87.

e) The early stages of processing in Cook County are reported by Donald M. McIntyre, Jr., "A Study of Judicial Dominance of the Charging Process," 59 *Journal of Criminal Law, Criminology and Police Science* 463 (1968).

f) The *Philadelphia Inquirer* published a special study of that city's criminal courts emphasizing the discrimination and irrationality of operations, Donald L. Bartlett and James B. Steele, "Crime and Injustice" (no date shown, 1973).

g) The role of the prosecutor in Chicago, Los Angeles, Brooklyn, Detroit, Baltimore and Houston are compared in general terms in Donald M. McIntyre, Jr. and David Lippman, "Prosecutors and Early Disposition of Felony Cases" 56 *Journal of the American Bar Association* 1154 (1970).

h) A detailed comparison of New York and California practice is Floyd F. Feeney and James R. Woods, "A Comparative Description of New York and California Criminal Justice Systems: Arrest Through Arraignment," 26 *Vanderbilt Law Review* 973 (1973). An older, but interesting study, also based on California practice is Edward L. Barrett, Jr., "Police Practices and the Law—From Arrest to Release or Charge," 50 *California Law Review* 11 (1962).

i) There have been a number of studies made of the Los Angeles system from different perspectives. The Rand Corporation published a largely statistical systems analysis: Peter W. Greenwood *et al., Prosecution of Adult Felony Defendants in Los Angeles County: A Policy Perspective* (Washington, D.C.: Law Enforcement Assistance Administration, 1973). A good sociological examination of Los Angeles plea bargaining is Lynn Mather, "Some Determinants of the Method of Case Disposition: Decision Making by Public Defenders in Los Angeles," 8 *Law and Society Review* 187 (1973). Two good legal studies of Los Angeles Courts are Kenneth Graham and Leon Letwin, "The Preliminary Hearing in Los Angeles: Some Field Findings and Legal-Policy Observations," 18 *UCLA Law Review* 635 (1971); and Comment, "Prosecutorial Discretion in the Initiation of Criminal Complaints," 42 *Southern California Law Review* 519 (1969).

j) Two short comparative descriptions of the Houston and Baltimore prosecutors' offices were written by a prosecutor from each of these cities who visited the other under an exchange program: Robert Fertitta, "Comparative Study of Prosecutors' Offices: Baltimore and Houston," 5 *The Prosecutor* 248 (1969); and Ted Busch, "Prosecution in Baltimore Compared to the Houston System," 5 *The Prosecutor* 253 (1969). A similar comparative view of Brooklyn and Los Angeles is found in John Meglio, "Comparative Studies of the District Attorneys' Offices in Los Angeles and Brooklyn," 5 *The Prosecutor* 237 (1969) and George Tramwell, III, "Control of System Policy and Practice by the Office of District Attorney in Brooklyn and Los Angeles," 5 *The Prosecutor* 242 (1969).

k) Two views of the system from the perspective of the defendant are John Irwin, *The Felon* (Englewood Cliffs, N.J.: Prentice-Hall, 1970) written with emphasis on prison and parole as seen in a California setting, and Jonathan Caspar, *American Criminal Justice* (Englewood Cliffs, N.J.: Prentice-Hall, 1972) based on studies in a Connecticut courthouse.

l) A book-length study of a California district attorney's office is Lief H. Carter, *The Limits of Order* (Lexington, Mass.: Lexington Books, 1974).

m) Two comparisons of British and American Practice are Jon L. Heberling, "Conviction without Trial," 2 *Anglo-American Law Review*, 428 (1973), and Anthony Davis, "Sentences for Sale: A New Look at Plea Bargaining in England and America," *Criminal Law Review* 150 (1971).

n) The operation of the system in the Netherlands and California are compared in Arthur Rosett, "Trial and Discretion in Dutch Criminal Justice," 19 *UCLA Law Review* 353 (1972).

31. The statement by a defendant that he was represented by a

public defender, not an attorney, has been heard by the authors in three different jurisdictions. It has always seemed one of the most powerful indictments of the legal services provided indigents accused of crime. The confusion apparently is quite general and has found its way into the literature: Jonathan Caspar, "Did You Have a Lawyer When You Went to Court? No, I Had a Public Defender," 1 *Yale Review Law and Social Action* 4 (1971). See also Donald Dahlin, "Toward a Theory of the Public Defender's Place in the Legal System," 19 *South Dakota Law Review* 87 (1974).

Chapter 3: The Story of the Courtroom.
1. For a recent study of a local community's system of criminal justice in Elizabethan times, see Joel Samaha, *Law and Order in Historical Perspective: The Case of Elizabethan Essex* (New York: Academic Press, 1974).
2. While volumes could be written about the meanings of due process of law, no comprehensive contemporary exploration is available. Two related reasons are not hard to find: it would be a very thick and confusing book, and it would be necessary for the author to undertake supplements every few years as new connotations of the concept developed. The most recent quantum jump in the concept is found in the Supreme Court decision holding it beyond the power of the state to forbid abortion early in pregnancy, *Roe* v. *Wade,* 410 U.S. 113 (1973).
3. A history of the guilty plea from tribal society to the present is surveyed in Jay Wishingood, "The Plea Bargain in Historical Perspective," 23 *Buffalo Law Review* 499 (1974). A French jurist in 1820 observed routine structural coercion toward guilty pleas (which he calls "incroyable clémence") in England, where the law punished by death the counterfeiting of banknotes and the passing of the false notes, but punished by transportation the possession of false notes. Counterfeiters were indicted for one or both capital offenses, as well as for possession, but if a defendant pleaded guilty to possession, the bank lawyer would tell the jury he could not produce witnesses to the capital crimes, and the jury would render a not guilty verdict. M. Cottu, *De L'Administration de la Justice Criminelle en Angleterre* (Paris: H. Nicolle, 1820), pp. 99–101. The classical English authorities are 2 M. Hale, *Pleas of the Crown* 225 (1736) and 4 W. Blackstone *Commentaries* *329. A fascinating early consideration of the problem in the United States includes historical statistics

from a number of states and tables on the use of the guilty plea in New York from 1839–1926: Raymond Moley, "The Vanishing Jury," 2 *Southern California Law Review* 97 (1928).

4. The first coerced confession case involving conviction of a state crime was *Brown* v. *Mississippi,* 297 U.S. 278 (1936). The earliest statement of a federal constitutional right to counsel in state criminal trials is *Powell* v. *Alabama,* 287 U.S. 45 (1932), which grew out of the notorious Scottsboro cases. A treatment of the historical development is found in Otis H. Stephens, *The Supreme Court and Confessions of Guilt* (Knoxville: University of Tennessee Press, 1973); see also Anthony Amsterdam, "The Supreme Court and the Rights of Suspects in Criminal Cases," 45 *New York University Law Review* 785 (1970) and "Developments in the Law—Confessions," 79 *Harvard Law Review* 935 (1966).

5. Two influential early studies were R. G. Weintraub and R. Tough, "Lesser Pleas Considered," 32 *Journal of Criminal Law and Criminology* 506 (1942); and Donald J. Newman, "Pleading Guilty for Considerations: A Study of Bargain Justice," 46 *Journal of Criminal Law, Criminology and Police Science* 780 (1956). The studies made by the American Bar Foundation had an important impact even before the five volumes listed in the note on page 201 were published. Also deserving mention is the Model Penal Code Project of the American Law Institute under the leadership of Professor Herbert Wechsler; this project produced between 1951 and 1962 the most comprehensive and scholarly examination ever made of the substantive penal law. Further, the American Bar Association's Standards Project has published eighteen volumes in the past decade, the last of which is a compilation of all of the standards: American Bar Association's Project on Standards for Criminal Justice, *The Administration of Criminal Justice* (New York: Institute of Judicial Administration, 1974).

6. The report on the guilty plea is The American Bar Association's Project on Minimum Standards for Criminal Justice, *Standards Relating to Pleas of Guilty* (New York: Institute of Judicial Administration, 1967) approved by the ABA House of Delegates, February 19, 1968.

7. The case is *Kercheval* v. *United States,* 274 U.S. 220 (1926). The citation of *United States* v. *Jackson* is 390 U.S. 570 (1968).

8. *McCarthy* v. *United States,* 394 U.S. 459 (1969).

9. Rule 11 of the Federal Rules of Criminal Procedure provides:

> A defendant may plead not guilty, guilty or, with the consent of the court, *nolo contendere*. The court may refuse to accept a plea of guilty, and shall not accept such plea or a plea of *nolo contendere* without first addressing the defendant personally and determining that the plea is made voluntarily with understanding of the nature of the charge and the consequences of the plea. If a defendant refuses to plead or if the court refuses to accept a plea of guilty or if a defendant corporation fails to appear, the court shall enter a plea of not guilty. The court shall not enter a judgment upon a plea of guilty unless it is satisfied that there is a factual basis for the plea.

10. *Boykin* v. *Alabama*, 395 U.S. 238 (1969).
11. *Brady* v. *United States*, 397 U.S. 742 (1970).
12. *McMann* v. *Richardson*, 397 U.S. 759 (1970); *Parker* v. *North Carolina*, 397 U.S. 790 (1970).
13. *Brady* v. *United States*, 397 U.S. at 750.
14. *Ibid.* at 751.
15. *McMann* v. *Richardson*, 397 U.S. at 770.
16. *North Carolina* v. *Alford*, 400 U.S. 25 (1970), footnote 2 to the Court's opinion at 28.
17. *Santobello* v. *New York*, 404 U.S. 257 (1971).
18. *Ibid.* at 260 and 262.

Chapter 4: Judge Perkins Considers the Law

1. Over 80 percent of the judicial positions in the United States are elective. In nineteen states, candidates for the bench run in partisan elections after having won a primary election or after having received their party's nomination at a political convention. In other states, candidates run without party designation. See The President's Commission on Law Enforcement and Administration of Justice, *Task Force Report: The Courts* (Washington, D.C.: U.S. Government Printing Office, 1967), p. 66.
2. The problems of disparity in sentence have been the source of much recent concern and a number of observational and statistical studies have documented its existence. Many of these are reviewed in The President's Commission, *Task Force Report: The Courts, op. cit.,* pp. 23–24. See also Robert O. Dawson, *Sentencing: The Decision as to Type, Length and Conditions of Sentence* (Boston: Little, Brown, 1969), Chapter 8; John Hogarth, *Sentencing as a Human Process* (Toronto: University of Toronto Press, 1971); James Johnson, "Sentencing in the Criminal District Courts," 9 *Houston Law Review* 944 (1972); Nigel Walker, *Sentencing in a Rational Society* (London: Penguin, 1972); and Sol

Rubin, *Law of Criminal Correction,* second ed. (Minneapolis, Minn.: West Publishing Co., 1973), pp. 128–145. The problems of sentencing seen from the perspective of an experienced and perceptive federal trial judge are described in Marvin Frankel, *Criminal Sentences: Law Without Order* (New York: Hill & Wang, 1973).

3. A short and exceptionally clear statement of the differences between distributive and retributive justice has been made by a distinguished Norwegian legal scholar: Torstein Eckhoff, "Justice, Efficiency, and Self-Made Rules in Public Administration," *New York University Institute of Comparative Law—First Copenhagen Conference* (Copenhagen: New York University Law Association in Scandinavia, 1960), pp. 52–69.

4. The career and work of Bob Pollitzer is based on an empirical study which characterized probation-parole personnel as punitive officers, protective agents or welfare workers: Lloyd E. Ohlin, Herman Piven, and Donnel M. Pappenfort, "Major Dilemmas of the Social Worker in Probation and Parole," 2 *National Probation and Parole Association Journal* 211 (1956). Probation officers ordinarily are employed by the judicial branch of government, on a county level, while parole officers usually are employed by the executive branch of state government.

5. *United States* ex rel. *Elksnis* v. *Gillegan,* 356 F. Supp. 244 (S.D.N.Y. 1966). See also Chief Judge Bazelon's opinion in *Scott* v. *United States,* 419 F. 2nd 264, 274–77 (D.C. Cir. 1969).

6. The quotation is from Arlen Spector's review of Donald J. Newman's book *Conviction: The Determination of Guilt or Innocence Without Trial,* 76 *Yale Law Journal* 605, 607 (1967).

7. Several studies of the degree to which judges follow the probation officer's recommendation are reported in Robert M. Carter and Leslie T. Wilkins, "Some Factors in Sentencing Policy," 58 *Journal of Criminal Law, Criminology and Police Science* 503 (1967). The findings are confirmed by a later study of Harris County, Texas (Houston) in Johnson, "Sentencing in the Criminal District Courts," *op. cit.,* pp. 982–984, Table G.

Chapter 5: Joe Carbo Negotiates the Facts
1. A study of a California prosecutor's office is presented in Lief H. Carter, *The Limits of Order* (Lexington, Mass.: Lexington Books, 1974). The views of a federal prosecutor

turned law professor are found in John Kaplan, "The Prosecutorial Discretion—A Comment," 60 *Northwestern University Law Review* 74 (1965). See also Newton Baker, "The Prosecutor—Initiation of Prosecution," 23 *Journal of Criminal Law and Criminology* 770 (1933); Note, "Prosecutor's Discretion," 103 *University of Pennsylvania Law Review* 1057 (1955): David Worgan and Monrad Paulsen, "The Position of a Prosecutor in a Criminal Case," 7 *Practical Lawyer* 44 (November 1967); Albert Alschuler, "The Prosecutor's Role in Plea Bargaining," 36 *University of Chicago Law Review* 50 (1968); and Frank W. Miller, *Prosecution: The Decision to Charge a Suspect with a Crime* (Boston: Little, Brown, 1969); and Donald J. Newman and Edgar Nemoyer, "Issues of Propriety in Negotiated Justice," 47 *Denver Law Journal* 367 (1970).

2. A comparative examination of prosecutorial role and discretion in the United States, France, Canada, West Germany and Japan is found in a symposium published in XVIII *The American Journal of Comparative Law,* No. 3 (1970). See also Jonas Myhre, "Conviction Without Trial in the United States and Norway," 5 *Houston Law Review* 647 (1969); Anthony Davis, "Sentences for Sale: A New Look at Plea Bargaining in England and America," (1971) *Criminal Law Review* 150; Bernard M. Dickens, "The Prosecuting Roles of the Attorney-General and Director of Public Prosecutors," (1974) *Public Law* 50; John Langbein, "Controlling Prosecutorial Discretion in Germany," 41 *University of Chicago Law Review* 439 (1974); and Joachim Herrmann, "The Rule of Compulsory Prosecution and the Scope of Prosecutorial Discretion in Germany," 41 *University of Chicago Law Review* 468 (1974). The Canadian prosecution is described in Brian A. Grosman, *The Prosecutor: An Inquiry into the Exercise of Discretion* (Toronto: University of Toronto Press, 1969).

3. The "subculture of justice" concept was developed from sociological writings on reciprocity and exchange in social relationships. For examples of this literature, see George C. Homans, "Social Behavior as Exchange," 63 *American Journal of Sociology,* 597 (1958); Alvin W. Gouldner, "The Norm of Reciprocity: A Preliminary Statement," 65 *American Journal of Sociology,* 161 (1960); and Peter M. Blau, *Exchange and Power in Social Life* (New York: John Wiley & Sons, 1964). A Canadian study characterized what we call a subculture of justice as follows: "There may exist a continu-

ing high level of conformity to behavioral norms which could be said to represent laws in a functional sense without the usual available authoritative sanction. These habitual modes of interaction are subject neither to commands nor to controls in the conventional sense. Rather than control by a superior or independent authority, the stability of the relationship is preserved by these norms. They constitute a form of self-regulation within the limitations set by the system . . . Adversarial conflict and its ritualization at trial is incompatible with the more satisfactory conciliatory adjustments which assure more consistent and reliable outcomes. As long as reciprocal relationships and compromise provide more benefits to defense and prosecution than those provided by the trial process, criminal cases will continue to be adjusted outside the courtroom." Brian A. Grosman, *The Prosecutor: An Inquiry Into the Exercise of Discretion* (Toronto: University of Toronto Press, 1969), pp. 93–96.

4.   The material on groups with conflicting interests in courthouse operations is derived from a general statement by Lloyd E. Ohlin, "Conflicting Interests in Correctional Objectives," Chapter 6 in Richard A. Cloward, Donald R. Cressey, George E. Grosser, Richard McCleery, Lloyd E. Ohlin, Gresham M. Sykes, and Sheldon Messinger, *Theoretical Studies in Social Organization of the Prison* (New York: Social Science Research Council, 1960). The analysis is extended in Lloyd E. Ohlin, Robert B. Coates, and Alden D. Miller, "Radical Correctional Reform: A Case Study of the Massachusetts Youth Correctional System," 44 *Harvard Educational Review* 74 (1974).

5.   American Bar Association's Project on Minimum Standards for Criminal Justice, *The Prosecution Function and the Defense Function* (New York: Institute of Judicial Administration, 1970). The function of office policy as a guide to the prosecutor in performing his tasks is discussed in Norman Abrams, "Internal Policy: Guiding the Exercise of Prosecutorial Discretion," 19 *UCLA Law Review* 1 (1971).

6.   The idea that social order stems from accommodations between conflicting interest groups is elaborated in Donald R. Cressey, "Bet Taking, Cosa Nostra, and Negotiated Social Order," 19 *Journal of Public Law* 13 (1970).

7.   "Flunked the attitude test" is a phrase used commonly in the Los Angeles Police Department to indicate improper demeanor on the part of a suspect confronted by the police. For empirical evidence that demeanor is an important variable in

police decisions to arrest, see Irving Piliavian and Scott Briar, "Police Encounters with Juveniles," 7 *American Journal of Sociology* 206 (1964); James R. Hudson, "Police-Citizen Encounters that Lead to Citizen Complaints," 18 *Social Problems* 190 (1970); and Donald J. Black, "Production of Crime Rates," 35 *American Sociological Review* 733 (1970).

8. The notion that facts are negotiated, not discovered, in legal and other social affairs follows the presentation of Thomas J. Scheff, "Negotiating Reality: Notes on Power in the Assessment of Responsibility," 16 *Social Problems* 3 (1968); David Sudnow, "Normal Crimes: Sociological Features of the Penal Code in a Public Defender's Office," 12 *Social Problems* 255 (1965); and Richard Quinney, *Criminology: Analysis and Critique of Crime in America* (Boston: Little, Brown, 1975), pp. 33–41.

9. Henry T. Lummus, *The Trial Judge* (Chicago: Foundation Press, 1937), p. 46.

10. An experienced attorney has written a provocative analysis of litigation as a combative game, James Marshall, "Lawyers, Truth and the Zero-Sum Game," 47 *Notre Dame Lawyer* 919 (1972).

11. Alschuler, "The Prosecutor's Role in Plea Bargaining" *op. cit.*, pp. 50, 54–56.

12. Donald J. Newman, *Conviction: The Determination of Guilt or Innocence Without Trial* (Boston: Little, Brown, 1966), 74.

13. Blumberg's study is summarized in "The Practice of Law as Confidence Game: Organizational Co-option of a Profession," 1 *Law and Society Review* 15 (1967). It is also reported in Abraham Blumberg, *Criminal Justice* (Chicago: Quadrangle Books, 1967), Chapter 4.

14. The prosecutor survey is reported in Note, "Guilty Plea Bargaining—Compromises by Prosecutors to Secure Guilty Pleas," 112 *University of Pennsylvania Law Review* 865 (1964).

15. Alschuler, "The Prosecutor's Role in Plea Bargaining," *op. cit.;* pp. 50, 59–60.

16. *Ibid.*, p. 58.

17. Lewis M. Steel, "The Losers in Plea-Bargaining," *New York Times*, February 24, 1975.

Chapter 6: Steve Ohler Tangles with Bureaucracy
1. For a good general survey of studies relating organizational structure to policy, see Theodore Caplow, *Principles of Organization* (New York: Harcourt Brace Jovanovich, 1964).

2. There is a considerable body of scholarly literature examining criminal lawyers. The best book-length treatment is Arthur Lewis Wood, *Criminal Lawyer* (New Haven: College & University Press, 1967). However, that study was completed before the explosion in criminal defender programs that followed constitutional rulings greatly expanding the right of poor defendants to a lawyer at public expense.

   Noteworthy studies of public defenders include: David Sudnow, "Normal Crimes: Sociological Features of the Penal Code in a Public Defender's Office," 12 *Social Problems* 255 (1965); Jerome Skolnick, "Social Control in the Adversary System," 11 *Journal of Conflict Resolution* 52 (1967); Jackson B. Battle, "In Search of the Adversary System—Cooperative Practices of Private Criminal Defense Attorneys," 50 *Texas Law Review* 60 (1971). See also Jean G. Taylor, *et al.,* "An Analysis of Defense Counsel in the Processing of Felony Defendants in Denver, Colorado"; Carol Kocivar, *et al.,* "The Right to Effective Counsel: A Case Study of the Denver Public Defender"; and Jackson B. Battle, "Comparison of Public Defenders' and Private Attorneys' Relationships with the Prosecution in the City of Denver," all of which are 50 *Denver Law Journal* 1-136 (1973).

   A critical evaluation of defense counsel's role in plea bargaining based on extensive field observation and interview is Albert Alschuler, "The Defense Attorney's Role in Plea Bargaining," 84 *Yale Law Journal* 1179 (1975). The literature is reviewed in a monograph by Olavi Maru, *Research on the Legal Profession* (Chicago: American Bar Foundation, (1972); and in Donald Dahlin, "Toward a Theory of the Public Defender's Place in the Legal System," 19 *South Dakota Law Review* 87 (1974).

3. The disparity of investment in prosecution and defense is documented by the Department of Justice and Department of Commerce Census, *Expenditure and Employment Data for the Criminal Justice System 1971–72* (Washington, D.C.: U.S. Government Printing Office, 1974). This survey of fifty states, 3,044 counties and 6,010 municipalities indicates that during the fiscal year ending 1971–1972 the nation spent in excess of 11.7 billion dollars on criminal justice. About 473 million dollars was spent on government legal services and prosecution while 87 million dollars was spent on defense of the indigent. In terms of manpower, prosecution at all levels of government employed nearly 44,000 employees while indigent defense employed slightly more than 4,000.

4. Robert F. Kennedy, *Collected Works of Robert F. Kennedy.*
5. The development of a judicial constitutional obligation to appoint counsel for poor defendants in criminal cases has followed a twisted path. The basis of the right is the Sixth Amendment to the U.S. Constitution which provides: "In all criminal prosecutions, the accused shall enjoy the right . . . to have the assistance of Counsel for his defense." In *Powell* v. *Alabama,* 287 U.S. 45 (1932) this right was held to be an aspect of due process of law binding on the states as well as the federal government, and was held to require that counsel be provided defendants who cannot afford a lawyer and who face a possible death penalty in state court. In *Johnson* v. *Zerbst,* 304 U.S. 458 (1938) it was held that counsel must be provided all indigent defendants in federal prosecutions, but in *Betts* v. *Brady,* 316 U.S. 455 (1942) the Supreme Court declined to extend this right to all state defendants. *Betts* v. *Brady* was overruled and counsel for indigents required in all felony prosecutions in *Gideon* v. *Wainwright,* 372 U.S. 335 (1963). The *Gideon* case is an interesting tale by itself and is the subject of Anthony Lewis' fascinating book *Gideon's Trumpet* (New York: Vintage Books, 1964). Finally, in *Argersinger* v. *Hamlen,* 407 U.S. 25 (1972) the Supreme Court held that the states must afford counsel to indigent defendants in petty offense trials when the accused faces imprisonment or jail. Counsel also must be granted children facing delinquency charges in juvenile court, *In re Gault,* 387 U.S. 1 (1967) and in some probation or parole revocation hearings, *Gagnon* v. *Scarpelli,* 411 U.S. 778 (1973). The right to counsel continues to develop, and its application in a variety of other proceedings is uncertain.

   Studies of the comparative merits of different methods of providing legal services to the indigent are generally inconclusive. See Lee Silverstein, *The Defense of the Poor in Criminal Cases in American State Courts* (Chicago: The American Bar Foundation, 1965).
6. Transformation or displacement of organizational goals is a central concern of many sociologists. Three studies that have attained classic status are: Robert Michels, *Political Parties* (Glencoe, Ill.: The Free Press, 1949); Philip Selznick, *TVA and the Grass Roots* (Berkeley: University of California Press, 1949); and Seymour M. Lipset, *Agrarian Socialism* (Berkeley: University of California Press, 1950). Earlier analyses of how instrumental values become terminal values are cited in Rob-

ert K. Merton, "The Unanticipated Consequences of Purposive Social Action," 1 *American Sociological Review* 894 (1936); and also in the chapter on "Bureaucratic Structure and Personality," in Robert K. Merton, *Social Theory and Social Structure* (Glencoe, Ill.: The Free Press, 1957), pp. 195–206. The transformation process has been studied in hundreds of settings, including institutions for juveniles, law enforcement agencies and prisons.

7. A good discussion of some of the advantages and disadvantages of ambiguous organizational goals, using the Soviet industrial system as an example, is Andrew Gunder Frank, "Goal Ambiguity and Conflicting Standards: An Approach to the Study of Organization," 17 *Human Organization* 8 (1958).

8. The classic statement about the effects of statistical measurement on goals and behavior is V. F. Ridgway, "Disfunctional Consequences of Performance Measurements," 2 *Administrative Science Quarterly* 240 (1956).

9. The discussion of "hierarchical bureaucracy" and "expert-oriented" bureaucracy follows the distinction made by the noted German sociologist and lawyer, Max Weber [Hans Gerth, ed., *From Max Weber* (New York: Oxford University Press, 1946), p. 246] as elaborated by Talcott Parsons [A. M. Henderson and Talcott Parsons, eds., *Max Weber: The Theory of Social and Economic Organization* (New York: Oxford University Press, 1947), p. 49]; and by Alvin W. Gouldner, *Patterns of Industrial Bureaucracy* (Glencoe, Ill.: The Free Press, 1954), pp. 20–24, 187–206. This distinction helps make sense of organizational behavior in which some participants are both persons of superior rank and persons of superior knowledge. See Donald R. Cressey, "Prison Organizations," Chapter 25 in James G. March, ed., *Handbook of Organizations* (Chicago: Rand McNally, 1965), pp. 1023–1070.

10. On the inevitability as well as the importance of autonomy in various forms of bureaucracy, see Fred E. Katz, *Autonomy and Organization: The limits of Social Controls* (New York: Random House, 1968). A popular area of comparative sociological analysis consists of examining the substitution of bureaucratic conditions of governmental administration for nonbureaucratic ones. In a short encyclopedia article, a leading authority on the subject traces this pattern of social change to the royal households of medieval Europe, to the

eventual employment of university-trained jurists as administrators, to the civilian transformation of military control on the continent, and to the civil-service reforms in England and the United States in the nineteenth century. "These several changes," it is noted, "were related to other social trends, especially the development of the universities, a money economy, the legal system, and representative institutions." Reinhard Bendix, "Bureaucracy," *International Encyclopedia of the Social Sciences* (New York: Macmillan, 1968), 2:201–219.

11. The "ridiculous" and "useless" aspects of bureaucratic forms was long ago analyzed in an article which has become a sociological classic: Alvin W. Gouldner, "Red Tape as A Social Problem," in Robert K. Merton, *et al.*, eds., *Reader in Bureaucracy* (Glencoe, Ill.: The Free Press, 1952), pp. 410–418. Thompson has given the name "bureaupathology" to behavior patterns which exaggerate organizational tendencies toward routinization, impersonality, resistance to change, categorization and so on: Victor A. Thompson, *Modern Organization* (New York: Alfred A. Knopf, 1961), pp. 152–177. Gerald D. Bell has constructed a set of theoretical propositions and hypotheses which account for his observation that flexible, loosely organized enterprises are just as efficient as tightly knit ones. Bell, "Formality Versus Flexibility in Complex Organizations," in Gerald D. Bell, ed., *Organizations and Human Behavior* (Englewood Cliffs, N.J.: Prentice-Hall, 1967), pp. 97–106.

12. Lawyer-client relationships and the ambiguities and conflicts inherent in them are analyzed in Douglas E. Rosenthal, *Lawyer and Client: Who's in Charge?* (New York: Russel Sage Foundation, 1974). This study suggests a variety of models for professional-client relationships, building on the sociological literature concerning doctors and others. A notable conclusion is that clients who do not accept the dependent role assigned to them but participate actively in the conduct of their case get significantly better results than clients who passively delegate decision responsibility to their lawyer. Concerning the conflicting obligations of defense counsel in criminal cases, see Monroe Freedman, "Where the Bodies are Buried: The Adversary System and the Obligation of Confidentiality," 10 *Criminal Law Bulletin* 979 (1974).

13. The relationship between uncertainty as to facts and likely outcome and the guilty plea process was illuminated by

Arnold Enker in a study for the National Crime Commission, *Perspectives on Plea Bargaining,* in The President's Commission on Law Enforcement and Administration of Justice, *Task Force Report: The Courts* (Washington, D.C.: U.S. Government Printing Office, 1967), pp. 108.

Chapter 7: Acquiescence and Severity

1. This chapter is based on Arthur Rosett, "Discretion, Severity and Legality in Criminal Justice," 46 *Southern California Law Review* 12 (1972).
2. Donald J. Newman, *Conviction: The Determination of Guilt or Innocence Without Trial* (Boston: Little, Brown, 1966), p. 15.
3. *North Carolina* v. *Alford,* 400 U.S. 25, 37 (1970).
4. A good short analysis of crimes committed out of moral conviction is Stephen Schafer, *The Political Criminal: The Problems of Morality and Crime* (New York: The Free Press, 1974).
5. Jonathan Caspar, *American Criminal Justice* (Englewood Cliffs, N.J.: Prentice-Hall 1972), p. 67.
6. *Tally* v. *Stevens,* 247 F. Supp. 683 (E.D. Ark. 1965)
7. Statement of Raymond J. Procunier, Hearings, Subcommittee of the House Judiciary Committee on Corrections, Part II, p. 123 (Washington, D.C.: U.S. Government Printing Office, 1972). Two recent examinations of the function of the prison are Norval Morris, *The Future of Imprisonment* (Chicago: University of Chicago Press, 1974) and Paul Keve, *Prison and Human Worth* (Minneapolis: University of Minnesota Press, 1974).
8. Over the last twenty years social scientists have studied inmate participation in some detail, and they have established as fact the idea that whether any particular inmate becomes "reformed," or becomes "hardened," or remains essentially unchanged during his prison experience depends upon the specific nature of his participation in the prison community. Alternative theoretical models are presented in Gresham M. Sykes, "Men, Merchants and Toughs: A Study of Reactions to Imprisonment," 4 *Social Problems* 130 (1956); and John Irwin and Donald R. Cressey, "Thieves, Convicts and the Inmate Culture," 10 *Social Problems* 142 (1962). For a good bibliography of the extensive literature in this area, see Esther Hefferman, *Making it in Prison: The Square, the Cool, and the Life* (New York: John Wiley & Sons, 1972).

9. Ralph W. England, Jr., "New Developments in Prison Labor," 41 *Prison Journal* 21 (1961). The general situation is described in Daniel Glaser, *The Effectiveness of a Prison and Parole System* (New York: Bobbs-Merrill, 1964).

10. The statutory punishments for particular acts vary from jurisdiction to jurisdiction. The examples are taken from the California Penal Code 487, 487a and 489; and Title 18, United States Code, 495. Other examples are recounted in the American Bar Association Project on Minimum Standards for Criminal Justice, *Sentencing Alternatives and Procedures* (New York: Institute of Judicial Administration, 1967), pp. 49–50.

11. The quotation is from Charles Breitel, "Controls in Law Enforcement," 27 *University of Chicago Law Review* 427 (1960). After more than twenty-five years on the bench, Judge Breitel was recently elected Chief Judge of the New York Court of Appeals, the highest court in that state.

12. Kenneth Culp Davis, *Discretionary Justice* (Baton Rouge, La.: Louisiana State University Press, 1969), p. 170.

13. The discussion of social trends is an elaboration and modification of themes noted by Edwin H. Sutherland and Donald R. Cressey, *Criminology*, ninth ed. (Philadelphia: J. B. Lippincott Company, 1974), pp. 336–339.

Chapter 8: The Path to Reform

1. What we call "real reform" was specifically called for by The American Assembly over a decade ago, but few, if any, of the responses can be characterized as "boldly imaginative." "There are widening discrepancies between the formal law in the books and the law in action in the courts. These are not cracks to be painted over but faults that imperil the structure of American justice. We are going to have to be searching and candid in our appraisal of existing judicial procedures and boldly imaginative in reconstructing traditional institutions to meet the challenges of our own time." Harry W. Jones, "Introduction" to Harry W. Jones, ed., *The Courts, the Public and the Law Explosion* (Englewood Cliffs, N.J.: Prentice-Hall, 1965), p. 3.

2. The misleading assumption was long ago noted by Chief Judge Breitel in the following terms: "Recourse to rule of law in an effort to eliminate or reduce discretion is a natural reaction to the abuse of discretion; but it is, nevertheless, a naive reaction. For, in recognizing the place of discretion we

perforce accept the limitations on verbalized law." Charles D. Breitel, "Controls in Criminal Law Enforcement," 27 *University of Chicago Law Review* 427 (1960).

3. This sort of simplistic calculus has recently been popping up in economists' cost-benefit analyses of deterrence. An example is Gordon Tullock, "Does Punishment Deter Crime?" (Summer, 1974) *The Public Interest* 103.

4. Early reports suggest that the felony drug arrests in New York declined 75 percent following passage of the law. It has been suggested that this is in part the result of the "police looking the other way." (*Trial*, p. 55, November/December 1973). Another report indicates arrests were down 30 percent from a year earlier. Robert Jones, "Effects of N.Y. Narcotics Law Appear Slight," *Los Angeles Times*, December 9, 1973, p. 1–2, Sec. 1-A.

5. The Supreme Court case equating the foreshortened trial on the transcript and the guilty plea is *In re Mosley*, 1 Cal. 3d 913, 926 (1970). The procedure is described by Kenneth Graham and Leon Letwin, "The Preliminary Hearing in Los Angeles," 18 *UCLA Law Review* 635, 931 (1971); and Lynn Mather, "Some Determinants of the Method of Case Disposition: Decision-making by Public Defenders in Los Angeles," 8 *Law and Society Review* 187 (1973).

6. The President's Commission on Law Enforcement and Administration of Justice, *Task Force Report: The Courts* (Washington, D.C.: U.S. Government Printing Office, 1967).

7. An excellent analysis of the judicialization process is found in Philippe Nonet, *Administrative Justice: Advocacy and Change in A Government Agency* (New York: Russell Sage Foundation, 1969). This study traces the history of California's Industrial Accident Commission as it is transformed from a welfare agency into a court of law: "Designed as an administrative authority, the early commission had a mandate for social action, aimed at improving the welfare of disable workers by means of relief and rehabilitation. It had broad discretion in making and interpreting its policies, and enjoyed considerable freedom from procedural restraints and judicial review. Fifty years later, the agency had lost most of its early sense of initiative and public mission; it has acquired the outlook of a passive arbitrator, responsible only to those private interests of labor and industry it was originally meant

8. Mather, "Some Determinants of the Method of Case Disposition," *op. cit.*, p. 204.

to regulate. The IAC has become a highly self-conscious judicial body, largely removed from the concrete problems of welfare policy and governed by exacting standards of procedure. Its primary function is to hear and decide claims of right under a determinate set of laws." (p. 1)

9. *Ibid.,* p. 189.

10. Restitution as a response to crime has ancient roots. Exodus 21:37. A modern attempt to enhance the role of restitution as an alternative to other punishment is described in David Fogel, Burt Galaway, and Joe Hudson, "Restitution in Criminal Justice: A Minnesota Experiment," 8 *Criminal Law Bulletin* 681 (1972). See also Stephen Schafer, *Compensation and Restitution to Victims of Crime,* second ed. (Montclair, N.J.: Patterson Smith, 1970); Gerhard O. W. Mueller, and H. H. A. Cooper, *The Criminal, Society and The Victim* (Washington D.C.: National Criminal Justice Reference Service, 1973); and Mary E. Baluss, *Integrated Services for Victims of Crime: A County Based Approach* (Washington, D.C.: The National Association of Counties Research Foundation, 1975).

11. The possibilities and difficulties of decentralization of the urban courthouse are reviewed in Richard Danzig, "Toward the Creation of a Complementary, Decentralized System of Criminal Justice," 26 *Stanford Law Review* 1 (1973). See also Richard Danzig and Benjamin Heinemann, "Decentralization in New York City: A Proposal," 8 *Harvard Journal of Legislation* 407 (1971). A more general study of the decentralization of urban municipal services is Howard W. Hallman, *Neighborhood Government in a Metropolitan Setting* (Beverly Hills, Calif.: Sage Publications, 1974).

12. Lay persons are used as judges in England, where most criminal cases are disposed of by Justices of the Peace, most of whom are not professional judges, and in many nations of Western Europe, where lay assessors sit with the professional judges. In the socialist countries of Eastern Europe "Comrade's Courts" are used to bring the offender and the community closer together. Harold Berman and Jane Spindler, "Soviet Comrade's Courts," 38 *Washington Law Review* 842 (1962); George Feifer, *Justice in Moscow,* (New York: Dell Publishing Co. 1965); Edith Rogovin, "Social Conformity and Comradely Courts in the Soviet Union," 7 *Crime & Delinquency* 303 (1971); and Gordon Smith, "Popular Participation in the Administration of Justice in the Soviet

Union: Comades' Courts and the Brezhnev Regime," 49 *Indiana Law Journal* 238 (1974).

13. This manipulation in Washington, D.C., Baltimore and Philadelphia is reported in several articles in the June/July 1972 issues of *Justice Magazine:* William Morrissey, "Balancing the Scales," p. 4, "Nixon Anti-Crime Plan Undermines Crime Status," p. 8 "Philadelphia Take Heart," p. 11; and Roger Twigg, "Downgrading of Crimes Verified in Baltimore," p. 15.

14. See Herbert L. Packer, *The Limits of the Criminal Sanction* (Stanford, Calif.: Stanford University Press, 1968), pp. 249–364; Edwin M. Schur, *Crimes Without Victims: Deviant Behavior and Public Policy* (Englewood Cliffs, N.J.: Prentice-Hall, 1965); Sanford Kadish, "The Crisis of Overcriminalization," 374 *Annals of the American Academy of Political and Social Science* 157 (1967); Jerome Skolnick, "Coercion to Virtue: The Enforcement of Morals," 41 *Southern California Law Review* 588 (1968).

15. The President's Commission, *Task Force Report: The Courts, op. cit.,* p. 107.

16. This tragedy of decriminalization was eloquently stated by Justice Thurgood Marshall in a decision upholding the constitutionality of drunk laws. *Powell* v. *Texas,* 1968 392 U.S. 514, 528–30:

... facilities for the attempted treatment of indigent alcoholics are woefully lacking throughout the country. It would be tragic to return large numbers of helpless, sometimes dangerous and frequently unsanitary inebriates to the streets of our cities without even the opportunity to sober up adequately which a brief jail term provides. Presumably no State or city will tolerate such a state of affairs. Yet the medical profession cannot, and does not, tell us with any assurance that, even if the buildings, equipment and trained personnel were made available, it could provide anything more than slightly higher-class jails for our indigent habitual inebriates. Thus we run the grave risk that nothing will be accomplished beyond the hanging of a new sign—reading "hospital"—over one wing of the jailhouse.

One virtue of the criminal process is, at least, that the duration of penal incarceration typically has some outside statutory limit; this is universally true in the case of petty offenses, such as public drunkenness, where jail terms are quite short on the whole. "Therapeutic civil commitment" lacks this feature; one is typically committed until one is "cured." Thus, to do otherwise than affirm might subject indigent alcoholics to the risk that they may be locked up for an indefinite period of time under the same conditions as before, with no more hope than before of receiving effective treatment and no prospect of periodic "freedom."

Faced with this unpleasant reality, we are unable to assert that the use of the criminal process as a means of dealing with the public aspects of problem drinking can never be defended as rational. The picture of the penniless drunk propelled aimlessly and endlessly through the law's "revolving door" of arrest, incarceration, release and re-arrest is not a pretty one. But before we condemn the present practice across-the-board, perhaps we ought to be able to point to some clear promise of a better world for these unfortunate people. . . .

17. Much of the evidence on deterrent effects of punishment is summarized in Franklin Zimring and Gordon Hawkins, *Deterrence* (Chicago: University of Chicago Press, 1973). The literature on the relationship of severity of punishment to effectiveness is reviewed in George Anjunes and A. Lee Hunt, "The Impact of Certainty and Severity of Punishment on Levels of Crime in American States," 64 *Journal of Criminal Law and Criminology* 486 (1973).

18. A vision of a criminal process based upon what is described as a "family model" is presented by John Griffiths, "Ideology in Criminal Procedure or A Third 'Model' of the Criminal Process," 79 *Yale Law Journal* 359 (1970).

19. One of our university colleagues has pinpointed the very limited conditions under which the repressive policy is desirable: "Absolute enforcement is only desirable where the society is absolutely confident that the rule it has passed should be observed." Monroe E. Price, "Criminal Law and Technology: Some Comments," 16 *UCLA Law Review* 120, 134 (1968).

index

224